"Participatory budgeting offers citizens a greater voice in the allocation of resources, but public managers are often skeptical of public involvement in financial decision-making. *Participatory Budgeting in the United States* helps abate these concerns by offering scholars and practitioners of public administration an explanation of how the method is working in a handful of local governments throughout the nation."

William Hatcher, Augusta University, USA

"This book is a welcome addition to the field of public administration due to the practical approach the authors take in examining citizen participation in the budgeting process, which graduate students will find insightful. The work also emphasizes the importance of public budgeting theories and practices in an evolving system of governance, where citizen input and representation are more than merely democratic principles, but essential elements of good governance."

Beth M. Rauhaus, University of North Georgia, USA

"Participatory budgeting sounds good in theory, but how does it work in practice? Through interviews with community leaders in five U.S. localities that have implemented participatory budgeting, this book provides an insider's view on the opportunities and challenges that arise. This book will be a valuable resource for communities that are using or considering participatory budgeting, as well as for students, scholars, and others who are interested in democratic values and citizen engagement."

Beverly Bunch, University of Illinois Springfield, USA

"*Participatory Budgeting in the United States* is a needed addition to the field with good value for students, academics, and practitioners. The text offers a thorough understanding of participatory budgeting, five interesting American case studies, comparisons with international efforts, assessment of efforts of citizen participation in budgeting, lessons learned, and a how to guide. It is a good complementary text for budgeting courses, a valued text for discussion of public engagement in more general public administration and policy courses, and a useful resource for practitioners and researchers in the field."

Larkin Dudley, Virginia Polytechnic Institute, Emeritus, USA

Participatory Budgeting in the United States

Although citizen engagement is a core public service value, few public administrators receive training on how to share leadership with people outside the government. *Participatory Budgeting in the United States* serves as a primer for those looking to understand a classic example of participatory governance, engaging local citizens in examining budgetary constraints and priorities before making recommendations to local government. Utilizing case studies and an original set of interviews with community members, elected officials, and city employees, this book provides a rare window onto the participatory budgeting process through the words and experiences of the very individuals involved. The central themes that emerge from these fascinating and detailed cases focus on three core areas: creating the participatory budgeting infrastructure; increasing citizen participation in participatory budgeting; and assessing and increasing the impact of participatory budgeting. This book provides students, local government elected officials, practitioners, and citizens with a comprehensive understanding of participatory budgeting and straightforward guidelines to enhance the process of civic engagement and democratic values in local communities.

Victoria Gordon is Associate Professor in the Department of Political Science and Director of the Master of Public Administration program at Western Kentucky University, USA.

Jeffery L. Osgood, Jr. is Professor of Public Policy and Administration, Vice Provost, and Dean of Graduate Studies at West Chester University, USA.

Daniel Boden is Assistant Professor in the Department of Political Science at Western Kentucky University, USA, and has professional experience in the public, private, and nonprofit sectors.

American Society for Public Administration

Series in Public Administration & Public Policy
David H. Rosenbloom, Ph.D.
Editor-in-Chief

Mission: Throughout its history, ASPA has sought to be true to its founding principles of promoting scholarship and professionalism within the public service. The ASPA Book Series on Public Administration and Public Policy publishes books that increase national and international interest for public administration and which discuss practical or cutting edge topics in engaging ways of interest to practitioners, policy makers, and those concerned with bringing scholarship to the practice of public administration.

Recent Publications

Adaptive Administration
Practice Strategies for Dealing with Constant Change in Public Administration and Policy
by Ferd H. Mitchell and Cheryl C. Mitchell

Non-Profit Organizations
Real Issues for Public Administrators
by Nicolas A. Valcik, Teodoro J. Benavides, and Kimberly Scruton

Sustaining the States
The Fiscal Viability of American State Governments
by Marilyn Marks Rubin and Katherine G. Willoughby

Using the "Narcotrafico" Threat to Build Public Administration Capacity between the US and Mexico
by Donald E. Klingner and Roberto Moreno Espinosa

Environmental Policymaking and Stakeholder Collaboration
Theory and Practice
by Shannon K. Orr

Organizational Assessment and Improvement in the Public Sector Workbook
by Kathleen M. Immordino

Challenges in City Management
A Case Study Approach
by Becky J. Starnes

Local Economic Development and the Environment
Finding Common Ground
by Susan M. Opp and Jeffery L. Osgood, Jr.

Case Studies in Disaster Response and Emergency Management
by Nicolas A. Valcik and Paul E. Tracy

Participatory Budgeting in the United States

A Guide for Local Governments

Victoria Gordon
Jeffery L. Osgood, Jr.
and Daniel Boden

Routledge
Taylor & Francis Group

NEW YORK AND LONDON

First published 2017
by Routledge
711 Third Avenue, New York, NY 10017

and by Routledge
2 Park Square, Milton Park, Abingdon, Oxon OX14 4RN

Routledge is an imprint of the Taylor & Francis Group, an informa business

© 2017 Taylor & Francis

The right of Victoria Gordon, Jeffery L. Osgood, Jr., and Daniel Boden to be identified as authors of this work has been asserted in accordance with sections 77 and 78 of the Copyright, Designs and Patents Act 1988.

Library of Congress Cataloging in Publication Data
Names: Gordon, Victoria (Associate professor), author. | Osgood, Jeffery L., Jr., author. | Boden, Daniel P.
Title: Participatory budgeting in the United States : a guide for local governments / by Victoria Gordon, Jeffery L. Osgood, Jr., and Daniel Boden.
Description: New York, NY : Routledge, 2016. | Series: ASPA series in public administration & public policy | Includes bibliographical references and index.
Identifiers: LCCN 2016006450| ISBN 9781498742078 (hardback : alk. paper) | ISBN 9781315535296 (ebook)
Subjects: LCSH: Municipal budgets—United States—Citizen participation—Case studies. | Local government—United States—Citizen participation—Case studies. | Public administration—United States—Case studies.
Classification: LCC HJ9147 .G67 2016 | DDC 352.4/82160973—dc23
LC record available at http://lccn.loc.gov/2016006450

ISBN: 978-1-4987-4207-8 (hbk)
ISBN: 978-1-315-53529-6 (ebk)

Typeset in Times New Roman
by Book Now Ltd, London

Dedication

For my grandchildren—Maggie Ann, Greyson Alexander, Gemma Rosalind, and Luca Deegan—and for my other grandbabies yet to arrive—VG (GiGi)

For my mother and grandparents—Donna, Richard and Mary Lou—my success is your sacrifice fulfilled—JO

For my parents, Richard and Carolyn Boden—DB

Contents

Illustrations and Appendices

Figures

Tables

Appendices

Foreword

In the year 2000, Janet Denhardt and I published an article in the *Public Administration Review*, titled "The New Public Service: Serving or Steering?" That article and a subsequent book with the same title challenged several assumptions about what we called the "old public administration," and those of the emerging "new public management." With respect to the latter, we recognized the significance of the technical and managerial aspects of the approach, but we also faulted that view of public administration for its reliance on a business/economic model for the public sector, and especially the assumption that individual citizens could be treated as "customers" rather than "citizens."

As an alternative, the New Public Service provided a framework for discussing democratic values, the role of citizens in the governmental process, and the concept of public service. Specifically, the book was organized around a set of seven core principles: 1) serve citizens, not customers; 2) seek the public interest; 3) value citizenship and public service over entrepreneurship; 4) think strategically, act democratically; 5) recognize that accountability isn't simple; 6) serve rather than steer; and 7) value people over productivity. We also pointed out the gap between public administrators and citizens and argued for 1) a greater role for citizens in the process of policy development and implementation; and 2) public administrators taking the initiative in creating opportunities for civic engagement. Basically, we made an argument for restoration of democratic values and civic engagement in the process of policy formulation and implementation.

At that time, ours was probably a minority opinion, but over the ensuing years, it has become much more central to public deliberations at all levels of government. We now recognize that public involvement in governmental decisions, at both the political and the administrative levels, is essential in coming up with the best ideas, in gaining broad public support for those ideas or proposals, and in establishing close working relationships between administrative agencies and the public generally. These were technical reasons for advancing the New Public Service, but we also did so because we simply felt it was consistent with democratic values. That is, in our view, citizen engagement is a "smart thing" for governments to undertake, and it is also the "right thing" to do to achieve effective democratic governance.

In the last 15 or so years, the New Public Service and activities consistent with its ideals have moved to a new prominence in the governance process. At the federal level, there have been active programs of public participation in decision-making, many based around the use of newly available applications of social media. At the same time, there have been new calls for transparency and openness with respect to public policy and administration. Similar developments have occurred at the state level. For example, many highway and transportation departments are using citizen forums to help design the routing and aesthetics of new highways, especially those through environmentally and historically sensitive areas. But perhaps the greatest numbers of applications of the New Public Service have occurred at the local level. Local governments have traditionally been recognized for their closeness to their citizens, and so it is not unexpected that they would lead the move to even closer connections. Again a wide variety of civic engagement activities, ranging from citizen-initiated performance assessment to surveys about citizen support of proposed bond measures, to grassroots ecosystem management, have been explored by local governments in the United States and well beyond.

Let me comment briefly on three of these applications, the third of which will be the one that is the focus of this book. As we reported in *The New Public Service*, in the mid-to-late 1990s, the Chairman and governing body of Orange County, Florida, undertook what they called the "Targeted Communities Initiative" (TCI). The idea was that the governing body would set aside a large sum of money to be devoted to a particular community that had been identified as traditionally underserved. The county chairman, Linda Chapin, convened a series of public meetings, the first of which led to her announcement of the TCI for the community of Bithlo, a small town east of Orlando. At a second meeting, they assembled citizens and created drawings of the community as it existed at that point and a second set of drawings of the community that they desired. Included in the first set of drawings were animals running wild through the neighborhoods, and included in the second set of drawings were community centers and recreation facilities.

The remaining four meetings were devoted to specifying priorities for the community, a commitment from the county to carry out the projects, and the establishment of oversight committees to make sure that the county was acting in a way consistent with community interest. A couple of years later, I actually saw the community center that I had first seen illustrated by a rough drawing done in black marker on a large sheet of chart paper. One thing that was especially interesting about the entire process is that when it began the department heads all agreed that the top priority for the citizens of Bithlo would be a bridge over a highway that divided the town into two areas otherwise disconnected. The bridge was actually not even in the top 10 priorities when ranked by the citizens of the community, who preferred that attention be given to a community center and recreation facilities and to eliminating some of the wild dogs running through the neighborhoods!

A second and much more recent illustration of a community becoming sensitive to the needs of citizens occurred in the City of Santa Monica. In 2013,

Santa Monica was one of five recipients of the Bloomberg Philanthropies award for innovation in local government. The Santa Monica proposal was to: "First, define what a city needed to thrive. Second, get the data that would show how the city measured up. Third, get the community and the city government together to take action on what needed to be improved."

The data gathering phase involved an examination of quantitative data resources from the city and state, a survey of some 2,200 citizens, and the mining of data from such sources as Twitter and Foursquare. The results were focused on five primary areas of interest: community, place, learning, health, and economic opportunity. According to then city manager Rod Gould, the city worked with partners such as the Rand Corporation and the University of Southern California's Price School of Public Policy to gather and analyze the data so as to make it useful in the public decision process. According to Gould, the most difficult part of the process was and remains translating the data concerning well-being into specific action processes that the city and its partners could undertake. But clearly now there is a baseline that will give local government officials an understanding of what their citizens are interested in with respect to their happiness and well-being.

A third illustration of the New Public Service in action concerns the application of participatory budgeting in local governments, first in Brazil and more recently in the United States. Participatory budgeting involves local citizens engaged in extended activities to examine budgetary constraints and priorities, then making recommendations to local government decision-makers. In this current book, Victoria Gordon, Jeff Osgood, and Daniel Boden describe participatory budgeting through the experiences of those involved in such activities in various cities in the United States. The cities could be considered early adopters of participatory budgeting, and based on their experiences, Gordon, Osgood, and Boden have identified a set of lessons or guidelines that other cities might use in deciding whether to use participatory budgeting and, if so, how. This revealing work continues an important tradition of study and practice with respect to civic engagement, and the lessons that it contains and the straightforward guidelines it offers will surely enhance the process of civic engagement in other communities. In this way, this volume makes a substantial contribution to restoring the prominence of democratic values (as opposed to the values of the marketplace) in the governance of local communities.

Robert B. Denhardt
Sol Price School of Public Policy
University of Southern California

Preface

The purpose of the book is twofold: to describe participatory budgeting as it exists in the United States today and to describe participatory budgeting through the words and experiences of individuals involved in the process. To accomplish this second objective, we interviewed 14 individuals to garner a variety of perspectives and perceptions. We spoke with community members, elected officials, and city employees in five communities—the 49th ward in Chicago, Illinois; the 6th ward in St. Louis, Missouri; Boston, Massachusetts; Greensboro, North Carolina; and Clarkston, Georgia. The importance of this book is found in the detailed descriptions of the experiences of these community members. The central themes that evolved from the interviews focus on three areas: creating the participatory budgeting infrastructure; increasing citizen participation in participatory budgeting; and assessing and increasing the impact of participatory budgeting.

Since our first visit to the 49th ward in Chicago in 2012, the number of communities and organizations that have implemented and adapted the participatory budgeting process for their communities has grown and spread to several U.S. states. The White House Office of Science and Technology Policy has brought national attention to participatory budgeting through the publication of the Open Government National Action Plan and by the hosting of White House events supporting and exploring the challenges and potential of participatory budgeting.

We hope that this volume will help all readers—but especially local government elected officials, practitioners, and citizens—to gain a more comprehensive understanding of participatory budgeting and consider its applicability for their respective communities. We hope that local governments will embrace and draw on the lessons learned from the experiences of these five cities as they develop participatory budgeting practices. It is also our hope that students and scholars will see the connections within the process of participatory budgeting to both the theory and the practice of public administration. We encourage other researchers from a variety of disciplines to study participatory budgeting.

Acknowledgments

The authors would like to thank Taylor & Francis, and editors Lara Zoble and Laura Stearns, for ensuring the timely publication of our research. Special thanks go to Cecilia Salinas for sharing her photographs of the participatory budgeting process in the 49th ward in Chicago and to Gary Gordon and Dennis Kouba for providing technical support. Dr. Osgood would like to acknowledge and thank copyeditor Paula Dohnal for bringing her talent and skills to the production of a second volume. Special appreciation from Dr. Gordon and Dr. Boden also goes to Western Kentucky University, Potter College of Arts and Letters for providing financial support under PCAL Faculty Research Grant Award #15-015; and the Department of Political Science for providing help through the efforts of excellent MPA graduate assistants—Kennedy Prather and Ashleigh Barker. Dr. Gordon would like to acknowledge the IBM Center for The Business of Government for providing financial support for her initial research on this topic. And most importantly, the authors would like to thank the interviewees for sharing their time and their experiences with participatory budgeting. Thank you to all!

About the Authors

Victoria Gordon is Associate Professor in the Department of Political Science, and serves as the director of the Master of Public Administration program at Western Kentucky University, Bowling Green, Kentucky. She earned her Doctor of Public Administration degree from the University of Illinois—Springfield. Her areas of research interest include municipal finance, regional economic development, and human resources management. Dr. Gordon's most recent book is *Maternity Leave: Policy and Practice* (CRC Press/Taylor and Francis, 2013).

Jeffery L. Osgood, Jr. Ph.D. MPA is Professor of Public Policy and Administration and currently serves as Vice Provost and Dean of Graduate Studies at West Chester University. He served as founding chair of the department and successfully led the Master of Public Administration program through the accreditation process. Additionally, he was responsible for the development of the Doctor of Public Administration, the university's first research doctorate. Dr. Osgood's research focuses on local government and economic development. His most recent book is *Local Economic Development and the Environment*, published in the ASPA Public Administration and Public Policy series (CRC Press/Taylor & Francis, 2013).

Daniel Boden holds a bachelor's degree from Brigham Young University and a MPA and Ph.D. from Virginia Tech. He has professional experience in the public, private, and nonprofit sectors. His research interests are interdisciplinary in nature and revolve around concerns with collaborative management, nonprofit management, and higher education policy.

1   Introduction

Participatory budgeting is a tool for public administrators to engage citizens in the process of resource decision-making and allocation, which yields greater public involvement. Its goals are increased transparency and accountability. A product of the emerging Brazilian democracy of the latter part of the 1980s, participatory budgeting was born of a desire to "confront social and political legacies of clientelism, social exclusion, and corruption by making the budgetary process transparent and public" (Wampler 2007, 23). Subsequently, this method of citizen engagement has materialized in more than 1,500 governments across the globe (Baiocchi and Ganuza 2014; Gordon 2014). The United States, often at the forefront of such democratic experiments, was uncharacteristically late in its exploration of participatory budgeting. Since 2009, more than 20 examples have been implemented in American localities. This volume describes five of those cases: Chicago, Illinois; St. Louis, Missouri; Boston, Massachusetts; Greensboro, North Carolina; and Clarkston, Georgia.

Through these American examples, we seek to understand the perceptions and experiences of community leaders involved in participatory budgeting. At the same time, we look to these localities for lessons regarding the use of social media, a tool that can be leveraged to enhance citizen engagement, in the implementation of participatory budgeting and overcoming common barriers to participation. Perhaps most important, through the responses of community leaders, we provide important information about the variety of tactics, strategies, and processes used to implement participatory budgeting. By presenting their answers to these questions, this volume seeks to provide readers with both a more general description of participatory budgeting and a representative set of experiences that fully describe the variation that exists when implementing such initiatives.

From Minnowbrook to Public Service Values

Since the Minnowbrook conference in 1968, public administration scholars have sought to inject democratic values into the discipline (Rossmann and Shanahan 2012, 65). Over time, a significant amount has been written about the practice of public administration within the framework of democratic, ethical, and social equity values. These overlapping and complementary ideals have been brought together under the larger category of public service values. In 2000, one of the more definitive pieces describing the increasing prominence of values-based public administration was published. Robert and Janet Denhardt (2000) identified a change in the means of achieving policy objectives to build "coalitions of public, nonprofit, and private agencies to meet mutually agreed upon needs" and the shift in organizational emphasis to "collaborative structures with leadership shared internally and externally" (554).

In response to the increasing hegemony of public service values, the Network of Schools of Public Policy, Affairs, and Administration (NASPAA) revised the standards of accreditation for master's level public service education programs. Included in these revisions were requirements that a program's "mission, governance, and curriculum ... demonstrably emphasize public service values" (NASPAA 2014, 2). The standards set forth that graduates of such programs have the ability "to articulate and apply a public service perspective" (7).

This research and attention to public service values has not yet led to a consensus on what role the values of administrators play in the way they behave and the decisions they make (Molina and McKeown 2012, 376). One such example is participatory budgeting, which provides a well-defined and road-tested method of how values can impact an administrator's conduct and decisions. In this same vein, we call for public administration scholars and practitioners to understand how their day-to-day activities should be influenced by a conception of the public interest as the "result of a dialogue about shared values" (Denhardt and Denhardt 2000, 554). As researchers, scholars, and practitioners contribute to the literature on public service values, the resources available to current and future administrators will be greater and more democratic than was the case for previous generations.

This volume is evidence of the increasing realization of values-based public administration. Calls for enhanced democracy in the administration of government that serves the public interest are not new. This literature has largely been dominated by theoretical works that have convincingly argued for the incorporation of values into public administration. Missing, however, is a critical mass of research and literature that advances praxis. Here we present real-world examples of tactics designed to inject public service values into the tension-filled arena of competition for and allocation of scarce public resources.

The Road Ahead

This book is organized into eleven chapters. Following this introduction, the second chapter provides an overview of participatory budgeting and its place within public sector values. It also provides a brief comparison of participatory budgeting in other countries as compared with the United States.

Chapter 3 explores the digital and physical spaces of participatory budgeting with regard to direct public engagement. Citizen participation in the budgetary process occurs both face-to-face and virtually via web-based technologies. Regardless of the medium, citizen participation requires space. Local government administrators must consider the impact the physical and the virtual space will have on citizens' participation in the budget process.

Chapter 4 describes the research questions and the research approach used to conduct this study and offers a brief description of the participants that were interviewed. Chapters 5–9 present profiles of the cities studied and focus on the individual interviews presented in the participants' voices. The cities chosen for study were Chicago, Illinois; St. Louis, Missouri; Boston, Massachusetts; Greensboro, North Carolina; and Clarkston, Georgia.

Chapter 10 focuses on the voices and perspectives of those who are absent from the core interviews. Last, Chapter 11 offers lessons learned and practical recommendations for local government officials and citizens interested in adopting participatory budgeting in their own communities. Included in this chapter are some of the themes that developed from the interviews in the five cities under study.

A Future for Public Administration

We see the increasing adoption of participatory budgeting and similar strategies by administrators at all levels of government as positive developments. President Barack Obama set a new tone for such initiatives by stating, "the way to solve the problems of our time, as one nation, is by involving the American people in shaping the policies that affect their lives" (White House 2014, n.p.). We are optimistic that future presidential administrations will see the value of the U.S. Open Government National Action Plan, which calls for participatory budgeting and other similar initiatives to be implemented.

The future of public administration may be one where members of the public have a dual role: citizen and administrator. This conceptualization of the public's rights and responsibilities is better suited to yield government action that more closely aligns with the public interest than is currently the case. Until we see what the future holds, in the pages that follow, we offer this work in the pursuit of furthering the praxis of public service values. We look forward to the time when these strategies and processes are commonplace in classrooms and town halls across the globe.

References

Baiocchi, G., and E. Ganuza. 2014. Participatory budgeting as if emancipation mattered. *Politics and Society* 42 (1): 29–50.

Denhardt, J. V., and R. B. Denhardt. 2000. The new public service: Serving, not steering. *Public Administration Review* 60 (6): 549–559.

Gordon, V. 2014. *Participatory budgeting: Ten actions to engage citizens via social media*. IBM Center for The Business of Government.

Molina, A. D., and C. L. McKeown. 2012. The heart of the profession: Understanding public service values. *Journal of Public Affairs Education* 18 (2): 375–396.

NASPAA. 2014. Accreditation standards. https://naspaaaccreditation.files.wordpress.com/2015/02/naspaa-accreditation-standards.pdf (accessed November 20, 2015).

Rossmann, D., and E. A. Shanahan. 2012. Defining and achieving normative democratic values in participatory budgeting processes. *Public Administration Review* 72 (1): 56–66.

Wampler, B. 2007. A guide to participatory budgeting. In Anwar Shah (Ed.), *Participatory Budgeting*, 21–54. Washington, D.C.: World Bank.

White House. 2014. Promoting innovation in civic engagement: Celebrating community-led participatory budgeting. https://www.whitehouse.gov/blog/2014/06/02/promoting-innovation-civic-engagement-celebrating-community-led-participatory-budget (accessed December 1, 2015).

2   Participatory Budgeting in Context

Participatory budgeting is a process of public engagement designed to solicit feedback and input and, in some cases, produce decisions regarding the allocation of financial resources. While there is a growing list of examples of organizations outside government utilizing this deliberative decision-making technique, the vast majority of examples of participatory budgeting are in the public sector. In particular, participatory budgeting has primarily been a municipal phenomenon.

The larger context in which participatory budgeting has developed is the "shift from government to governance and its emphasis on facilitating and enabling the role of public authority" (Pieterse 2001, 408). As governments face the daunting budget realities of fewer resources, communities across the globe are seeking new institutional methods of addressing public problems and issues.

In a number of examples the governing of civil society has transitioned from a singular focus on government to an emphasis on governance. *Governance* describes arrangements of both formal and informal institutions coalescing and entering into partnerships for the purpose of addressing public policy issues. This is exemplified by an emergent trend whereby governments provide fewer direct services and nonprofit organizations fill the gap left by government retrenchment. In some cases, governments provide these civil organizations with partial funding. The relationship between the two sectors in pursuit of addressing a policy objective is a textbook example of governance.

In adopting participatory budgeting, governments are decentralizing their authority under the banner of democracy. Involvement of the public in the deliberative decision-making process is one approach to governing outside the formal structures of government. It is, as Pieterse (2001) points out, an approach to enhancing the role of public authority in the governing process. Where others have limited their conception of governance to a possible coalition of three sectors (public, private, and nonprofit), participatory budgeting offers an additional actor in governance: the public. It expands governance to include participatory approaches to democracy.

Participatory budgeting is gaining ground as an innovative approach to creating governance in localities where government has operated as the sole or primary actor in addressing public problems (Rodgers 2010). Ultimately, the involvement of the public in the political process is likely to yield significant and positive outcomes that are more in keeping with the public interest versus a purely technocratic and bureaucratic approach (Stone 2011).

Evolution of Participatory Budgeting

Since its appearance in 1989, participatory budgeting has evolved over three phases: experimentation, consolidation, and extension and diversification (Global Campaign on Urban Governance 2004). Participatory budgeting's birthplace is generally agreed on as Porto Alegre, Brazil, in 1989. At the same time, a limited number of other Brazilian cities served as laboratories where communities experimented with this new form of democracy. Participatory budgeting then experienced a consolidation of those early experiences into an established approach to citizen engagement, which led to further adoption by other cities in Brazil. This modern take on participatory governance is slowly infiltrating town halls and government buildings across the globe. With each locality adapting participatory budgeting to its own political culture and realities, this later and more recent phase is characterized not only by expansion but also by diversification in this democratic experiment.

Municipalities worldwide have used participatory budgeting at varying levels, with some implementing this form of democratic involvement throughout the entire locality and others limiting it to a particular ward or district. Examples are found in towns both large and small.

Political and Environmental Preconditions

Any municipality could adopt participatory budgeting, but enabling statutory requirements may be necessary in cases where participatory budgeting cedes decision-making power directly to its citizens. Outside the legal requirements, other preconditions that have been found necessary for implementation include political will on the part of elected officials; interest and active participation by citizens and civic organizations; clearly delineated procedures and a shared understanding of purpose; sense of capacity and support needed to train officials, staff, and citizens; effective and efficient means to disseminate information; and a means of resolving differences between competing demands and limited resources (Global Campaign on Urban Governance 2004).

Support of Public Officials and Citizens

Participation in participatory budgeting is a two-sided equation, with elected officials and municipal staff as one side. Without even the smallest amount of support from elected officials, participatory budgeting will yield nothing more than a one-way communication from the citizens to politicians about the people's budgetary preferences. Elected officials must be committed to taking seriously both the process and the resulting recommendations. Political will is also necessary to establish legitimacy and sustainability. In cases where citizens are making recommendations instead of the decisions themselves, it is critical that politicians adopt the recommendations to demonstrate to the community that the practice has an appreciable impact on policies. As citizens begin to see the results, the larger community will become more interested, which in turn contributes to the long-term sustainability of the process. In this way, political will must be present with regard to both a commitment to providing the necessary resources and a good-faith effort at implementing the recommendations or decisions of the public.

The other part of the participation equation is civic capacity and interest on the part of citizens and civil organizations. Municipalities may find that early attempts at participatory budgeting yield greater levels of participation on the part of community organizations than on individuals. In addition, some individual participants will contribute to the process without a connection to a civic organization. Early participants, if convinced of their individual and collective efficacy in influencing policy outcomes, are likely to become process evangelists, assisting in generating additional participants in subsequent budget cycles (Aragones and Sánchez-Pagés 2009).

Procedures and Training

Clearly delineated procedures and a shared understanding of purpose are critical conditions for an effective process. Note that the designing of the process is an opportunity to involve the public. Participatory budgeting planned by elected officials or political elites stops short of realizing the full potential by which the public can be empowered to influence their government. Instead, a truly participatory process will involve the public from ideation through implementation. Involvement across the development continuum increases the likelihood that citizens and government will reach a shared understanding of purpose and procedures.

In the design and implementation of the participatory budgeting process, it is critical that those participating are representative of the larger population. Without this representation, there is an increased risk of the political elites or more affluent citizens capturing the process. If this occurs, the outcomes of participatory budgeting are unlikely to serve the greater public interest.

Understanding the capacity and support needed to educate officials, staff, and citizens is critical to the success of the participatory budgeting process. Citizens must have channels through which their voices will be heard by the local government and its representatives. Just as important, the government must be able to respond to citizens' needs—which may require staff members to adopt new behaviors and attitudes (Gaventa 2004, 17).

There may be an impulse to move directly from the design phase to execution. Doing so may contribute to systemic failure as the process is rolled out and decisions are being considered without having addressed deficiencies in knowledge about the budget. Instead, there is an intermediary step that is informed by an assessment of the capacity of the officials, staff, and citizens to make informed decisions. By undertaking this examination, officials and citizens can determine the extent to which training on the components of the budget is necessary. While the learning curve is likely to be steeper for the average citizen compared to local officials, it is worth considering including both groups in the same training. This will promote group cohesion before citizens and members of government begin working together in the decision-making phase.

Communication

An effective and efficient means of information dissemination must ensure that the general population, even those not directly participating, can easily find out what is occurring. Information can be communicated passively, such as on a locality's website. Alternatively, active dissemination strategies may include mailings (both postal and electronic), use of digital and social media, and even traditional mass media. Exemplars will use a combination of active and passive approaches to disseminate information. By leveraging both types of tactics, a municipality is more likely to inform more participants and ensure that information is not limited just to those who participate. In many ways, ensuring equal access to information increases the democratic qualities of the process.

Conflict Resolution

The process of participatory budgeting must include a means of resolving differences between competing demands and limited resources. The mechanism for reconciling the disparity between limited resources and an ostensibly unlimited number of demands for funding should be addressed during the design phase of implementation. It should be established early on that there will be criteria by which resolution will be reached. Technical approaches that include predetermined criteria are more likely to lead to outcomes that distribute resources fairly (Global Campaign on Urban Governance 2004, 31).

While each of these preconditions are necessary for effective implementation of participatory budgeting, it is not the case that each needs to be fully fleshed out before the process begins. Localities may find value in the process of addressing these conditions with public involvement. Doing so provides greater opportunity for both involving the public in the process and creating positive group dynamics. Understanding the context in which participatory budgeting is likely to be successful will allow localities to design better processes as well as those that are sensitive to the local culture.

Five Dimensions of Participatory Budgeting

Participatory budgeting is characterized by five dimensions, or areas of focus (Global Campaign on Urban Governance 2004): financial, participatory, normative/legal, spatial, and political. Considering each of these dimensions helps to clarify the ways a municipality could arrange and benefit from participatory budgeting.

Financial Dimension

The financial dimension of participatory budgeting includes components related to the categories and amount of the budget impacted by the process (Scherer and Wimmer 2012, 100). Previous attempts at participatory budgeting have involved anywhere from 1 to 100 percent of the budget in the decision-making process. However, exposing a higher percentage of the budget to the process is increasingly difficult given the significant monies generally reserved for personnel costs and other mandatory expenses. Thus, participatory budgeting is usually limited to the discretionary parts of budgets. Often it is the case, especially in early attempts, that only a small portion of the budget is decided via participatory budgeting. The portion of the budget involved can be focused in a particular area (e.g., parks and recreation, economic development) or it can be a percentage of the entire budget.

Participatory Dimension

Participatory budgeting has two main components with regard to the type of participation and power exercised by the community. In relation to participation, community members can contribute either directly or indirectly to the process. Direct approaches to participatory budgeting are those instances where community members are individually involved, in contrast to indirect approaches, where representatives are either elected or selected from the community to act as delegates for the public (Nabatchi and Amsler 2014, 65S).

Nabatchi and Amsler (2014) make an important distinction between public participation and public engagement. Public participation is a limited form of involvement during which community members have an opportunity to provide feedback and comments. It is in this context that participatory budgeting's power dimension becomes clear. Public engagement elevates involvement from a point of soliciting feedback to the active incorporation of that input into final policy choices.

Supporting this distinction between participation and engagement is the discussion surrounding the differences between deliberative and participatory democracy. Deliberative democracy focuses on the creation of opportunities for the public to be engaged in deliberations about public decisions. Participatory democracy, on the other hand, focuses on institutionalizing the structures of direct public involvement in government decision-making. To borrow a phrase from Carole Pateman (2012, 10), participatory democracy is about "democratizing democracy" (see also Santos 2005). Put another way, participatory democracy focuses on creating processes and structures that push the inclusivity of the deliberative process to its full extent.

The power dimension is more clearly understood as a continuum between informing and empowering, which is the basis of the International Association for Public Participation's Spectrum of Public Participation (Figure 2.1). At one end of the spectrum, the goal of involving the public is limited to informing citizens about the problem and possible approaches for addressing the issue. In this case, power is absent from the participation equation. Moving along the continuum, the public's power or influence over the final result increasingly expands from a place of feedback to the ultimate expression of authority, where decisions are entirely in the purview of the public.

While one could interpret this spectrum as a set of mutually exclusive goals, they are, in fact, complementary, with each building on the previous. The spectrum not only helps to identify the role of the public in the policy process but also synthesizes the goals of participatory budgeting: to inform, consult, involve, collaborate with, and empower citizens. These goals are more than just aspirations; they provide a framework around which to build a participatory budgeting process that achieves the highest levels of democratic participation.

Three explanatory factors have been identified with regard to citizen involvement (Verba, Schlozman, and Brady 1995; Ganuza and Francés 2012). The first factor is whether individuals have the desire to take part in the workings of their government. The second factor is whether material or symbolic barriers exist to prevent them from taking part. Third is whether the public is asked to take part in a way that indicates that their participation is important.

Research is needed to determine whether the amount of money allocated by participatory budgeting and the level of involvement by the public are related (Global Campaign on Urban Governance 2004). In other words, there is nothing to suggest that starting with smaller portions of the budget, as a proof-of-concept approach, will lead to lower public involvement. Until further research is done in this area, there is little information on which to base a recommendation for optimizing the parameters of involvement in pursuit of increased participation.

Some argue that a certain rate of citizen participation must be reached before participatory budgeting can be seen as legitimately addressing the needs of the public. Similarly, the overall representativeness of the participants raises concerns regarding how much the outcome will reflect the true will of the population, not just a small segment of the population that is more likely to participate.

Normative/Legal Dimension

The process of involving the public in budgeting decisions may require enabling legislation. This is especially true in cases where a locality assigns decision-making authority to the participatory budgeting process. In these instances, such approaches are more akin to participatory democracy than deliberative democracy. Little or no legislation is necessary in cases where citizen involvement is limited to a non-binding advisory role to elected officials, which is more consistent with a deliberative approach to participatory budgeting.

	Inform	Consult	Involve	Collaborate	Empower
Public participation goal	To provide the public with balanced and objective information to assist them in understanding the problem, alternatives, opportunities and/or solutions.	To obtain public feedback on analysis, alternatives and/or decisions.	To work directly with the public throughout the process to ensure that public concerns and aspirations are consistently understood and considered.	To partner with the public in each aspect of the decision including the development of alternatives and the identification of the preferred solution.	To place final decision-making in the hands of the public.
Promise to the public	We will keep you informed.	We will keep you informed, listen to and acknowledge concerns and aspirations, and provide feedback on how public input influenced the decision.	We will work with you to ensure that your concerns and aspirations are directly reflected in the alternatives developed and provide feedback on how public input influenced the decision.	We will look to you for advice and innovation in formulating solutions and incorporate your advice and recommendations into the decisions to the maximum extent possible.	We will implement what you decide.
Example techniques	• Fact sheets • Web sites • Open houses	• Public comment • Focus groups • Surveys • Public meetings	• Workshops • Deliberative polling	• Citizen advisory committees • Consensus-building • Participatory decision-making	• Citizen juries • Ballots • Delegated decision

Increasing Level of Public Impact

Figure 2.1 Spectrum of Public Participation

Source: Courtesy of IAP2.

Localities that want the outcomes of these processes to be binding must adopt the required statutory language. Without a legal framework affirming the authorities of the process, elected officials are free to modify or disregard the budgetary decisions of the citizens.

Spatial Dimension

Participatory budgeting creates "new public spheres" (Hordjik 2009, 45) in which citizens come forward with their ideas and get involved in the workings of their government. The public spheres of participatory budgeting are tied spatially in terms of their scope; they can encompass an entire municipality or be limited to a district within a municipality. According to the Global Campaign on Urban Governance (2004, 80), participatory budgeting is strongly connected to the decentralization of political power to sub-areas in the government.

It is important to understand the appropriate scale for participatory budgeting (Fung 2003). Building on public choice theory, it is rational to expect that approaches to participatory budgeting that subdivide the government into smaller units may result in outcomes that best reflect the needs of participants. This argument mirrors Elinor Ostrom's thesis that "public good problems are best resolved at the most local level through a system of voluntary collective organization" (Warner 2015, 8). Local issues are more likely to be understood and to create a sense of urgency in community members than are issues of a larger scope (Nabatchi and Amsler 2014, 65S).

Political/Governance Dimension

While the origins of participatory budgeting are rooted in political objectives, the technique has transformed from a political tool to a political-administrative practice (Ganuza and Baiocchi 2012). When the participation of the public extends to oversight of the budget, corruption is reduced (Global Campaign on Urban Governance 2004). Participatory budgeting also contributes to high transparency—a hallmark of good governance. However, officials must disseminate information with good intentions. In *opaque transparency*, the government appears to behave transparently, but the information distributed does not tell citizens how decisions were actually reached or what the true results were (Fox 2007, 667). *Clear transparency* provides exact information about processes, outcomes, and the individuals involved. Clear transparency about budgeting provides information about who does and gets what (667). Transparency leads to a democratic process in which elected officials are less likely to act in self-interest and more likely to allocate resources fairly (Kavanagh, Johnson, and Fabian 2010, 4).

Like transparency, the following five aspects of participatory budgeting enhance the quality of governance within a municipality (Hadden and Lerner 2011; Lerner 2011).

- *Democracy.* Participatory budgeting institutionalizes direct democracy. It also provides an environment in which members of the community have more meaningful interactions with their elected officials, which can engender legitimacy in the governmental process.
- *Education.* Budgetary knowledge allows community members to monitor governmental operations. Even participatory budgeting that does not situate members of the public as decision-makers still leads to greater access to relevant information and better informed citizens.
- *Efficiency.* Governmental decisions informed by public participation are inherently more representative, which increases the efficiency of the policy process. By soliciting input from all citizens, participatory budgeting acknowledges that policy issues are complex and multifaceted, and it asks citizens to help resolve conflicts (Nabatchi 2010, 377).
- *Social justice.* Participatory budgeting provides a way to get citizens involved in government and broadens participation to include more segments of the community, including those who are typically denied access (Wampler 2008, 62; Ganuza and Francés 2012, 285). If groups not typically active in government, such as the poor, get involved, budgetary decisions are more likely to benefit them (Gaventa 2004, 21).
- *Community.* Participatory budgeting engenders a sense of community by bringing together individuals who are unlikely to interact otherwise. Moreover, it provides an opportunity to connect community members to civic organizations, which strengthens the civic fabric of a municipality.

Each of these aspects contributes to good governance and a greater sense of civic cohesion in communities. Participatory budgeting can be the remedy for the citizenship deficit that is common in contemporary municipalities.

Phases of Participatory Budgeting

While standard operating procedures do not exist for participatory budgeting, there are five phases representative of previous implementations: 1) initiation and design; 2) preparation; 3) implementation; 4) realization; and 5) evaluation (Scherer and Wimmer 2012, 100–101).

During the initiation, design, and preparation phases, three specific areas are discussed: focus, scope, and regular effort (Scherer and Wimmer 2012, 100). These early phases include the political and community conversations necessary to determine the acceptability of implementing participatory budgeting. With regard to focus, the municipality engages in decisions concerning which parts of the budget will be subject to the process. This could be either a percentage of the budget or a particular area of expenditure. At the same time, questions of scope need to be answered. In particular, it must be decided if the participants will participate on a municipality-wide basis or in sub-units such as wards, districts, or boroughs. In the same vein, it must be decided if citizens will participate as a quasi-committee of the whole or if they will elect delegates or representatives.

Perhaps most important, the goals and objectives of participatory budgeting must be decided during the design phase. Is the goal to engage more people in the civic process? Are there hopes of greater citizen satisfaction with public spending? No matter the objective or objectives, it is important that these be explicitly discussed, debated, and determined, as they will inform the evaluation phase of the process.

Questions of frequency and schedule must be decided. Without an established schedule of interactions, participatory budgeting may become a one-off effort and this will raise questions of sustainability and legitimacy. Another design aspect important to determine is the criteria or "technical tools" used to make decisions (Scherer and Wimmer 2012). These criteria can be structured in such a way as to create a process by which projects are selected for consideration by the public during the deliberative process and before a public vote. Some of the benefits of well-crafted criteria intended to create fairer distributions of resources include better quality of life for citizens with lower incomes and other marginalized groups (Marquetti, da Silva, and Campbell 2012, 80). Thus, the benefits of a well-designed process that seeks to achieve larger societal outcomes cannot be understated.

Implementation has always been the most difficult area of public policy. While it may seem like the easiest phase of the process, implementation is actually the most difficult, as implementation tests theoretical discussions. During this phase it is important that officials and citizens alike keep accurate records and collect feedback. This information will yield a more robust evaluation and lead to improvements in subsequent iterations of the process. During the evaluation phase, citizens and elected officials should determine whether the participatory budgeting process met the stated objectives. Evaluation is an opportunity to determine which parts of the process can be improved during the next budget cycle (Scherer and Wimmer 2012).

Public Service Values

According to Denhardt and Denhardt (2011, 172), citizen engagement is at the core of public service values, because it is consistent with democratic ideas and helps to create community and shared responsibility. As the values of the discipline of public administration have evolved from Old Public Administration through New Public Management, and now to a growing acceptance of New Public Service, the emphasis has shifted to "collaborative structures with leadership shared internally and externally" (29). Participatory budgeting is about sharing leadership with the public in an area of great public importance.

Citizen engagement is also a form of co-production. According to Boyle and Harris (2009, 11):

> Co-production means delivering public services in an equal and reciprocal relationship between professionals, people using services, their families and their neighbors. Where activities are co-produced in this way, both services and neighborhoods become far more effective agents of change.

Co-production is not simply about the delivery of public services. Instead, it can include aspects of government work such as the budget, evaluation of public services, and policy development and implementation. In co-production citizens are situated as both agents of change and partners in achieving and realizing value for the public. Participation strategies designed to foster higher levels of citizen engagement are attempts to move individuals from passive to active citizenship (Wampler 2012).

As co-producers, citizens can be explorers, ideators, designers, and diffusers (Nambisan and Nambisan 2013, 6). As explorers, citizens can help to define and clarify the extent of a policy problem or issue. They can generate ideas in the pursuit of solutions. Citizens can aid in the design of public policies and government services. They can also act as diffusers by supporting or facilitating the adopted solution or policy. Participatory budgeting has the unique ability to engage citizens in each of these roles, which allows them to increase their level of democratic engagement.

Although citizen engagement is a core public service value, many public administrators need training in how to share leadership with people outside the government. According to Hornbein and King (2012), few graduate-level programs include public participation as the central topic of a course or part of the formal curriculum. This volume can serve as a primer for those looking to understand a classic example of participatory governance.

Benefits of Participatory Budgeting

The benefits of participatory budgeting are derived from the inclusionary aspects of the process. Participation has been linked to the promotion of the public interest, enhanced social capacity, and sense of community (Owen, Videras, and Willemsen 2008). With regard to capacity and community, participatory activities have been linked to the creation of both bonding and bridging capital (Wampler and Hartz-Karp 2012). *Bonding capital* is the linkages and networks between similar groups, while *bridging capital* is the connection of dissimilar groups of individuals. Without being dismissive of bonding capital, the potential of creating bridging capital within a community is likely among the greatest of the benefits and incentives for pursuing activities such as participatory budgeting. Activities that strengthen the bonds within a community, especially those among differing groups, should be valued tools in the repertoire of public officials.

Participatory budgeting also serves the necessary function of educating the citizenry (Bräutigam 2004, 667). As citizens interact with the process, if it is designed well, they will become more informed about the resources, constraints, and overall budgetary picture in their community (Sintomer, Herzberg, and Röcke 2008). Information transfer from officials and staff to the citizens allows individuals to become better consumers of such information. Participatory budgeting is a permeable activity, meaning that the knowledge acquired by individuals has the potential to be transferred outside to citizens not actively involved in the process. The potential for this flow of information beyond active participants is more likely to be present when community leaders and civil organizations share the information with their segments of the community.

Participatory budgeting also has the opportunity to enhance accountability in a locality. According to Wampler (2004, 76):

> Participatory institutions have the potential to act as a check on the prerogatives and actions of mayoral administration (horizontal), to allow citizens to vote for representatives and specific policies (vertical), and to rely on the mobilization of citizens into the political process as a means to legitimate the new policymaking process (societal).

The presence of all three types of accountability is significant when one considers that most activities exert only one type. Participatory budgeting encourages horizontal accountability by allowing citizens to provide feedback and control parts of the government that once were the domain of elected and municipal officials. It allows citizens to be actively engaged in the selection of policy options and alternatives. It also allows citizens, through their participation, to enhance societal accountability. Increased accountability is one reason that local governments that have implemented such processes have been found to be better managed and to have fewer issues with audit reports (Zamboni 2007; Speer 2012).

While there are many possible benefits of participatory budgeting, one is worth highlighting. Decisions involving the public have a higher likelihood of being closer to the public interest than those not including the public in deliberations. Thus, even if a decision is ultimately judged to be misguided, the magnitude of error with regard to its impact on the public is likely to be smaller, because it will have been informed by public participation (Aragones and Sánchez-Pagés 2009). In other words, it is likely that the decisions resulting from a participatory process will be closer to the actual solution or less likely to negatively impact the public, even when a suboptimal policy choice has been made.

Participatory Budgeting Around the World

Examples of participatory budgeting can be found on all six inhabited continents, ranging from Brazil in South America, Cameroon in Africa, Pune in Asia, Freiburg in Europe, Heathcoate in Australia, and even New York City in North America (Cabannes 2004, 27). More than 1,500 municipalities are currently engaged in some form of participatory budgeting (Baiocchi and Ganuza 2014; Gordon 2014). Even though participatory budgeting is a democratic instrument, the benefits of participation have had an appreciable impact in a non-democratic country, instilling a sense of legitimacy in the budgetary process in two Chinese communities (Wu and Wang 2011; 2012).

The World Bank has taken an active role in spreading participatory budgeting around the globe. Since 2002 the World Bank has provided at least $280 million in financial resources to fund participatory budgeting and related projects in at least 15 countries (Goldfrank 2012, 3). The same organization published a report on participatory budgeting in 2007, which was followed by the first international conference on participatory budgeting in 2010 (Pateman 2012, 7).

Even with the diffusion of this policy tool throughout the globe, it has been absent from the U.S. political agenda until recently. To be sure, participatory budgeting has been a lesson learned from the Global South (Sintomer, Herzber, and Allegretti 2010). As this policy approach evolved and traveled from continent to continent, it has adapted to the political culture of each area. The motivations for implementation may differ vastly in each place, but participatory budgeting has significant potential for "democratizing democracy" (Pateman 2012, 14), or in the Chinese example, inserting some democratic principles into local government operations.

Participatory Budgeting in the United States

While the United States has lagged in adopting participatory budgeting, there are emerging signs that this approach is engendering higher levels of democracy throughout cities. In the summer of 2014, the White House's Office of Science and Technology Policy hosted individuals from throughout the United States to discuss their experiences with participatory budgeting. In the Second Open Government National Action Plan (Open Government Partnership 2013, 10), the Office of the President called for city government and nonprofit organizations to:

> create tools and best practices that communities can use to implement projects; raise awareness among other American communities that participatory budgeting can be used to help determine local investment priorities; and help educate communities on participatory budgeting and its benefits.

Despite a slow start, there are lessons to be learned from participatory budgeting experiences in the United States (Lerner and Secondo 2012). Since 2009 more than 20 municipalities have experimented with participatory budgeting (Gordon 2014). The chapters that follow provide insight into attempts at participatory budgeting in the following cities: Chicago, Illinois; St. Louis, Missouri; Boston, Massachusetts; Greensboro, North Carolina; and Clarkston, Georgia.

References

Aragones, E., and S. Sánchez-Pagés. 2009. A theory of participatory democracy based on the real case of Porto Alegre. *European Economic Review* 53 (1): 56–72.
Baiocchi, G., and E. Ganuza. 2014. Participatory budgeting as if emancipation mattered. *Politics and Society* 42 (1): 29–50.

Boyle, D., and M. Harris. 2009. *The challenge of co-production*. London: New Economics Foundation.

Bräutigam, D. 2004. The people's budget? Politics, participation and pro-poor policy. *Development Policy Review* 22 (6): 653–668.

Cabannes, Y. 2004. Participatory budgeting: A significant contribution to participatory democracy. *Environment and Urbanization* 16 (1): 27–46.

Denhardt, J. V., and R. B. Denhardt. 2011. *The new public service: Serving, not steering*. Abingdon: Routledge.

Fox, J. 2007. The uncertain relationship between transparency and accountability. *Development in Practice* 17 (4–5): 663–671.

Fung, A. 2003. Thinking about empowered participatory governance. In Archon Fung and Erik Olin Wright, *Deepening democracy: Institutional innovations in empowered participatory governance*, 3–44. London: Verso.

Ganuza, E., and G. Baiocchi. 2012. The power of ambiguity: How participatory budgeting travels the globe. *Journal of Public Deliberation* 8 (2).

Ganuza, E., and F. Francés. 2012. The deliberative turn in participation: The problem of inclusion and deliberative opportunities in participatory budgeting. *European Political Science Review* 4 (2): 283–302.

Gaventa, J. 2004. Strengthening participatory approaches to local governance: Learning the lessons from abroad. *National Civic Review* 93 (4): 16–27.

Global Campaign on Urban Governance. 2004. *72 frequently asked questions about participatory budgeting*. Nairobi: UN-HABITAT.

Goldfrank, B. 2012. The World Bank and the globalization of participatory budgeting. *Journal of Public Deliberation* 8 (2): 7.

Gordon, V. 2014. *Participatory budgeting: Ten actions to engage citizens via social media*. Washington, D.C.: IBM Center for The Business of Government.

Hadden, M., and J. Lerner. 2011, December 3. How to start participatory budgeting in your city. http://www.shareable.net.

Hordijk, M. A. 2009. Peru's participatory budgeting: Configurations of power, opportunities for change. *Open Urban Studies Journal* 2: 43–55.

Hornbein, R., and C. S. King. 2012. Should we be teaching public participation? Student responses and MPA program practices. *Journal of Public Affairs Education* 18 (4): 717–737.

Kavanagh, S., J. Johnson, and C. Fabian. 2010. *Anatomy of a priority-based budget process*. Chicago: Government Finance Officers Association.

Lerner, J. 2011. Participatory budgeting: Building community agreement around tough budget decisions. *National Civic Review* 100 (2): 30–35.

Lerner, J., and D. Secondo. 2012. By the people, for the people: Participatory budgeting from the bottom up in North America. *Journal of Public Deliberation* 8 (2): 2.

Marquetti, A., C. E. S. da Silva, and A. Campbell. 2012. Participatory economic democracy in action: Participatory budgeting in Porto Alegre, 1989–2004. *Review of Radical Political Economics* 44 (1): 62–81.

Nabatchi, T. 2010. Addressing the citizenship and democratic deficits: The potential of deliberative democracy for public administration. *American Review of Public Administration* 40 (4): 376–399.

Nabatchi, T., and L. B. Amsler. 2014. Direct public engagement in local government. *American Review of Public Administration* 44 (4 supp): 63S–88S.

Nambisan, S., and P. Nambisan. 2013. *Engaging citizens in co-creation in public services: Lessons learned and best practices*. Washington, D.C.: IBM Center for The Business of Government.

Open Government Partnership. 2013, December 5. Second Open Government National Action Plan for the United States of America. https://www.whitehouse.gov/sites/default/files/docs/us_national_action_plan_6p.pdf.

Owen, A. L., J. Videras, and C. Willemsen. 2008. Democracy, participation, and life satisfaction. *Social Science Quarterly* 89 (4): 987–1005.

Pateman, C. 2012. Participatory democracy revisited. *Perspectives on Politics* 10 (1): 7–19.

Pieterse, J. N. 2001. Participatory democratization reconceived. *Futures* 33 (5): 407–422.

Rodgers, D. 2010. Contingent democratisation? The rise and fall of participatory budgeting in Buenos Aires. *Journal of Latin American Studies* 42 (1): 1–27.

Santos, Boaventura de Sousa (Ed.). 2005. *Democratizing democracy: Beyond the liberal democratic canon.* London: Verso.

Scherer, S., and M. A. Wimmer. 2012. Reference process model for participatory budgeting in Germany. In *Electronic participation*, 97–111. Berlin: Springer.

Schugurensky, D., and J. Lerner. 2005. Learning citizenship and democracy through participatory budgeting: The case of Rosario, Argentina. Paper presented at Democratic Practices as Learning Opportunities Conference, Teacher's College, Columbia University.

Sintomer, Y., C. Herzberg, and G. Allegretti. 2010. Learning from the South: Participatory budgeting worldwide: An invitation to global cooperation. *Dialog Global* 25.

Sintomer, Y., C. Herzberg, and A. Röcke. 2008. Participatory budgeting in Europe: Potentials and challenges. *International Journal of Urban and Regional Research* 32 (1): 164–178.

Speer, J. 2012. Participatory governance reform: A good strategy for increasing government responsiveness and improving public services? *World Development* 40 (12): 2379–2398.

Stone, D. A. 2011. *Policy paradox: The art of political decision making.* New York: W. W. Norton.

Verba, S., K. L. Schlozman, and H. E. Brady. 1995. *Voice and equality: Civic voluntarism in American politics*, Vol. 4. Cambridge, MA: Harvard University Press.

Wampler, B. 2004. Expanding accountability through participatory institutions: Mayors, citizens, and budgeting in three Brazilian municipalities. *Latin American Politics and Society* 46 (2): 73–99.

———. 2008. When does participatory democracy deepen the quality of democracy? Lessons from Brazil. *Comparative Politics* 41 (1): 61–81.

———. 2012. Participatory budgeting: Core principles and key impacts. *Journal of Public Deliberation* 8 (2): 12.

Wampler, B., and J. Hartz-Karp. 2012. Participatory budgeting: Diffusion and outcomes across the world. *Journal of Public Deliberation* 8 (2): 13.

Warner, M. 2015. Municipal size, resources, and efficiency. In A. Henderson (Ed.), *Municipal shared services and consolidation: A public solutions handbook*, 3–16. New York: Routledge.

Wu, Y., and W. Wang. 2011. The rationalization of public budgeting in China: A reflection on participatory budgeting in Wuxi. *Public Finance and Management* 11 (3): 262.

———. 2012. Does participatory budgeting improve the legitimacy of the local government? A comparative case study of two cities in China. *Australian Journal of Public Administration* 71 (2): 122–135.

Zamboni, Y. 2007. *Participatory budgeting and local governance: An evidence-based evaluation of participatory budgeting experiences in Brazil.* Clifton, U.K.: University of Bristol.

3   The Physical and Digital Space of Participatory Budgeting

Participatory budgeting establishes "new public spheres" (Hordijk 2009, 45) with the capacity to increase dialogue between citizens and government representatives. Positive and recurrent discourse between citizens and government officials is critical to sound government administration (Stivers 2001) in a democracy (Barber 2003). Participatory budgeting, like other citizen engagement activities, promises both citizen and government participants a meaningful opportunity to become "coproducers" of public goods and services (Stivers 1990). Such co-production does not occur spontaneously; positive relationships are not formed simply when government officials invite citizens to participate in the local government budgeting process. Collaboration requires space (Amey and Brown 2004).

Many participatory budgeting activities occur within government buildings and at the request of government officials. Inherent in the invitation extended to citizens to participate in the budgeting process is the invitation to share space. This shared space creates an opportunity for citizens and government officials to have a dialogue about priorities and possibilities. Successful citizen participation requires officials who are willing to convert "management spaces into *political* spaces" (Cornwall and Coelho 2007, 14; emphasis in original). Professional administrators must recognize the importance of space and its impact on the process of participatory budgeting.

Charles Goodsell (1981) explained that "the public encounter," or "the interaction of citizen and government official" (3), does not occur by happenstance but rather is purposeful in nature. Such human experiences require both setting and medium to take place (7). Participatory budgeting, as well as other public policy tools, is affected by the medium and setting of collaboration (Domahidy and Gilsinan 1992). Participatory budgeting activities occur in both physical (i.e., municipal buildings) and virtual (i.e., Internet) settings. The medium of participatory budgeting in physical spaces is often face-to-face meetings, such as town hall meetings or smaller work groups. The Internet and information technologies, such as social networking sites, present new mediums and settings for public participation in the governance process to occur (Toregas 2001). This chapter explores both the physical and the digital settings of participatory budgeting and the accompanying mediums of these interactions.

Physical Space

More than simply providing space for actors to operate, physical space influences human behavior (Hatch and Cunliffe 2013). Winston Churchill famously said, "We shape our buildings, and afterwards our buildings shape us" (quoted in Goodsell 2001, 11). That is, physical space structures social interaction (Harrison and Dourish 1996). Built environments have a "mnemonic" quality about them, instructing individuals and groups on the appropriateness of certain actions therein and, perhaps more important, the impropriety of others (Rapoport 1982, 80–81). The physical layout of a space—room size, furniture, and equipment—not only dictates the appropriateness of certain actions but also limits which actions are possible.

Elements of a particular built environment that influence human interaction might be permanent, such as walls or other such physical barriers, or they might be temporary, such as the arrangement of chairs within a room. Regardless of their mobility, elements related to the layout of physical space impact personal interactions (Hatch and Cunliffe 2013, 200–228). Additionally, the characteristics of a particular physical setting affect the medium of human interaction. Presumably, in-depth and extended conversations between citizens and administrators are less likely to occur in public forums held in large halls than in work groups held in smaller rooms.

In addition to restricting or facilitating certain actions, the physical environment sends powerful signals concerning which actions are acceptable for specific actors. Physical space that restricts personal interaction and reinforces hierarchical social structures cues individuals as to the expected roles they take on in certain social settings (Bitner 1992). As content experts and officials of the government, administrators must recognize the potential impact their presence may have on participatory budgeting activities (Cornwall and Coelho 2007). Complicating the realities of preexisting social structures, many face-to-face initiatives focused on improving citizen engagement occur within government buildings.

Holding public meetings related to participatory budgeting in government buildings is often both unavoidable and desirable. Regardless of why citizen engagement meetings take place in government buildings, it is important for administrators to recognize that their interactions with citizens in government buildings are not neutral (Domahidy and Gilsinan 1992). Citizens less familiar with government buildings may be overwhelmed by architectural elements purposively designed to evoke feelings of respect regarding the public institutions housed therein (Goodsell 1988). Government buildings are a part of a public administrator's daily routine; any sense of awe an official might have held regarding a public building understandably fades over time (Goodsell 2001). In addition to the advantage familiarity with government buildings gives public administrators over citizens in participatory governance, officials often consider the buildings they work in on a daily basis to be "their space" (Cornwall and Coelho 2007, 1). This realization is important as officials invite citizens to participate in the budgeting process.

Inherent in the invitation to citizens to participate is the opportunity administrators have to frame the physical space where the collaboration will take place. Seemingly mundane decisions, such as room size and seating arrangements within a given space, send important messages to citizens about the sincerity of the invitation to participate. Seeing budgeting activities as occurring in a collaborative space requires administrators to see the budget itself as an artifact or as politics rather than management (Cornwall and Coelho 2007, 14). Such a perspective shifts citizens from consumers to co-creators of public goods and services (Stivers 1990).

Central to the goal of finding a collaborative space is to create an "intellectual neutral space," where all participants are free to express their thoughts and perspectives openly. At the very least, however, administrators should seek to develop "a demilitarized zone" (Amey and Brown 2004, 44) where conflicting viewpoints "exist parallel to each other" (42). In an effort to create such a space, administrators must consider the components of physical space available to them and the impact such spaces will have on the participatory process.

Elements of Physical Space

The physical layout of a space establishes expectations for action (Parish, Berry, and Lam 2007). The environmental aspects of a specific space, such as room size, seating arrangements, and audiovisual equipment, have been found to affect public participation in local government settings (Koehler 1980). Bitner (1992) identifies ambient conditions, spatial layout and functionality, and signs, symbols, and artifacts as three key elements of the physical layout that impact human behavior.

The *ambient conditions* of a space refer to the background elements of a physical setting, "such as temperature, lighting, noise, music, and scent" (Bitner 1992, 66). The ambient conditions of a particular space have an impact on all parties; importantly, the effects of these conditions are not always immediately discernible, nor are they always consciously detected. The purposeful nature of participatory budgeting activities heightens the importance of the *spatial layout and functionality* of the spaces where they occur (65–66). These elements of physical space relate to such things as the seating arrangements, audiovisual technologies, walkways and aisles, podiums or rostrums, and lecterns. Each of these elements dictates how citizens and officials will interact with one another and, just as important, how citizens will interact with one another. Decisions about these elements of space are often devalued as questions of efficiency regarding the human interactions that will take place. In concerning themselves with issues related to how the physical space will affect citizen engagement, administrators will be forced to consider the nature of engagement they desire to facilitate.

The *signs, symbols, and artifacts* of physical space provide both implicit and explicit cues to all parties about the purpose and expectations of a particular space (Bitner 1992, 66). Citizen engagement activities such as participatory budgeting should utilize proper signage. Appropriate signage can communicate a welcoming atmosphere reinforcing the expectation of collaboration. Symbols and artifacts of a physical space include artwork, decorations, furnishings, and building material. Many symbols and artifacts of a physical space are permanent to a specific site and beyond the control of administrators. Regardless of their mobility, administrators should recognize the existence of such symbols and artifacts and the messages they may convey to specific communities.

Much of this discussion has centered on the importance of administrators considering the impact space can have on citizens in participatory budgeting activities. It is true that shared physical space allows citizens to engage with government officials; however, and of equal importance, physical space dedicated to collaboration also allows administrators to interact with citizens. Constructive interactions of administrators with citizens in the governance process have the potential to alter negative and reinforce positive perceptions of citizen engagement activities. Administrators who are fully convinced of the benefits of participatory budgeting are more likely to have not only a greater respect for citizens but also an increased inclination to listen to and respond positively to citizens' perspectives in the future (Cornwall and Coelho 2007).

Virtual Space

In an effort to facilitate greater citizen participation, governments, at all levels, have attempted to implement e-governance initiatives. Although scholars disagree about a precise definition, it is clear that e-governance is less about how government does its work and more about the structures that influence what government does (Bannister and Connolly 2012). Proponents of e-governance see the Internet as an effective tool in facilitating increased citizen engagement. E-governance provides the space where citizens and government officials can collaboratively shape government action. Information and communication technologies (ICTs), such as social networking sites, create virtual space that has the potential to break down barriers to citizen engagement in the political process (Baumgartner and Morris 2010).

Efforts by government officials to employ e-governance measures are driven largely by attempts at greater transparency and citizen engagement (Justice, Melitski, and Smith 2006). ICTs allow for citizens and government officials to "create and exchange content" in a meaningful way (Gainous and Wagner 2014, 1). In this way, e-governance does more than simply automate existing government processes (Bannister and Connolly 2012); its true capacity is found it its ability to "redefine the relationship between citizens and government and help foster more engaged citizens" (Scott 2006, 349).

Proponents of e-governance see ICTs as facilitating the transition of the United States into "an electronic republic," a system of governance where "elements of direct democracy" are more fully embraced by "our traditional representative form of government" (Grossman 1995, 3). ICTs have had an undeniable impact on the production and delivery of government goods and services (Zheng, Schachter, and Holzer 2014) and on how citizens and government officials communicate (Toregas 2001). E-governance purports to address two of the largest challenges to direct citizen participation: time and effort (Boulianne 2009, 205). E-governance promises to improve government efficiency and effectiveness while simultaneously encouraging and refining citizenship (Johnson 2015). As such, e-governance has the potential to increase both the number of citizens engaged in the governance process and the frequency of interactions between digital citizens and officials. Face-to-face meetings can require significant investments of time for both citizens and government officials. E-governance reduces the time required for citizens and officials to dialogue (Roberts 2004). A key aspect of e-governance, then, is the relationship between ICTs and increased citizen engagement. This relationship is of particular importance when considering attempts to engage younger citizens in the governance process. Younger Americans are often more familiar than their parents and grandparents with ICTs, and they expect to interact with government officials via "participation channels" supported by e-governance (Dalton 2008).

Skeptics of e-governance caution viewing electronic means of participation as a panacea for civic engagement (Baumgartner and Morris 2010; Boulianne 2015). The ubiquity of ICTs notwithstanding, scholars disagree about the impact e-governance initiatives in the United States have had on civic engagement (Boulianne 2009; Theocharis and Lowe 2015). Although ICTs have altered the way citizens access and consume political news (Boulianne 2015), questions remain about the ultimate impact such technologies have on political activity (Gainous and Wagner 2014). Baumgartner and Morris (2010) argue that the effects of ICTs on public participation have been overstated and that the "hype" associated with newer, interactive ICTs is similar to "earlier developments in mass communication" (38). Regardless of the impact on civic engagement, many local governments continue to use e-governance initiatives (Johnson 2015).

Opportunities for e-governance vary greatly among municipalities. Researchers have found a positive relationship between higher wealth in municipalities and the number and extent of e-governance interactions (Zheng, Schachter, and Holzer 2014, 655). This is not surprising considering the expectations ICTs create for instantaneous dialogue. Localities with few employees might not have the human resources necessary to monitor and respond to social media communications. Additionally, government officials must decide which department will administer e-governance initiatives: "the IT department, the chief administrator's office or elsewhere" (Reddick and Norris 2013, 459). IT staff may have a better understanding of the ICTs used to create the virtual space necessary for citizens and government officials to collaborate effectively; however, they may not have the time or the policy expertise necessary to administer e-governance activities competently.

Concerns that e-governance has little impact on who participates in citizen engagement are real (Schlozman, Verba, and Brady 2010). Social media technologies are user driven, which means individuals can opt out of communication networks they find unpleasant or uninteresting (Gainous and Wagner 2014, 1). Such facts highlight the concern that e-governance is simply traditional politics by other means (Gainous and Wagner 2014). The primary concerns for e-governance initiatives are citizens' access to ICTs and their ability to use them effectively (van Dijk and Hacker 2003). ICTs such as computers and mobile devices are costly, which makes them financially inaccessible for some members of society. Even as ICTs become less expensive and more accessible, many people lack the skills to use new technology effectively. In addition to asking questions related to citizens' access to ICTs and their ability to operate existing and emerging technologies, government officials must directly ask citizens if they desire e-governance services and, if so, how would they like to receive them (Gauld, Goldfinch, and Horsburgh 2010).

In considering e-governance, administrators must recognize that engagement with citizens in virtual space is significantly different from collaborations in physical space. As discussed in the previous section, many of the interactions between citizens and government officials in physical space occur in government buildings. Government ownership of these buildings allows officials to influence, if not control, many elements of the physical space. ICTs generally, and social media websites specifically are dynamic in nature, allowing users to generate and distribute content instantly. ICTs are generally not the property of the government engaged in e-governance; as a result, government officials do not have the ability to control dialogue in virtual space as they might be able to in a physical setting. Government officials engaged in e-governance should consider the distinct benefits and challenges of virtual space to citizen participation.

Kaplan and Haenlein (2010) offer several points to consider when using ICTs to engage with an external audience. First, administrators should realize that being active on social media sites is essential for success and that activity requires effort. Administrators should be strategic about which virtual settings they choose to engage with citizens (65). Second, administrators should realize that social media is about collaboration. Government officials cannot use ICTs as a virtual message board, but must see them for what they are, an opportunity to share and dialogue with citizens (65). Third, administrators must realize that the messages broadcast in virtual spaces must be consistent with those in the physical world. Inconsistency breeds confusion, which reduces legitimacy (65). Fourth, administrators should resist the urge to see the dialogue in virtual space as separate from that held in physical space because citizens will see them as the same (65). Last, administrators need to make sure social media efforts are accessible to all (66).

Even as critics question the effectiveness of e-governance, it continues to be an important means by which citizens and government officials interact. The promises of e-governance are in its ability to remove barriers to citizen engagement. It is understandable, then, that governments could look to e-governance as a means of creating virtual space for positive interactions between citizens and officials. As e-governance expands and evolves, government officials and citizens must remember ICT's "chief virtue and vice is its speed" (Barber 2001, 44). The immediacy of Internet communication allows administrators to receive prompt feedback from citizens; however, administrators must consider the benefits and drawbacks of the space e-governance creates for collaborating with citizens. Although e-governance does create new spheres of interaction between citizens and government, it is significant that individuals "interact with cyberspace by a solitary interface" (44). In considering e-governance it is imperative that administrators reflect on the effect virtual space has on the interaction between citizen and government official.

Conclusion

As more governments attempt to engage with citizens online, it becomes clear that citizen participation efforts in virtual space are distinct from those in physical spaces (Bode, Vraga, Borah, and Shah 2014). The interactions between citizens and government officials are purposeful in nature. Regardless of whether participatory budgeting activities occur in physical or virtual settings, administrators must consider the impact space will have on the interactions. In Chapter 4 we explore the major research questions driving this project as well as the methods we used to gather data about participatory budgeting initiatives within the United States.

References

Amey, M. J., and D. F. Brown. 2004. *Breaking out of the box: Interdisciplinary collaboration and faculty work*. Greenwich, CT: Information Age Publishing.

Bannister, F., and R. Connolly. 2012. Defining e-governance. *e-Service Journal* 8 (2): 3–25.

Barber, B. R. 2001. The uncertainity of digital politics: Democracy's uneasy relationship with information technology. *Harvard International Review* 23 (1): 42–47.

———. 2003. *Strong democracy: Participatory politics for a new age*. Berkeley: University of California Press.

Baumgartner, J. C., and J. S. Morris. 2010. MyFaceTube politics: Social networking web sites and political engagement of young adults. *Social Science Computer Review* 28 (1): 24–44.

Bitner, M. J. 1992. Servicescapes: The impact of physical surroundings on customers and employees. *Journal of Marketing* 56 (2): 57–71.

Bode, L., E. K. Vraga, P. Borah, and D. V. Shah. 2014. A new space for political behavior: Political social networking and its democratic consequences. *Journal of Computer-Mediated Communication* 19 (3): 414–429.

Boulianne, S. 2009. Does internet use affect engagement? A meta-analysis of research. *Political Communication* 26 (2): 193–211.

———. 2015. Online news, civic awareness, and engagement in civic and political life. *New Media & Society*. doi: 10.1177/1461444815616222.

Cornwall, A., and V. Schattan Coelho. 2007. Spaces for change? The politics of participation in new democratic arenas. In Andrea Cornwall and Vera Schattan Coelho (Eds.), *Spaces for change? The politics of participation in new democratic arenas*, 1–29. New York: Zed Books.

Dalton, R. J. 2008. Citizenship norms and the expansion of political participation. *Political Studies* 56 (1): 76–98.

Domahidy, M. R., and J. F. Gilsinan. 1992. The back stage is not the back room: How spatial arrangements affect the administration of public affairs. *Public Administration Review* 52 (6): 588–593.

Gainous, J., and K. M. Wagner. 2014. *Tweeting to power: The social media revolution in American politics*. New York: Oxford University Press.

Gauld, R., S. Goldfinch, and S. Hirsburgh. 2010. Do they want it? Do they use it? The "demand-side" of e-government in Australia and New Zealand. *Government Information Quarterly* 21 (2): 177–186.

Goodsell, C. T. 1981. The public encounter and its study. In Charles T. Goodsell (Ed.), *The public encounter: Where state and citizen meet*, 3–20. Bloomington: Indiana University Press.

——. 1988. The architecture of parliaments: Legislative houses and political culture. *British Journal of Political Science* 18 (3): 287–302.

——. 2001. *The American statehouse: Interpreting democracy's temples*. Lawrence: University of Kansas Press.

Grossman, L. K. 1995. *The electronic republic: Reshaping democracy in the information age*. New York: Viking.

Harrison, S., and P. Dourish. 1996. Re-place-ing space: The roles of place and space in collaborative systems. Proceedings of the 1996 ACM conference on Computer Supported Cooperative Work, Boston, Massachusetts.

Hatch, M. J., and A. L. Cunliffe. 2013. *Organization theory: Modern, symbolic, and postmodern perspectives*. 3rd ed. Oxford: Oxford University Press.

Hordijk, M. A. 2009. Peru's participatory budgeting: Configurations of power, opportunities for change. *Open Urban Studies Journal* 2: 43–55.

Johnson, C. 2015. Local civic participation and democratic legitimacy: Evidence from England and Wales. *Political Studies* 63 (4): 765–792. doi: 10.1111/1467-9248.12128.

Justice, J. B., J. Melitski, and D. L. Smith. 2006. E-Government as an instrument of fiscal accountability and responsiveness: Do the best practitioners employ the best practices? *American Review of Public Administration* 36 (3): 301–322.

Kaplan, A., and M. Haenlein. 2010. Users of the world, unite! The challenges and opportunities of social media. *Business Horizons* 53 (1): 59–68.

Koehler, C. T. 1980. City council chamber design: The impact of interior design upon the meeting process. *Journal of Environmental Systems* 10 (1): 53–79.

Parish, J. T., L. L. Berry, and S. Y. Lam. 2007. The effects of the servicescape on service workers. *Journal of Service Research*. doi: 10.1177/1094670507310770.

Rapoport, A. 1982. *The meaning of the built environment: A nonverbal communication approach*. Beverly Hills, CA: Sage.

Reddick, C., and D. F. Norris. 2013. E-participation in local governments: An examination of political-managerial support and impacts. *Transforming Government: People, Process and Policy* 7 (4): 453–476.

Roberts, N. 2004. Public deliberation in an age of direct citizen participation. *American Review of Public Administration* 34 (4): 315–353.

Schlozman, K. L., S. Verba, and H. E. Brady. 2010. Weapon of the strong? Participatory inequality and the internet. *Perspectives on Politics* 8 (2): 487–509.

Scott, J. K. 2006. "E" the people: Do U.S. municipal government web sites support public involvement? *Public Administration Review* 66 (3): 341–353.

Stivers, C. M. 1990. Active citizenship and public administration. In Gary L. Wamsley (Ed.), *Refounding public administration*, 246–273. Newbury Park, CA: Sage.

——. 2001. The listening bureaucrat: Responsiveness in public administration. In Camilla M. Stivers (Ed.), *Democracy, bureaucracy and the study of administration*, 222–234. Boulder, CO: Westview Press.

Theocharis, Y., and Lowe, W. 2015. Does Facebook increase political participation? Evidence from a field experiment. *Information, Communication & Society*, 1–22.

Toregas, C. 2001. The politics of e-gov: The upcoming struggle for redefining civic engagement. *National Civic Review* 90 (3): 235–240.

van Dijk, J., and K. Hacker. 2003. The digital divide as a complex and dynamic phenomenon. *Information Society* 19 (4): 315–326.

Zheng, Y., H. L. Schachter, and M. Holzer. 2014. The impact of government form on e-participation: A study of New Jersey municipalities. *Government Information Quarterly* 31 (4): 653–659.

4 Research Approach

Research Framework and Questions

This research project first offers an opportunity to demonstrate how the challenges of citizen participation are handled by local governments in the context of introducing a new approach to the budgeting process, an approach that has the potential to significantly alter the traditional rules of local government budgeting. Second, it offers an opportunity to realize a better understanding of direct citizen participation in the budgeting and decision-making processes through actual field research, an area that, according to Nabatchi (2010, 390–392; see also Guo and Neshkova 2013) is missing in this body of literature. Finally, this project offers an opportunity to demonstrate the benefits of the participatory budgeting process as it relates to municipalities, encouraging an increase in accountability, transparency, trust, and legitimacy. Participatory budgeting provides the opportunity for more citizens to be engaged and active in government through the use of social media platforms, thus strengthening and enhancing governance (Gordon, Osgood, Jr., and Boden 2016).

The overall research question guiding this project is: what are the perceptions and experiences of community leaders in the participatory budgeting process? The secondary questions are: 1) what are the perceptions and experiences of community leaders in using social media platforms to engage citizens in the participatory budgeting process?; and 2) what are the ways in which these community leaders use social media to overcome obstacles of public participation in the budgetary process? Drawing upon interviews with community leaders in Chicago, Illinois; St. Louis, Missouri; Boston, Massachusetts; Greensboro, North Carolina; and Clarkston, Georgia, this research presents these communities' experiences in interacting with both citizens and elected officials through the participatory budgeting process (Gordon, Osgood, Jr., and Boden 2016).

The Methodology: Why Qualitative Research?

Many scholars agree that citizen participation in the budgeting process is beneficial and important, but understudied (see Guo and Neshkova 2013, 343).

Further, many scholars agree that research on social media's impact on governance is also limited and understudied. Perlman (2012) found that "the promises of SMS [social media sites]—greater connectivity among citizens themselves in the coalescence of policy preferences, faster iteration, and communication of these preferences between citizens and representatives, and higher citizen participation in representative forums—have been touted but not yet delivered or well-studied" (71; Gordon, Osgood, Jr., and Boden 2016).

This research project attempts to address a broad understanding of participatory budgeting in practice and also one aspect of the gap in these interrelated bodies of literature by understanding the use of social media platforms in the participatory budgeting process. This project utilizes a qualitative approach for gathering data, due to the very limited number of cities in the U.S. that have adopted the use of participatory budgeting (Gordon, Osgood, Jr., and Boden 2016).

A lack of generalizability is often a criticism leveled against qualitative research designs (Johnson, Reynolds, and Mycoff 2008). Although the results of qualitative research may not be generalized they may be transferable to other research contexts (Anfara, Brown, and Mangione 2002). Qualitative studies permit researchers to explore complex problems with a "depth of analysis" (Gerring 2004, 348) that may not be obtainable through other means (Marshall and Rossman 2010; Gordon, Osgood, Jr., and Boden 2016).

Interviews are a valuable means of understanding the "perspectives and experiences" of interviewees to "build a solid, deep understanding" of the participatory budgeting process and the interactions between citizens and their elected officials (Rubin and Rubin 2011, 38). The best way to assure that we are presenting reliable and valid results is to listen to these interviewees, and pursue high standards of accuracy and verifiability in the presentation and analysis of their words, and in the conclusions we draw from these interviews. While we in no way expected that each community member would describe their individual experiences with participatory budgeting in the same way, we did find some convergence among the interviews and we believe this will be useful to other communities interested in understanding participatory budgeting as they work through the process of deciding whether participatory budgeting should be implemented in their own communities.

The interviews were conducted, recorded, and transcribed verbatim by one of the authors. A second person reviewed each tape and the accompanying transcripts for accuracy. Based on previous experience with qualitative research, the interviews conducted appeared to give us a good sense of what is going on with participatory budgeting in these particular communities (Gordon, Osgood, Jr., and Boden 2016).

The Participants: Who are these Community Leaders?

The individuals who were asked to participate were based on a purposive sample. Representatives in several communities that are utilizing participatory budgeting were contacted and referrals were obtained to potential interviewees who had the most knowledge about the use of social media tools in the participatory budgeting process. Each individual was first contacted by email or telephone to ascertain whether he or she was willing to participate. All of the interviews were conducted by the same person and each interview lasted about one hour (Gordon, Osgood, Jr., and Boden 2016). Each of the interviewees agreed to be identified; however, the 49th ward employees in Chicago are identified by job title only as some staffing changes have taken place and one individual no longer has an affiliation with the ward office.

A total of 14 interviews were conducted. Four interviews were conducted regarding participatory budgeting in Chicago; one interview was conducted in St. Louis; two interviews were conducted in Boston; four interviews were conducted in Greensboro; one interview was conducted in Clarkston; and two interviews were conducted with people who had a broad knowledge of participatory budgeting in several cities. Specific details on each interviewee and why they were asked to participate is presented in the subsequent six chapters.

Rarely when presenting qualitative data is one given the opportunity to present the entire content of multiple interviews and usually the researcher must summarize, organize, or give some context within which to place the interviewee's words (Sandelowski 1998). In the subsequent six chapters, each of the interview transcripts are presented with minimal interpretive and analytical intrusion (Sandelowski 1998, 377), and the reader has the luxury of listening to the words of the interviewees and drawing his or her own conclusions about participatory budgeting (Gordon 2013, 149). An analysis of the themes and the commonalities that developed from the interviews across all of the cities represented are discussed in the concluding chapter, along with the lessons learned related to creating the infrastructure needed for participatory budgeting, increasing citizen participation, and methods of assessing and increasing the impact of the participatory budgeting process.

Description of the In-Depth Interview Questions

The interview questions were used as a guide, but each interview was tailored for the particular interviewee and his or her specific realm of expertise, involvement, and experience with participatory budgeting. The interview questions were developed in part by reviewing previous research on participatory budgeting (Hadden and Lerner 2011; Gordon 2012). The questions used to guide the interviews are presented in Table 4.1.

Study Limitations

It must be noted that there are missing voices. Participatory budgeting, where it exists in the United States, is most prevalent in larger cities and has not made its way into smaller cities. Clarkston, Georgia, is the one exception. This study does not include input from cities of every population size, nor every

Table 4.1 Interview Questions

How did you first get involved in participatory budgeting and why?
As a community, do you think your community was ready for PB?
Who were the original leaders? Who is involved now? Has that changed?
Who are the stakeholders in the PB process?
What new relationships have been built? Strengthened?
What role do city employees play in the PB process?
What gets people in the room? Why do people participate? Why not?
Do you get better participation results if you ask people in person to attend?
What are the challenges to getting people together?
What are barriers to meaningful citizen participation? Transportation, lost wages, food, child care?
Does public participation remain strong throughout the process or does it fall off when work must be done?
What most surprised you about PB?
Have you been happy with the process? The projects? The outcomes?
How have you seen the process change over time?
What have been the projects that you think most impacted the community or which have been the most meaningful in building a sense of community? Which most impacted you?
How has the use of social media in the process changed over time?
How do you think you could increase the use of social media in the process?
How effective is Facebook? Twitter? Email, postcards, flyers?
The voting process? Paper ballots? Do you have online voting?
What is the early voting process like?
What will you do next year that is different than this year? In terms of use of social media platforms?
What do you see as the characteristics or benefits of PB?
Do you think PB is democratic?
Do you think PB is transparent?
Do you think PB is efficient?
Do you think PB provides education to citizens?
Do you think PB provides a sense of social justice?
Do you think PB builds community? Is inclusive of all of the diversity in your neighborhoods? Who is left out?
Do you think PB builds trust? As trust increases, does participation go up? Or as participation goes up, does trust increase?
Do you think PB builds a belief that meaningful change can occur?
Do you use or collect any feedback or survey the participants?
How will another community know if they are ready for PB? What advice would you give to another city or ward considering the implementation of PB?
What would you like other cities to know?

type or form of government, nor does it cover every geographic region in the United States. However, two of the interviewees had knowledge of the participatory budgeting process as it has developed in several cities. While we did reach out to other referrals for interviews, some either did not respond to initial emails or chose not to be interviewed. For those who declined, their reasons for declining to be interviewed were due to scheduling conflicts, not an unwillingness to be interviewed for this project (Goldstein 2002). Further, limitations of resources—time constraints and a limited travel budget of the authors, for example—also impacted the number of interviews conducted in each location (Gordon, Osgood, Jr., and Boden 2016).

Despite these limitations, the in-depth interview approach of collecting data provides a diverse and rich type of probing into our research questions, and we believe this is better than what we might have achieved using a survey instrument. The very nature of qualitative research demands that the researcher listen to the interviewee and let the "words" of the interviewee speak for him or her. The text—the transcribed words—is the data with which the researcher works. It is bulky and cumbersome and the researcher must be careful not to over-weigh or under-weigh her understanding of the words (Miles and Huberman 1994). Without overstating the results, at the very least, we can find value in the lessons learned from listening to the experiences of others about participatory budgeting. Although the results of this research cannot be fully generalized, the results can be shared with others so that they may use the information to make informed decisions about participatory budgeting within their own communities (Gordon, Osgood, Jr., and Boden 2016).

References

Anfara, V. A., Jr., K. M. Brown, and T. L. Mangione. 2002. Qualitative analysis on stage: Making the research process more public. *Educational Researcher* 31 (7): 28–38.

Gerring, J. 2004. What is a case study and what is it good for? *American Political Science Review* 98 (2): 341–354.

Goldstein, K. 2002. Getting in the door: Sampling and completing elite interviews. *PS: Political Science and Politics* 35 (4): 669–672.

Gordon, V. 2012. *Striking a balance: Matching the services offered by local governments with the revenue realities.* Washington, D.C.: ICMA.

Gordon, V. 2013. *Maternity leave: Policy and practice.* Boca Raton, FL: CRC Press/ Taylor & Francis.

Gordon, V., J. L. Osgood, Jr., and D. Boden. 2016. The role of citizen participation and the use of social media platforms in the participatory budgeting process. *International Journal of Public Administration.* doi: 10.1080/01900692.2015.1072215.

Guo, H., and M. Neshkova. 2013. Citizen input in the budget process: When does it matter most? *American Review of Public Administration* 43 (3): 331–346.

Hadden, M., and J. Lerner. December 3, 2011. How to start participatory budgeting in your city. http://www.shareable.net/blog/how-to-start-participatory-budgeting-in-your-city (accessed July 18, 2012).

Johnson, J. B., H. T. Reynolds, and J. D. Mycoff. 2008. *Political science research methods.* 6th ed. Washington, D.C.: CQ Press.

Marshall, C., and G. B. Rossman. 2010. *Designing qualitative research.* 5th ed. Thousand Oaks, CA: Sage.

Miles, M., and A. Huberman. 1994. *An expanded sourcebook: Qualitative data analysis.* Thousand Oaks, CA: Sage.

Nabatchi, T. 2010. Addressing the citizenship and democratic deficits: The potential of deliberative democracy for public administration. *American Review of Public Administration* 40 (3): 376–399.

Perlman, B. 2012. Social media sites at the state and local levels: Operational success and governance failure. *State and Local Government Review* 44 (1): 67–75.

Rubin, H. J., and I. S. Rubin. 2011. *Qualitative interviewing: The art of hearing data.* 3rd ed. Thousands Oaks, CA: Sage.

Sandelowski, M. 1998. Writing a good read: Strategies for re-presenting qualitative data. *Research in Nursing and Health* 21: 375–382.

5   Case One: 49th Ward in Chicago, Illinois

Since 2009, citizens in Chicago's 49th ward have voted on how to spend part of the $1.3 million dollars in discretionary funds that are made available annually for capital improvements in each of the city's wards. There are parameters on the type of projects that can be proposed as well as restrictions on how the funds can be spent. Each proposed project is subject to final approval by the city or relevant agencies operating in the ward. In the main, all projects have preliminary approval before going on the ballot (Gordon 2012; Moore 2012).

The steps taken to get to a decision each year include several neighborhood assemblies at which ideas are collected for possible projects. At each neighborhood assembly those in attendance are asked to volunteer to serve as community representatives. Once ideas for concrete and viable projects are further developed, community representatives who serve on steering committees begin the process of narrowing down the original list into a final list of the most promising ones. Eventually, this final list is voted on by a ward-wide assembly of citizens (Fortino 2013; Gordon, Osgood, Jr., and Boden 2016).

Anyone age 16 and older can cast a ballot, regardless of citizenship or voter registration status (Gordon 2012; Moore 2012). Proof of age and residency within the ward are required on voting day. Voting is conducted over a week-long period to provide ample opportunity to participate. The winning projects go through a final approval stage and are incorporated into the city's budget. Citizens can monitor and follow the progress of each of the projects from inception to implementation, and then on through completion (Gordon, Osgood, Jr., and Boden 2016).

The following interview with Alderman Joe Moore was conducted in 2012; the interview with Sheree Moratto, a member of the participatory budgeting leadership committee, was conducted in the spring of 2014; and the comments from city employees of the 49th ward were part of the roundtable presentation with Dr. Victoria Gordon at the American Society for Public Administration (ASPA) annual conference held in Chicago in spring 2015. Selected segments from the interviews are presented in Question and Answer format.

In the following section, the interview with Alderman Joe Moore in 2012 is presented.

Q.   One of the issues that came out of a research project regarding the fiscal health of municipalities and the "new normal" was the question, what do we know about participatory budgeting? I am particularly interested in the balance between how you get people interested in participating, and how you weigh the fact that there may be people who come out who have a particular interest or agenda, and how you get those people to look at the big picture with regard to local government finances and its limitations?

A.   Joe Moore.

An initial observation, I think a participatory budgeting model could serve well especially when government has to make very difficult decisions. I will say it's unfortunate though that government wants to get people involved when it's time to make politically unpopular decisions, rather than at a time when the question is not when you should cut, but what you should spend the money on. So, with that salvo, I would say what we have found is that people rise to the occasion and do look at the broader perspective especially if they are given real power to make real decisions. If it's simply just another "feel-good" exercise or people come and they share their opinions, but the elected officials go ahead and do what they were going to do anyway, it will have the same limited utility that those sort of processes have always had.

To a degree, what made participatory budgeting so unique is that it broke down that cynicism because we actually said to people, "you will participate in a process where you collectively are going to make decisions that the politician would honor." So I think that's the whole decision, if they're going to be involved in crafting difficult budgetary choices then for those recommendations, a system has to be set up in a way that those recommendations—that the elected officials and city officials agree to implement those recommendations of the process.

Q.   How did you get interested in participatory budgeting to begin with?

A.   Joe Moore.

I found out about it when I attended a conference in Atlanta, Georgia, back in 2007. I thought it was really neat. I had some reservations so I didn't get around to actually doing it until two years later, in 2009. But I'm glad I did. First of all it comports with my own philosophy of inclusion and giving people the power to make real decisions affecting their lives. And I also felt politically it would be very popular in a community such as mine which has a very strong history of community activism and people expressing their views in very vigorous and vocal ways.

Q.   Did you set up a committee? Tell me about the initial set-up.

A.   Joe Moore.

I knew that it wouldn't work unless everyone in our very diverse community felt that they were involved in being asked to participate. So I cast a wide net. I invited about 70 leaders from the community representing all of the different community factions from block clubs to community organizations to social service agencies to churches and other houses of worship, local school councils, park advising councils, respected leaders in various ethnic communities. I brought them all together, explained what I was thinking of doing, told them what participatory budgeting was all about, and then asked them to participate in establishing the rules for the process.

I explained that I had Josh Lerner from PBP and others from the same organization there to serve as my consultants to help guide the process, but that I would honor whatever the process and the rules were, whatever the process would come up with.

That's another important thing, you have to stretch yourself beyond the usual suspects, the media junkies I call them—the two or three hundred people that show up for anything. What made this process so unique is that we expanded beyond those folks to include people who ordinarily don't come to community meetings.

Q.   Did you have media support initially?
A.   Joe Moore.

No. It was very difficult to get the media to take us seriously. Even though there was very little—which is really unique for my neighborhood—very little cynicism among the residents in the community, there was a lot of cynicism in the media, which is I suppose what they are these days. There were a lot of questions about what if no one participates, why is it such a small percentage of the overall number? A lot of things like that. I responded to that saying, "look, this is the first year, I have no idea how this is going to work out." We may only have 100 people show up, and it was more than that, but even if it's 100 people, that's 99 more people than were making the decision before.

Ultimately, by the time we got to the election day we did get some pretty favorable media coverage that helped to boost the turnout on the actual election day, but leading up to that process it was very difficult. We only had a smattering of media attention before that time.

Q.   What is the population of your ward?
A.   Joe Moore.

We are about 56,000, a little over, almost 57,000.

Q.   Of that group that initially showed up beyond the committee that came out to vote, did you feel like they were representative of all of those groups that you described?
A.   Joe Moore.

It was a better representation than you would get at a community meeting. Not where I wanted it to be, but certainly more diverse than you normally see. And so the next two years, in particular this past year (2012), we doubled our efforts to increase participation by low-income communities, Latino communities in particular, and we have done a much better job. While it is not near the diversity of the ward, we have gotten much better at reflecting that diversity of the ward.

Q. In terms of the kinds of citizen participation that cities often point to—
they will do surveys, have a web presence. Do you use surveys to understand what people are thinking?

A. Joe Moore.

Those things are all well and good. The steering committee that
runs this process working with my office has done some outreach, taking surveys of what people want, as a way of helping to inform their
decision-making, and as to what projects they would like to propose on
the ballot.

Q. Do people normally though if they have an issue go to or through their
alderman?

A. Joe Moore.

Generally, yes. That's the Chicago way. Not everyone, but generally
we have this unique system in Chicago where people really look at us
as "mayors" of our communities, much more so than most communities
where city council members tend to have a large legislative role. Here
in Chicago, most of our responsibilities, most of the work that our staff
performs, are governmental service, housekeeping, the legislative is just
a very small portion of the overall. Even for someone like me who is a
chairman of a committee, who has a history of being an idea guy, a policy
guy, even I spend 80 to 90 percent of my time being the mayor of my
community, rather than working on policy.

Q. What do you think is the one project or thing that has come out of this that
you are the most proud of?

A. Joe Moore.

The process is what I am most proud of. The results are kind of interesting because there were a diversity of projects that were chosen by the people that are different from what I chose. When I made the decisions it was
by and large traditional nuts and bolts infrastructure. And well over half,
65 to 70 percent of the funds supported by the voters through the projects were those traditional projects. But there were also non-traditional
projects, lots of arts things were funded, a dog-friendly area was funded.
Things that I think the people, when given the power to make those decisions, have taken a much broader view of what constitutes quality of life
in the city. There are a lot of challenges about living in an urban area and
having artwork, having a place to take the dog, having community gardens to plant your vegetables, those are all pursuits that add to the quality
of life in the city. And so I think more than anything else, and when I do
presentations, I show different pie charts representing how the money
was spent when I was making decisions, and then I compare the pie chart
after the voters weighed in. Theirs was multi-colored with all these different projects and categories, and mine was one-half to streets, one-quarter
sidewalks, and one-quarter street lights.

Q. If you were to give advice to a community who was going to undertake participatory budgeting from the approach that you have taken, as

opposed to how to get rid of or limit services, what advice would you give them? Is there anything you would do differently?

A. Joe Moore.

Don't be afraid to give up power, that's my advice to the elected officials and city managers. You'll find that a process that is properly run, where if the ground rules are set clearly at the beginning, and if it is done in a transparent fashion, people will embrace it and it will make your job as a city manager, your job as the mayor, or a city council member, a little bit easier because if a particular project of someone's doesn't get done they don't blame you for that, for not getting it done, they accept it as part of this process. It really is a remarkable exercise in democracy. I think it really helps restore the connection to local government, particularly, that people have lost.

Q. Have you had any interest from other wards in Chicago?

A. Joe Moore.

I have. In fact this year (2012) we are expanding participatory budgeting to several other wards.

Q. And they would be using their money that is set aside also?

A. Joe Moore.

Yes, their discretionary funds. The same funds I had.

Q. The research in the area of citizen participation has shown that obstacles of getting people to participate are things like somebody doesn't have the knowledge, they don't think their opinion is going to be valued by the elected officials, or they don't feel that they trust the elected officials, or they have time constraints, or they are apathetic, do you buy into that? Do you get beyond that with this process?

A. Joe Moore.

This gets beyond that. It gets beyond some of that. The lack of trust, the cynicism, those sort of things, if you run the process and are confident that you are going to support your results of that process, people will rise to the occasion and you will get more participation. The big thing for me is that we have a lot of new people energized and brought into the process that have not been to a community meeting or been active in their block. Somehow they decided to participate.

In terms of time constraints, a lot of it depends on how serious this city wants to be to do it. One of the things that I am bothered by is that I don't have the vast amount of resources to provide the support needed to make this process work. In my ideal situation, you would have day care and babysitters provided so people could come to meetings. We would have food served at the meetings to attract more people or at the election day. Certain things that are a huge burden for me, but for a municipal government it's a drop in the bucket. So providing that sort of support and the outreach addresses some of those concerns. Having people to go knocking on doors, to say "come to the meeting, come on out, come and vote, this is important," that sort of thing does help.

Q. Do you think you ever will be successful in getting corporate support for that kind of thing?

A. Joe Moore.

It is possible. Right now we are working on getting private foundation support for our city-wide effort. So yes, we haven't really worked on private corporations or individuals yet.

Q. Another finding from the research on participation is that councils would say that participatory budgeting just slows the process down too much. How would you counter that?

A. Joe Moore.

I would say for people to see our government operate, they would ask "how much slower could it get?" Really, every year we have to submit to the city the same funding requests to the city, and we are able to do it. It's more time intensive, it's more work, but the payout is worth it.

Q. Any chance you would ever see this be a city-wide thing?

A. Joe Moore.

I think we are doing it incrementally. We show it worked in our ward, and so that should show that it will work in different parts of the city, and my hope is eventually the Mayor will see the wisdom of doing it and expand it.

Q. In terms of your process, is it a short enough time frame with regards to the budget that it's doable?

A. Joe Moore.

It's a year process. We have meetings in September, then community representatives appointed in December, then we have committees that come up with policy proposals in January, February, and March, and then another round of community meetings where we present the ideas to get final input from the communities, then we have the vote in May. And then our evaluation process after that.

Q. And you have been happy so far with the progress of the projects that were approved?

A. Joe Moore.

Well, it takes forever to get anything done, it's frustrating, but the money is there, it's a matter of getting the city to fund it and do it.

Q. If a city was going to start the process, would you say start about two years out? Would that be reasonable to start the process and introduce it to citizens?

A. Joe Moore.

Yes, I would say ideally six months to really educate the public, begin the process, the process it's a little over a year. So say you want to look at the calendar year budget, if they started now, they could begin the public education process in time for coming up with proposals for the next budget.

In the following section, the interview with Sheree Moratto is presented. At the time of the interview, Sheree Moratto was the chair of the participatory budgeting leadership committee for the 49th ward.

Q. How did you first get involved in the participatory budgeting process and why?

A. Sheree Moratto.

I have lived here for 20 years and my day job is that I am the sustainability director at the Rogers Park Business Alliance. We do a variety of things around economic development in the community and we learned something interesting about Rogers Park a couple of years ago. We had the councilors of real estate who came in and did a study of one of our commercial corridors and they discovered that Rogers Park has a unique demographic makeup. The community is about half old timers like me and about half newcomers like people who are either immigrants, or just coming here out of college or are moving here as students or maybe it is their first apartment away from home.

So, that being said, I own a house here, I work in the community, and so when Joe Moore started participatory budgeting, I will be honest, I at first thought it was a savvy political move, and maybe that's what it is, but there was something interesting about it.

I was not involved in the first year, other than as an observer. I went to a couple of meetings, not to share ideas for what I wanted to have done, but to hear what my neighbors had come up with. And then my whole family went to the vote because my son was old enough—he was 16 so he could vote. So that was my whole experience the first year, and I thought it would be interesting to get involved. It was also motivated by the fact that I work here as well, so I do have some vested interest in certain things happening around the community beyond being a resident.

The next couple of years I was on a committee that used to be called Arts and Other, which we successfully renamed Arts and Innovation. My committee was really vibrant and we had a great experience of working together. I knew one other person on the committee when I started, and other than that everybody was completely brand new to me and I was to them.

It was exciting and frightening to figure out how to best work together, how to go through the process of looking at what the community is asking for, and then looking at what is realistic, and then learning how the city responds or not to ideas. I enjoyed it and so I did it again the following year.

Then, I had some complaints about how the leadership committee operated and got really mad about it and had a long conversation with Joe Moore because I didn't like the way they were communicating with the committee members. I thought it was not very transparent and they were making a lot of decisions at the last minute, and then implementing them after people had already developed projects that were going to be hampered by the leadership committee's decisions because they were removed from the committees' activities themselves. So now I am the chair of the leadership committee.

Q.   And that was in the second year of your involvement?

A.   Sheree Moratto.

So the first year I wasn't involved, then two years running I was doing the Arts and Innovation Committee, and then I came onto the leadership committee this year as the chair. I have been involved for the last three years very intensely.

Q.   In terms of the leadership committee, has it evolved and changed? Who were the original leaders? Has that changed?

A.   Sheree Moratto.

This is my first and only year on the leadership committee. I came in and I don't know exactly what all was happening in the past. They had a person who did chair I think for the first couple of years. When you have an initiative that is new, that has never existed before, anything you do when you start from nothing—is something, it is fantastic. You are just in motion.

So there was something in that transition period where from my outside point of view it felt like the leadership committee was working in total isolation. So there are all of these committees of community representatives and each committee had a staff member from the 49th ward assigned to it, as well as a mentor from the leadership committee, but not all leadership committee members were involved in the committee work. So, you would have maybe five committees, fifteen people on the leadership group, and maybe three of the mentors would consistently go to the community meetings. So that you would have these groups of well-meaning citizens just working to make a great project come together, and then some crazy decision from "on high" would come down and people would just get irritated. So there was a lot of strife amongst the committees and apparently there was strife amongst the leadership committee as well although I was not there to see that.

I think it was during this transition time from the original chair to the next chair, between her and me when this happened. When I came on board as the chair it was not an easy moment in time. People did not know me, those on the leadership committee.

So, it took a couple of meetings to get people on my side. I will tell you that. But the process that I went through was to almost address it like a strategic planning process or a SWOT analysis. Just to say, you don't know me and I don't know you, so what are the strengths of this group, what are the weaknesses, what are our opportunities, what are our threats, what about the process, where have things gone well, where have they gone badly? So, I approached it as a facilitator and then I framed their work in the way that they said they wanted it to be, and then in return they were willing to play a more active role in the committees.

So, now all leadership committee members are required to affiliate with one of our community committees, so that they have a direct relationship to all of the people that are working on stuff, they can bring concerns back to the whole group for consideration, so there is not that gap that there was between the actual feet on the street and the decision-makers that there was that I had experienced before. I think that has gone better. I think the leadership committee definitely does feel more strongly related to the work that the community is doing and sees themselves truly in the role of supporters and teachers, really. I think that has been a good change that I hope remains into the future.

Q.   From the standpoint of your job in the community, have you seen new relationships in the community be strengthened through this participatory budgeting process?

A.   Sheree Moratto.

I would say what I see more is cohesion in the community, and a willingness for people to engage with each other in a way that maybe they wouldn't normally. And that can be pretty messy and scary at times. I would say what is potentially the biggest challenge I think is that most people come at this with a vested interest and they are either going to the meeting because there is something specific that they want to see happen, or they are representing an organization that has an agenda. That does not work. People have to be willing to shed those things, that stuff. As to those organizational relationships, I would say I have not seen any expansion there.

Q.   So that is one of the criticisms from people about the participatory budgeting process—that the individual's self-interest is going to get in the way of community interests. What do you say to that?

A.   Sheree Moratto.

I would say that is where the process starts. I don't think anybody is going to show up unless they have an idea or have a worry, or a fear. So they either come at it with their ego—something that they want, or something that they are afraid they are going to lose, or something that they are fearful that somebody else is going to shove down their throats. So, in my opinion it is the motivator to get people there at the initial stages because the first stage of the process is where people can just throw out any idea that they have. There is no judgment, there is no stupid idea. So you can have any idea you want. We are not going to judge. We will take all of the ideas of everyone. And that is how they get their points across, right? So, all things are compiled in that way.

So where the rubber meets the road and where that shifts is in the committee meetings. If somebody is really passionate about a concept— really, you want them to stay passionate about it, because they have to work through a thousand things in order to see what it would take to get that idea together, and can they build support for it or is there support for it, or will the city even let you do it? So in a weird way I think I came at it too from the point of view that this is going to be "everyone being selfless and wonderful and sing Kumbaya and let's all join hands and drink a Coca-Cola or whatever." But you have to come at it as who you are, and so there is conflict and there is self-interest.

I guess I would say that is just part of the creative community development experience, and there can't be a voice that becomes too strong in the long run because if the group doesn't come to consensus about putting something on the ballot, or the city budget office won't approve it, or it is not a capital expenditure, then it doesn't matter how strongly you feel about it. It will not fly. It is not an unmessy process and it certainly is not without danger. I don't think it is bad for people to come in with the attitude "I want this."

Q. In your opinion, what have been the projects that got funded that you think most impacted the community or has been the most meaningful in building a sense of community?

A. Sheree Moratto.

I probably have a difference of attitude here than Joe Moore does, I look at PB as it is capital expenditures, some of which we have to do. Some of which are just totally cool. I tend to think of it in those two realms—as we have to do streets, we have got to do the sidewalks, we have got to do the streetlights, we have to have a viable infrastructure in our community, and we have to use this money to do it. That part I think just has to exist.

On the cool end—I think most people would say the murals, we have had huge success—the first of them were done before I was involved. I was chair on the Arts and Innovation committee at the time the rest of the viaducts were voted in, and I think the community in general is really proud of having all of those murals. People point them out and people want to do a book about them. I think it is a point of community pride and I think it is amazing that we were able to take city money and funnel it directly to artists, which I love cutting red-tape so that was really awesome.

I think in the long run, in the bigger picture, the thing that will have the most impact for generations to come I hope, is the tree planting initiative which I hope will come back to the ballot in a year or two to continue to replace the trees that we are going to be losing. They are both my projects. The big one is the murals, but the longer-term one is the trees.

Q. What is the role of social media in getting people to participate and in coming out to vote? How successful have you been with Facebook, Twitter, email, versus standing in front of somebody and say will you come to this?

A. Sheree Moratto.

I would say in terms of participatory budgeting I don't have access other than posting comments. I don't have administrative access to any of the social media accounts related to participatory budgeting. I would be maximizing their use if I did, however, I don't and the staff is not able to, or maybe don't know how to maximize social media use in my opinion. I use social media extensively in my other work. I think we have a couple hundred followers on Facebook for PB. It is just not being used adequately.

Going back to what I said originally, I think you know we have old timers and newcomers, and within those two segments each one has a huge component that are very social media savvy, and do respond to Twitter and Facebook more so than Pinterest or LinkedIn. Then you have the other group that don't have email, don't know the first thing about how to even turn a computer on, and then our new immigrant community who oftentimes are coming in with limited or no experience in using social media. Some people don't even have phones, let alone a computer. So, in our community, there is definitely a good percentage of people that you have to be standing in front of and speaking their language to say "please come to this." But we could make much more impact and we could have a larger impact on a much larger percentage of people in the community who do use social media. For example, Joe's email blasts are effective and people want to please him if they are a fan of his, so if he asks them to go someplace via email, and they follow him and you will definitely get a core group to come out to something. But I think we could do a lot more to enhance community engagement.

Q.   Could you talk about the actual voting process?

A.   Sheree Moratto.

Our process is very old school. So we go out with paper ballots, and go to where there will be a concentration of people. Grocery stores, CTA stations, rapid transit or the commuter line train stations. Since people age 16 and up can vote sometimes maybe a couple of stops at our two schools that have high school programs. We had the idea this year of going a little bit mobile and I am waiting to hear a final plan on that at our meeting coming up in a couple of weeks about really going out—getting a couple of magnetic signs that will fit on anybody's car and go out and drive around, and trying to use Twitter to announce ourselves. Not that it will be worth it because I am not sure how many followers there are but we will try to do something a little bit more hip as opposed to the paper ballot. It will still be a paper ballot, it will still be the tallying method and that is how the voting is going to go this year is my current understanding.

The Stanford University people, they came and talked to the leadership committee about a month ago, and described how this would work—sort of like a SurveyMonkey except it is specific to the PB process. They then came back for our last public expo, that is where the committees tell a community what projects they are thinking of putting on the ballot and take last ideas or concerns from the community about whether or not there is interest or should be refinement to them.

I think it looks like a totally fine system, and they are trying to accommodate the sort of idiosyncrasies that have developed with the tally system that it is hard for people to relinquish. Like allowing people to actually vote to spend more than $1 million dollars, but then only counting up to a million dollars. So somebody comes in and they vote 100 percent for streets, and they say well they told me I have four more votes. We say "go right ahead but it is not going to count." But they said, "well they said it would." Anyway, it seems like a pretty straightforward process that would be a fabulous alternative for people who are comfortable with computers.

However, a couple of our leadership committee members had a different view. They either are not themselves comfortable with working on a computer or work with communities like the Spanish-speaking community—many members of whom do not have computer savvy skills. When we saw the Stanford demonstration, people were like "awesome, let's do it" and these other folks were like "for you and me yes, but I know people who don't read English, don't speak English, maybe are illiterate in any language." So, figuring out ways to again make this accessible to the broadest community that we can will entail multiple formats to really be effective.

Q. The ballot, when they turn them in, is it anonymous?

A. Sheree Moratto.

When you come in you have to prove that you live in the ward, so although your name is not taken down and there is not a checklist, you just have to have an ID or even a household bill, just to prove you live in the ward and that you are over 16. That is just a check without any verification. Your ballot doesn't require any information. You just make your choices with a pencil on the ballot. They set up the portable voting booths like you are doing an actual election, which is fun. They put it in the big ballot box at the end.

Q. Do you try to collect email addresses or their addresses to know who is represented or which areas are represented by neighborhood, or are less represented?

A. Sheree Moratto.

At every community meeting, whether it's to gather ideas or to show people what we have in mind, there is always a sign-in sheet that requests telephone and email address, but not street address.

Q. With immigrants, any illegal immigrant issues?

A. Sheree Moratto.

We don't look at voter registration records at all, and in fact that is one of the big selling points that we say "you do not have to be a citizen, you do not have to be registered to vote, you only have to be 16 or over and live in the 49th ward."

Q. Next year when you get ready to start with project solicitations, how will you advertise that these are the dates and places you will meet?

A. Sheree Moratto.

There are flyers in English and Spanish, and Joe Moore will do an email blast. The 49th ward might post something on Facebook because emails are tied to that page. I think they do go out throughout the entire community, and there are a lot of unique regulations about how you can post flyers in residential communities in Chicago, so they have a person who knows the rules and regs who goes around and tapes these flyers to houses, apartment buildings throughout the entire ward, so it does go everywhere.

There have been five or six community meetings last fall to gather ideas in different areas throughout the ward, and they are usually park districts, a church, places that are not confrontational for people to go to. This definitely appeals to the Caucasian population, and it is really tough to get anybody involved in the immigrant population in the community. We do have a Spanish language committee that is headed up by two Spanish speakers, who are native Spanish speakers. They are trying to find how you bring this to the Hispanic community in a way that makes sense, and then how you take the ideas from that group and then pull them into the whole picture.

We also have a similar initiative with youth committees this year. In both cases we don't have a good model yet. So, what I would do personally, I would do a whole lot more with social media and with person-to-person conversations. I think social media is the low-hanging fruit.

Q.   Do you think the youth committee is open to using social media, that they would still be more likely to respond well to Facebook or Twitter?

A.   Sheree Moratto.

I think the youth concept needs an entirely different process, but I don't know what it is yet. I used to be a high school teacher and they are just a different thing. You cannot take an adult process and say "okay we are going to do the same thing." It is completely antithetical to everything that they stand for, so that to me needs a whole bunch of work. I don't think that pulling them into the process that currently exists with social media would have an impact. I think they need their own program.

Q.   Do you have somebody who is leading that charge?

A.   Sheree Moratto.

We have two great people who started leading that charge and it was depressing so they gave it up.

Q.   Can you think of young people who did get involved maybe more from wanting to be involved in the community?

A.   Sheree Moratto.

A couple, but from my experience, and I don't think this would be surprising to anybody that works with younger citizens, is that they have an idea, they see a need, have an idea about how to fix it or make it better or change it, and then they move on. It is hard for people to want to just keep standing there. This is a year-long process which is ridiculous, and in that year somebody is going to go from age 15 to 16, from a sophomore to the end of their junior year, they are getting ready for college, they can't relate to something that goes on that long, in my opinion.

Q.   At the end of the process, after the votes are tallied, is there a debriefing? How are winning projects announced?

A.   Sheree Moratto.

This is a party neighborhood, so yes, there will be a party—multiple parties. Joe does this thing called "Follow Me Friday's" and normally it is done at local businesses. The Friday before the big community vote, we have been doing the early voting at random locations leading up to this, so the Friday before, Joe has a huge bash at his office, you can come vote and eat free food. The next morning we go to set up the voting area in the school cafeteria that we use, and then after the voting the staff stays there and does all the tallying. The rest of us leave and wait for a tally. Results are announced there at the after party, and then Joe does post results on Facebook pretty immediately as well, and then Joe will do an email blast about the results the Monday after. Results are announced immediately.

Q.   And when the results are announced, how do you handle it if someone is really unhappy? Do they express that or do they just say "this is the participatory budgeting process"?

A.   Sheree Moratto.

You get a range of emotions—like the guy who didn't get funded, he didn't come to the after party. I think he knew it wasn't going to get selected, but we had a deal that I would let him know as soon as I knew the answer. I have never seen anybody go off or be real unhappy or upset. People get really sad if they don't get selected, but the nice thing is that eventually, in very short order, they release how many votes everything got so you can see, "wow if I just had two more votes, then my project would have surpassed this." So, what I have seen in most of those situations is that people are motivated to come back then the next year and try to get more votes.

Q.   I would like to ask you about the characteristics or benefits of participatory budgeting. Do you think participatory budgeting is transparent?

A.   Sheree Moratto.

Yes, I think it is true.

Q.   Is participatory budgeting efficient?

A.   Sheree Moratto.

No, because it takes forever and a day, just the time. Let's face it you could run this as a charrette. There is something to be said for getting back together a million times, but it is not efficient. It is not a bad thing, but that is what it is.

Q.   Does participatory budgeting provide education to citizens?

A.   Sheree Moratto.

True.

Q.   Does participatory budgeting contribute to a sense of social justice?

A.   Sheree Moratto.

Yes.

Q. Does participatory budgeting build community?

A. Sheree Moratto.

Yes.

Q. Is participatory budgeting inclusive of all of the diversity of immigrants in your neighborhoods? Who is left out of the process?

A. Sheree Moratto.

Not really left out, but I think the resident requirement thing is important, and good but at the same time we have many other people who have a vested interest in the community like business owners and people that are not really represented. Now, I don't know if that is a bad thing, but I have wondered if there is a way to get input from that community as well. They are not necessarily going to be able to be at a meeting at 7 p.m. if they have a restaurant, but they could share their ideas at the beginning of the process.

Q. Does participatory budgeting build trust?

A. Sheree Moratto.

Yes, I think that is true.

Q. Does participatory budgeting build trust in government?

A. Sheree Moratto.

In typical Chicago fashion, what it builds trust in is the attitude, "well yeah we knew the city operated like that."

Q. Does participatory budgeting build a belief that meaningful change can occur?

A. Sheree Moratto.

Yes.

Q. What advice would you give to another city or ward?

A. Sheree Moratto.

I have not been asked, but I think I should have been. I think the interesting thing here is that since this concept started in the 49th ward and even though we have miles to go before we really make this the best possible experience it could be, we are way far ahead of where the others are because we are going, and we are just a few years ahead of them in the process.

Q. Do you want to add anything?

A. Sheree Moratto.

It is not easy, and so it appeals to idealists, and then once you get into the muck and mire of the whole thing it can become overwhelming, and if you don't have political will behind it you are not going to get anywhere. We still see after five years of doing this, Joe's chief of staff is always in the position of contacting the city budget office, and saying "we would like to plant 100 trees, will you consider that a capital expenditure?" Trees, yes, shrubs, no. But it takes six months to get them to say that. And so staff keeps having to push the boundaries and the envelope and run the gamut of dealing with responses like "we are not going to let you spend money on that, it is a stupid idea."

For social media use, figuring out which outlets would be helpful. I have some ideas about how to do it in a way that it was not a daily thing—maybe something for scheduling, to write a script to plan this out a bit. Helping people understand how this could be a support rather than another layer of work is going to be the key.

Q. Were you encouraged by the Mayor's promise to create a position focusing on participatory budgeting in Chicago?

A. Sheree Moratto.

We will see! I think they will hire somebody, but it will just be somebody else that staff will have to talk to. Another layer, but that is my cynical self.

In the following section, selected comments by 49th ward staff members are presented. One is the staff assistant for Alderman Joe Moore, and has been in her position for four years, and the other is the chief of staff to Alderman Joe Moore and has been in her position since 2007. The staff members presented their information in question and answer format, so the questions they answered were based on the roundtable outline, or came directly from the conference audience. The staff members are referred to below by their job titles for ease of clarification regarding who is speaking during the roundtable presentation.

Q. What is Participatory Budgeting?

A. Chief of Staff.

It is a democratic process in which community members directly decide how to spend part of a public budget. I think the most important part here is the "directly." It's almost shocking actually that the elected officials, when they decide to do this process, they actually take themselves out of the process—they eliminate themselves, they are gone. And that is really scary for a lot of elected officials, maybe every elected official, because they say "I'm not going to make any decision whatsoever, the community is going to make the decision." And it's a binding decision. So it's not legislative democracy, it's not representative democracy, they aren't representing us anymore in terms of, "oh these people would like day care, these people would like more streets"—they say "I'm taking myself out of it and the people are going to decide." And I don't know if you could call it revolutionary, but it's certainly very different than how most people work with government within the United States.

Participatory budget is making real decisions about real money. That's super important. It's real money, it's a piece of a budget. It could be $100,000 or as little as maybe $25,000 or as much as one million dollars. I don't know of many places where it goes much above that.

It's not a consultation, but what I always tell people is that it's binding. You make this decision, even if you come up with some sort of whack-a-doodle project that the alderman thinks is not a good use of money, the alderman or the legislator or the mayor has said from the beginning that is what is going to happen. You decide it. It's going to happen, period.

And then you have to do that too because otherwise the trust that you have built with the community is going to be lost.

Q. Is it an annual cycle?

A. Chief of Staff.

It's usually an annual cycle, it can be shorter than that. There is a high school that's going to do it in probably a process of about two months, but usually annually. But the point is very important, that it's not a one-off event, like we are going to try it once and if it doesn't work we aren't going to try it again. Instead it's "we are going to try it once and we're going to make it better and better every year."

Q. Is it a part of a budget?

A. Chief of Staff.

Actually the first year that we did it with the whole budget, but it works best if it's part of a budget. The first year our budget for this was $1.3 million dollars, and that is what we get from the city for infrastructure. The alderman, we pleaded with him not to put up the whole $1.3 million but he thought that it would be just great to give everything to the people. We found ourselves then with repairs to be made, special projects that came up, cost overruns, and we had nothing extra then. So it's not a good idea to put up the entire budget to do participatory budgeting, it's normally part of a budget.

Q. How does it work? What are the stages of the process?

A. Chief of Staff.

In Chicago there are 50 wards, with about 50,000 to 60,000 people per ward. You get residents together of a ward. You get the people in whatever district together, you try to encourage people to come to these meetings, people sit down, volunteer to sit down and develop projects, come up with ideas, and then develop those projects. When the projects are developed, finally, it whittles down to what is on the ballots. These are the proposals that people really feel are important to put out there. People vote, whatever wins, wins, and then over the next period of time, for us it is annual, then you work with the city, or the state, or the county or whatever your legislative body is to actually reify those projects to make sure they are installed to the best of your ability.

Question from audience. Does that legislative body get a certain amount of money?

A. Chief of Staff.

Yes, every ward in Chicago gets $1.3 million dollars for infrastructure improvements. That's how it works here, it's going to work differently elsewhere. But this was pre-decided for 20 years. Chicago used to have a system where downtown made all the decisions about infrastructure. And so what happened was that the richer areas, and in particular the whiter areas of Chicago, got the streets paved with gold, and then there were dirt streets in other places. And so there was a push back in the early 1990s to equalize it. And so now every ward gets the same amount of money for infrastructure.

Q. Where else has participatory budgeting worked? What is the history of participatory budgeting?

A. Staff Assistant.

Alderman Moore brought it here in 2009 and it started here in the 49th ward in Chicago so this is the first time participatory budgeting has been in the United States. So from there, two years later, it went to New York City, where four districts took up PB, then spread out to eight districts, and today they have 24 districts that are working with participatory budgeting. We also have the city of Vallejo, California, where they started participatory budgeting after coming out of bankruptcy, and then in 2014 in St. Louis they also started another PB project. Boston created the first city-wide PB youth project.

Question from audience.   So it's general fund money, and not earmarked or special revenue money?

A.   Chief of Staff.

For us it is kind of special, actually it's a bond issue, but again every city is different. It's wherever someone is going to cough up a piece of a budget and make it available. So for us, though, it's actually limiting.

In Chicago these are funds for capital projects only. Because this is a bond issue, and whatever they put into that bond issue's limitations, we can only spend it on bricks and mortar. We cannot spend it on school teachers, we cannot spend it on laptops. Definitely not operating costs. It's a real limitation because if we could do things like get laptop computers or get iPads for the local schools, people would be running to join us in terms of their interest in it. It's a limitation for us in Chicago to get people interested because people think—it's streets, it's lights, why doesn't the alderman just make the decision? Why are you asking us? Isn't that your job?

On the other hand, some of the other projects that have come up are far more creative projects. But it is limited to, not even repairs, it has to be things that are bricks and mortar and that will stay there for at least ten years. So working backwards, it's $1 million dollars, of the actual budget which is $1.3 million and we have decided that the $300,000 would be used for emergencies, for cost overruns, for odds and ends that come up.

Where we are situated is northeast Chicago, we are at the top edge of Chicago, right by Evanston and the lake. We are the northeastern corner, and we have all the beaches along there too, which is fabulous. We have 57,000 residents. What's really important with the ward is the diversity. We have a very stable diversity there of African-Americans, whites, and Latinos, and Africans and Haitians and other Caribbean peoples. But it has been about 38–39 percent white, 28 percent African-American, 24 percent Latino, but has been that way for years and years. It's not a flash in time and then the property is all going to flip, we have a very stable diversity that we have there, which if you know anything about Chicago is very unusual.

Q. How does the process work?

A. Staff Assistant.

We start every year in the fall with neighborhood assemblies in October and November. We do nine assemblies, six in English, one in Spanish, and at two high schools that we have in the ward, and the idea is to identify project community needs, and then they listen to the community. We have some volunteers that will later develop these ideas into proposals.

These volunteers meet from December to April and they divide into different committees, we have parks and environment, traffic and public safety. We also have a committee of only Spanish language speakers and another group of youth. And the purpose of that is for them to develop proposals. They will look at presentations and refer back to the community at the project expos in April. And then after we do three project expos, two in English, one in Spanish. Then we get back together and we finalize and prepare the ballots for the vote.

The vote, we have an early voting week before the community voting day. During that time we go to different places of work, churches, parks, train stations, grocery stores, trying to capture the vote of the people that live in the ward. We also have voting every day in the office and people in the community can come. After that the projects that win up to $1 million dollars are implemented, and this is an on-going process that we also try to get the community involved in.

Q. What are some examples of the projects?

A. Staff Assistant.

Some projects are eligible and some are ineligible. We are limited in a way, we cannot use the money for operational costs, we cannot hire someone to work in a day care, we cannot provide services, we cannot buy computers, we cannot spend money on or repair private property or facilities. The eligible projects are the basic infrastructure, street resurfacing, lights, sidewalks, but we also can do park improvements, community gardens, and bike lanes.

Q. How do you involve the youth? What are the goals of involving the youth?

A. Chief of Staff.

High schools are really challenging, but we do want to involve youth in our programs. The idea of going to youth, at least what we have in mind, is first of all when you go there it gives them a sense of reality. I can't think of any other situation when they're going to get hands-on experience with real money and real government. I mean, when I went to school we had mock trials, we had mock supreme court, mock legislatures and all these kinds of things and everything was "mock." And that was supposed to teach us how to do things, and that's fine and we passed legislation but nothing ever meant anything. But here we are actually going to students and saying if you develop projects and vote on them along with the community, this is what's going to happen with $100,000 or with $50,000 or whatever it is that your projects are valued at. And we hope that inspires them into a whole different mindset.

Q.   What about empowerment?

A.   Chief of Staff.

Empowerment is something that UIC [University of Illinois at Chicago] has been working very closely with our efforts here in Chicago, and has been doing a lot of analysis of—do people in the regular PB process then become more empowered to get more involved in government? Do they vote more? Do they join neighborhood groups more? Do they do fundraising for neighborhood groups more?

Also with regard to empowerment, simply that in order to have the best projects that best serve the community, you want to have every group empowered to make those suggestions and to vote. You want seniors to vote, you want youth to vote, you want disabled people to vote, you want people who speak in different languages to vote, and in that way you can come closer to this holy grail of creating the best projects with the limited funds that you have, and so that's why it's so important for us to have youth.

And the best place to find youth is in the high schools. There are two high schools that we work with.

We've gone to each of them for several years and it has been challenging, there's no question about it. It's really, really challenging. I think one of the biggest challenges is simply getting people interested because it's about infrastructure. And you go in there, and they don't drive, some of them maybe they walk to school, they don't know the whole neighborhood, some of them are from outside of the neighborhood and they can participate in the decision-making process, but then they can't vote. So it's very challenging just to get them interested in what we're doing.

Where we have actually had the most success so far was last year in the "get out the vote" effort, so as opposed to the development of the projects, like what street here do you think has the most potholes—they don't drive on these streets. But when it got to the vote, we had laptops set up and a voting area in the main rotunda of the high school and they were really excited, they had t-shirts, and they had prizes and really got people out to vote.

The other thing that we found was that if you can work with another organization either inside the school or that comes to the school, it helps. We have an organization called Mikva Challenge, it's a city-wide organization, named after Abner Mikva, the federal judge. They use empowerment, they have all sorts of training with youth, they have classes during the year, they do research projects. In our office almost every summer we have a Mikva intern, a high school intern. They place them all throughout elected officials' offices in the summer. It is an amazing organization and they have adopted the neighborhood high school and to work with the PB process there. That is just amazing for us. We have limited time, and to be able to have this group that is there and has regular meetings there and they talk about process. It has really, really helped us.

The last thing about high schools, the principal who is enamored with the process, has made a decision that after the regular vote is over in April, the community vote, he is setting up a process for the students to vote on Chicago Public School money. He's going to put up $25,000 of his own budget for the students to develop projects and to vote on. And so there will finally be an all-high school project, actually it will be freshmen, sophomore, juniors, because seniors are going away. The other exciting thing about that is everything is going to be online—there will be no paper ballots. They can have as intense as possible the use of social media within the student body in order to build excitement and get ideas. I think this is unique, I don't believe this has happened anywhere else. It's going to be a very exciting thing to watch.

Q.   Can you tell us about the voting process and the ballots?
A.   Staff Assistant.

The ballots are in three languages. The ballot is in English, Spanish, and Russian. We also have six buildings where the people who live there are mainly Russian speakers, so we try to target the population and get them more involved so they can vote. So we went there and they cast the vote in those places.

In the ward everyone is able to vote, you just have to be 16 years or older regardless of immigration status, so everyone can vote. You just have to prove that you live in the ward. So how can you prove it? So you come with your ID, or if they don't have ID they may have a document issued from some central American countries, that the consulates issues that Visa, and it has an address on it, or they can also come with their lease or a bank statement or a piece of mail that has their name on it and also their address included.

The voters in this area, we always ask the voters to choose how to spend $1 million dollars of Alderman Joe Moore's discretionary money. We tell them that $300,000 is used for emergency or cost over-runs. Last year we set up the mobile vote at 31 sites, these are at the train stations. The purpose of this is we try to include as many people as we can in the process.

If you look at an actual ballot, it asks people to choose what percentage of the money from $0 to $1 million dollars they want to spend, and how they want to spend it on improving the streets, lights, alleys and sidewalks. They can choose 50 or 100 percent. We also include a place so they can prioritize the streets that need to be resurfaced.

On the other page, we are asking how the rest of the money should be spent. We are asking them to vote for up to four projects, and the projects with the most votes, up to the $1 million dollars, are the ones that are going to be implemented.

Question from the audience.   How are you developing the street paving priorities?

A.   Staff Assistant.

Through the year the members of that committee, the community reps, have been developing a database and they have been grading all the streets in the ward. We have 350 blocks. They go by blocks. So they have a system, they go from one to four. And they check every street and based on their standards to grade by, that is how we prioritize.

Question from audience.   How are other priorities set?

A.   Chief of Staff.

We always have a meeting once a year with water and transportation to find out where other work will be done. We try to work it around how the whole city is doing planning too, but they might be putting a new water line on one street a year from now and maybe that street is in terrible shape, then we don't put that on the ballot for that year because we know that street is going to get repaved anyway.

So it's this sort of game that we play back and forth about what would the city be doing with other projects that are coming in, occasionally federal money comes in, one of our biggest, Sheridan Road down by the lake got repaved several years ago, with Stimulus money, so all of a sudden we didn't have to do one project. That was huge.

Let me also say that if people are given a street or a dog park, or a street or a community garden or a street or an underpass mural to choose from, they're always going to go for the flashy stuff. Not always, but they would like that, because we don't have that in our community. This is what we really want. Then you forget there's no money left for the basics, and so we said okay we are going back to only basics.

And that's why there's this system, it's a little crazy, because how it works is you go from 0 percent to 100 percent on your vote, but it's confusing to people because if they vote for 100 percent of the budget, we still allow them to go over to the other side of the ballot and vote for projects. That doesn't disqualify them, we don't ask them to do the math. We don't say, okay you did $600,000, you have $400,000 left, we say just vote. We take the average of all those percentages, and it has come out to about 60 percent for streets at most since the first year, so that leaves the other 40 percent for the other side of the ballot.

Question from the audience. I imagine the street projects and costs go up and get priced out based on city contracts? How do the price estimates on other projects work? How do you get estimates?

A.   Staff Assistant.

We also work with the sister agencies because if it's park related we are in contact with the Chicago Park District. When the committee groups are meeting, the community reps, we set up meetings with an expert where people from the city come and meet with these groups, and explain how things work, and discuss their own projects that they want to develop. This is part of the research process that they work through at this time.

We have these meetings with the Chicago Park District, the department of transportation, and cultural affairs. We try to cover all this. Because our office is between the city and the community we also look for more information to help our volunteers with the proposals. We also have a database for the streets, alleys and the sidewalks. This year we incorporated alleys in the database because our alleys are in terrible shape. All these years we have been paying attention to the streets, so now that the streets are in better shape than before, we are putting more effort and emphasis into the alleys and sidewalks.

A.   Chief of Staff.

Let me add that we call it "menu" money. And it's really a menu. They send us this big thick menu. It is like going to a restaurant. And it shows you it's going to cost this much for a block of repaving, this much for a block of sidewalk, it is going to cost this much for bike lanes to be painted on, and you can flip through it. And that's what most aldermen do, is they flip through it, and say I'd like one of those, and I want two of those, and I would like that on the side, and I'm up to $1.3 million dollars. So most of the costs, anything to do with transportation, which is a lot including all sorts of bike-related things, come through this menu.

You just go to the menu for public transit, and for the parks, for cultural affairs, you go to those agencies to get special pricing for some of the projects. The thing that's shocking to the people is the prices. You would think $1.3 million dollars is going to go really far, but one block of repaving is over $60,000. It's shocking. We got a new playground, and it took two years and it cost $450,000. And people just go nuts, they say, "I just had some swings put in my backyard and that was $2,000, why don't I get that guy to come to the park and put the swings in?" We say you can't do that. Well, one swing in the city costs $10,000 so you can't do that. And it does. I don't know what to say. We are so immersed in it that we can say a swing costs $10,000, no problem, but it really is absurd. And of course that's paying for overhead and administration costs and they aren't getting enough tax funding. We know what's happening. So you're saying $1 million dollars you should get a whole lot done with that, but we really don't get a whole lot done with $1 million dollars.

Question from the audience. When people see that there is such difficulty, when they go home, and in my city you have these conversations, and you talk about having police officers versus a swimming pool in a crime-ridden area, but the light goes on in people's heads that says, "wow, we have to make a tough decision." Do people here come to these understandings?

A.   Chief of Staff.

In a way it's depressing how little you get with your money, on the other hand it is a real wake up that people say government really does cost money, this is really serious stuff that we are making decisions about. It kind of helps us at an alderman's office when people are saying, "oh why don't we have this in our ward" and then they come to these meetings and they go, "oh, we can only get this many streets paved, we can only get this many alleys fixed." In a way, it takes some of the pressure off us actually for people to be informed.

Q.   Let's move to a discussion of electronic voting.

A.   Chief of Staff.

This is so cool. This just started last year. This is quite new. The alderman, he ran into some people from Stanford University, and they were working on crowdsource democracy and they were really excited with participatory budgeting. What they wanted to do was create electronic platforms for voting and this is what we have done so far, but then ultimately electronic platforms could be used for all sorts of outreach and social media and that kind of stuff. But the first step is voting and that's what we did last year. It was an amazing team made up of a social scientist from Finland, an electrical engineer from India who was also one of the founders of Twitter, and a programmer from Thailand so this is the team they sent to us. They flew them in and out from Stanford, they came with laptops to share with us that we could keep during the process. And they developed this program to have an electronic ballot.

Q.   And what does an electronic ballot do versus a paper ballot?

A.   Chief of Staff.

For one thing it gives you a preview. People could go to this ballot and play around with it at home through a link. They could think about how they are going to vote in advance, talk about it with friends, share it. It's interactive, there is a map with it so when you're voting on streets, the map would highlight the different streets so you could see where the different projects would be.

So we have our favorite thing which is the randomization. Last year we had seven projects after streets and alleys, and ten this year. Every time the ballot popped up, the projects were in a different order. With this, then the seven projects got randomized. We all know from voting that in electoral politics if you have the first position in a ballot you get an automatic bump right there. It even turned out that there was a project, a little mini soccer field that was on the ballot, and with the randomized vote it made the cut for funding, and it was low on the paper ballot, and it didn't make the cut. It just shows that if you randomize you actually do get a different outcome. There's nothing we can do about it, because the paper ballot is the ballot.

I want to emphasize that it's electronic but it's not online. It's online in terms of the preview, because who cares who looks at it. But we have run up against that problem of residency that in order to vote you have to prove you are a resident. We have not figured out a way yet of having people sign up and prove if they live in the ward or not, and we have to have people who live in the ward in order to vote, and then we have to verify the age limit too.

So they are coming back and working again with us this year. They have also extended this platform and variations of the platform to Vallejo, to New York City, to other places. They eventually want to have an online platform that people can pick and choose how they make up the ballot from that. Their dream of course is to have an app, but that gets back to the residency situation. They're going to be working with us on the high school project where we're going to be using school money and that's where they can really let loose and have a real wrap-around project that has both social media and online voting.

Question from audience. So, you would establish residency first, and then go to early voting?

A. Chief of Staff.

You always have to show residency. We have talked about things like we'd mail you a postcard, like you registered with us, and then we mail you a postcard and that has a code on it, and it would come to your address which would have to be in the ward. Then you have the code to vote. But this stuff takes money. We haven't figured out a cost-effective way of doing that.

Question from audience. What is the cost of running this process?

A. Staff Assistant.

It take a lot of people. I'm dedicated to participatory budgeting, my time is not enough. I am doing more than 40 hours of work, I'm sometimes doing 60 hours of work when it is close to the voting time. I'm making sure that everything is in place. I do what people don't see. I'm invisible during the process. I make sure everything is working, making sure the volunteers are working and doing their job, and selecting projects. There are a lot of things in between, a lot of layers.

A. Chief of Staff.

I put 25 percent of time into this. There's another person in our office that deals with youth, we each do a little bit of it, but he really does a lot with the high schools. How aldermanic offices work, the alderman currently has a committee, just like in Congress, you get more staff when you have a committee. We are really lucky right now, we wish we could pay our staff assistant here more, but it's a decent job with benefits though. Before the alderman had a committee, we had students who had just graduated from college and they would work with us for a year for $24,000 per year with no benefits and then leave. We are in great shape with the committee, with the mayoral elections if there's any fall out and we lose the committee, then we are back to grad students doing it.

Like anything else, once you have the money and the staff you keep expanding, so we have the 31 voting sites, we are working with Stanford, we're working with two high schools, we wouldn't be able to do all those things if Alderman Moore didn't have a committee. It's expensive—staff wise. There's the printing, we get help on this from PB Chicago and they have allocated money to support participatory budgeting in Chicago and there are three wards that are doing it right now so they printed the ballots for us.

We don't know about final Mayoral election results, runoffs are still happening. The runoff is April 7th [2015] both for the Mayor and for 19 wards. So we don't know how many new people there will be committed to participatory budgeting. The problem is again the resources. A regular alderman's office has three staff people plus the money to get maybe a part-time person or a couple very low paid part-time people.

And you've got to do infrastructure, education, arts, licensing, zoning, all the stuff, and people say and PB? An alderman can go through that menu in like two days and hand it in and get their stuff done. Or we're going to use an entire year with nine neighborhood meetings, three project expos, and 31 voting sites. They look at that and think there's no way.

Question from the audience. How would this work with having another organization help?

A.   Chief of Staff.

Part of it really is creating a PB-lite that can be implemented that would work through maybe three neighborhood meetings, one expo, three days of voting. It's tough. Or work with another community.

A.   Staff Assistant.

The 22nd ward in Chicago is working with a community organization. This organization works very closely and is backing up the 22nd ward office. They are doing my job so it's easier for the office to maintain and support the process because otherwise it's very intensive and time-consuming. They do most of the outreach which is also very important in this process. They support the discussions and run the committees. I haven't seen my other counterpart because they are really swamped with work. It also has to do with the kind of community they do have. There are some communities that are more active than others, so when you have a good leader the work in the office is a little bit easier. This helps with the outreach. In some cases the wards have different communities and the way it is spread out it is difficult to do face-to-face outreach. These are things you have to take into account when you are trying to do this kind of process.

Q.   What are some of the projects that have been completed?

A.   Staff Assistant.

In 2010, the community voted for 13 mural underpasses and then it took two years to put it together, and why? Because the city and our office had to create the process to make it happen. After we got the proposals we used a voting system to choose the 13 murals, and this is one of the projects I've been working on.

In 2012, I was able to work with this again because the community voted for 20 more mural underpasses and we thought "oh this is good, we have this ready to go because we have the process done from before and have the experience behind us," but no we have to start all over again.

There was also a change of administration. It was tedious, but we were able to do it. Now, we have 33 mural underpasses in the ward. It is a beautiful collection from not only local artists, but also international artists.

We did a playground. The community voted to get this park done. While we were trying to implement it the cost went up, so we had to put it up again and get permission to try it again, and then we were able to build it. The playground cost $450,000.

Another project is the tree planting project. We planted more than 100 trees, and the project lasted only three months to implement so that was an easy project.

But Paw-ttawattomie Dog Park, located in Pottawattomie Park, this is a project that took two years to be implemented. With this project the community had to be involved, because there is maintenance and they also have a park board, and it sometimes doesn't end when the project is done.

The library carpet project is pretty much straightforward, but on top of that, deciding on the carpet, I also used this as an opportunity to get other things from the city for the library. We got the walls painted, we got the elevator repainted. So this was very exciting. So now we have a new carpet and a library that looks really nice. This was a very interesting project. This project was done in only three months.

Another project that we have in the ward is for beach access for people with disabilities. In the ward we don't have many people who are disabled, but in spite of that people were very concerned and tried to give the opportunity to other people to use the beaches. This project was on the ballot three times. And people are using it. The ramp can be used for wheelchairs, for mothers with strollers, and I've seen people practicing yoga there. It is really nice.

Figure 5.1 CTA Underpass Mural at Pratt, Tribute to the Fish of Lake Michigan painted by Amanda Paulson

Source: Courtesy of 49th Ward, Chicago, Illinois.

Figure 5.2 METRA Underpass Mural at Greenleaf, Faces of Rogers Park painted by Christopher Royal

Source: Courtesy of 49th Ward, Chicago, Illinois.

Figure 5.3 Touhy Park Playground

Source: Courtesy of 49th Ward, Chicago, Illinois.

Figure 5.4 Tree Planting

Source: Courtesy of 49th Ward, Chicago, Illinois.

Figure 5.5 Paw-ttawattomie Dog Park at Pottawattomie Park

Source: Courtesy of 49th Ward, Chicago, Illinois.

Figure 5.6 Rogers Park Library New Carpet

Source: Courtesy of 49th Ward, Chicago, Illinois.

Question from audience. Are there trade-offs sometimes where you buy the material and the park district does the labor and maintenance? Is there a lot of collaboration?

A.   Chief of Staff.
      Yes, and in some cases, they do maintenance.
A.   Staff Assistant.
      We have been learning how the city works in different ways than we did before. And now we know there are other things that we can ask for that we did not even know we could ask for it. This is leveraging other projects that we have now in the ward.

Question from audience. If I want something on the ballot do I need to know about community boards like with the dog park example?

A.   Chief of Staff.
      Dog parks are pretty rare actually. Community gardens and dog parks are the only two that require that, and it can't even go on the ballot unless you already have a committee in place. That has to come before it goes on the ballot.
Q.   What are the challenges of participatory budgeting?
A.   Chief of Staff.
      This is really important when you live in the ward and go to these meetings because people think that things happen magically, of course, when they don't. Each project takes one to three years to complete. Estimated costs are subject to change. The work of utility companies can often delay project completion. The PB process often introduces projects that have never been done before by the city agencies.

References

Fortino, E. 2013, October 2. 49th Ward residents kick off first 2014 participatory budgeting meeting. http://www.progressillinois.com (accessed October 6, 2013).

Gordon, V. 2012. *Striking a balance: Matching the services offered by local governments with the revenue realities*. Washington, D.C.: ICMA.

Gordon, V., J. L. Osgood, Jr., and D. Boden. 2016. The role of citizen participation and the use of social media platforms in the participatory budgeting process. *International Journal of Public Administration*. doi: 10.1080/01900692.2015.1072215.

Moore, J. 2012, July 5. Personal interview.

6   Case Two: 6th Ward in St. Louis, Missouri

Founded in 1764, St. Louis, Missouri, is known as the Gateway to the West. Its 2013 estimated population was 318,416, white persons comprising 43.5 percent of the population and black persons comprising 47.9 percent. The city covers 61.74 square miles and has 28 wards (City of St. Louis, Missouri 2015, A19–A20).

The pilot year for participatory budgeting in the city's 6th ward was 2014. Annually, each alderman in St. Louis is allocated a small budget for capital improvements within his or her respective ward. Alderwoman Christine Ingrassia agreed to set aside $100,000, which was 40 percent of the ward's capital improvement funds, for the participatory budgeting pilot project (Gordon, Osgood, Jr., and Boden 2016). In 2015, the 15th ward and the 27th ward also began the process of adopting participatory budgeting.

In the 6th ward, the participatory budgeting process began in late 2013 with a series of community brainstorming sessions to identify project ideas. The project idea lists were then sent to one of four committees—safety, streets, beautification, or parks—and each committee of volunteer delegates was charged with narrowing down the project list and identifying which projects were viable for further consideration. These delegates were given training and worked directly with the alderwoman to gather all information necessary to create the formal proposals and set project budgets. The delegates were connected with the proper city departments to make sure the project would be accepted and approved by the city for funding. Next, viable projects were presented at project expos in spring 2014. At the project expos the residents asked questions and made suggestions about which projects should be on the ballot (Participatory Budgeting St. Louis 2014; Gordon, Osgood, Jr., and Boden 2016).

The final projects were then voted on at multiple locations within the 6th ward over a period of eight days. The ballot contained the list of projects, along with a short description of the projects and anticipated costs. Votes were then tabulated, and results announced at a celebratory event. Anyone age 16 and older was allowed to cast a ballot for a project, regardless of citizenship or voter registration status. Proof of age and residency within the ward had to be provided in order to vote (Participatory Budgeting St. Louis 2014; Gordon, Osgood, Jr., and Boden 2016).

The winning projects for 2014 were installation of street lighting, installation of mobile security cameras that can be remotely monitored and relocated as security needs change, and installation of trash cans that include dog waste bag dispensers at bus stops and high pedestrian traffic areas (Participatory Budgeting St. Louis 2014). The ballot and the list of winning projects are presented in the Appendices.

The following interview with Zach Chasnoff was conducted in late spring 2014 immediately following the election process and tabulation of the ballots. Chasnoff co-founded Participatory Budgeting St. Louis along with Michelle Witthaus, and he is also a community organizer with Missourians Organizing for Reform and Empowerment. Selected segments from the interview with Chasnoff are presented in Question and Answer format.

Q.   Michelle Witthaus thought you might be the correct person to talk to about the use of social media in the participatory budgeting process. How did you first get involved in participatory budgeting and why did you get involved?

A.   Zach Chasnoff.

My executive director for the organization I work for had gone to a conference in New York where PB was brought up as a sidebar issue. He came back and said this was an interesting time for PB and I kind of latched on to it right away. I can't tell you exactly why, but intellectually it wasn't something that was high on my radar—the idea of providing spaces for people to vote on their tax dollars—that is something that had not really occurred to me until that point. But when I heard about it I just thought that it made so much common sense and that it was to me the next logical evolutionary step in the American approach for how citizens should be involved in decisions about their tax dollars. So it became something that I started looking into and I was just intellectually curious about this process. Then when there was an opportunity to actually advance it, as an issue in St. Louis, I kind of jumped on that.

Q.   How many districts or wards are currently participating in St. Louis?

A.   Zach Chasnoff.

The 6th ward had its pilot year start at the end of 2013 and then continued into the beginning of 2014, and it was the first in St. Louis and the sole participant. Now, we are actually bringing on board this year other wards as well, and I expect it to grow.

Also there is a bond issue being floated by the President of the Board of Aldermen and it is an $11 million dollar bond issue. One of the issues being brought up there was that the President of the Board of Aldermen in St. Louis is a big fan of PB. He and I had sat down and talked about how we might make this go city-wide. He is supporting this bond issue and one of his ideas was to set aside some money from the bond, and provide it to wards for capital expenditures, so long as they were willing to participate in the PB process to allocate that money. He is trying to incentivize it in a much stronger sense from his office. This would be in the next budget cycle I think.

Q. Have there been any city employees involved with helping you with the 6th ward participatory budgeting process in this initial year, whether it's in their budget office, or just anybody else answering questions, or helping in anyway?

A. Zach Chasnoff.

The short answer is no. Besides the alderwoman, and that's kind of a given. The aldermen are technically city employees, and definitely very helpful to us during this process. The alderwoman was not a hands-off person during the process. She was definitely very involved which was great. The dirty secret about St. Louis is that St. Louis is very broke, and none of our aldermen have any kind of staff whatsoever. So the closest thing to help is going to be that each ward has two neighborhood stabilization officers, and they can help with PB. I will say that one of the neighborhood stabilization officers did help us with some of the outreach with some of the neighborhood assemblies and things like that. That is another thing we are trying to tackle and that we identified as something that needs improvement for next year—what are the ways that the alderpersons or the city can really bring resources to the table, whether it is monetary resources or human resources?

Q. In terms of participation in general, what gets people in the room? Why do people participate? Why do they not?

A. Zach Chasnoff.

We used kind of the traditional ways—sort of the same things through all the phases of the PB process except for the delegate phase, that is a little different. But I would say getting people to neighborhood assemblies and getting people to the vote was very similar. So it was really about engaging the top leadership in the ward—so you could have one point of contact and they could get the word out to several people. We tried to identify those people right away and engage them. We also have a presence at every neighborhood improvement association meeting. We did door-to-door, we held special events, and also used social media as well.

Q. With regard to social media platforms—what did you rely on, what worked, what did not seem to have as much impact?

A. Zach Chasnoff.

What worked the best was getting on to the neighborhood forums, and there are several levels of active citizens. Some of them you just can't keep them away. They will come to every single thing you have for every topic and that is great. We utilize those people. But then there are a lot of other people who care about what is going on in the neighborhood. They will jump in if there is something that really concerns them, but mostly they just kind of monitor Facebook and look for updates on things going on. There are a good handful of these too, and three really active Facebook groups in the ward.

So, being on those forums we felt that it was important to not just be there and say, "hi, we are PB." We also tended to post other kinds of things that were relevant to us, but for us it was about becoming a known entity. So, we wanted to say "we are your friendly neighborhood PB St. Louis people" and we are just telling you about this thing you might not know about that is going on in the neighborhood. Also, we might say there is this information on these meetings, and so we would utilize the people that we had already engaged—the really active people—and they would "like" and "share" and "post" around and boost our profile online, and then we would get newer people who were paying attention to those forums, and they would say "oh, this is a great idea and I am excited about it." The neighborhood groups were I think the best for us.

Then Twitter is a funny thing. Twitter was probably the worst for us, so if we are posting from PB St. Louis and we were trying to get the word out. And we said "hey, this thing is happening." I think we had very little response from that. But when we get news articles or we had pictures to post and we could put them on Twitter, and then send them around using @ president of board of aldermen or @PBNEWYORK or @ and the name of a reporter I had established a relationship with, then I think you get more responses and you would get "shares" and "retweets" and things like that.

Here is the thing about Twitter, I think you can't not use Twitter in this day and age, but I also feel, if I were being honest, that if I had just called all of the people that I was tweeting I would have probably have had the same results. You are talking to a community organizer and I always believe that face-to-face or phone conversations work better.

Q. As you met with people were you collecting email addresses and phone numbers from them so you could contact them later?

A. Zach Chasnoff.

Yes, absolutely. I am a big fan of the software we use called Nation Builder. I don't think I went into this with this expectation. We started our list when we ran a candidate in the 6th ward whose sole platform practically was PB. [Referring to Michelle Witthaus.] We started our list there, and then had expanded it on each level of outreach, and it is about a 900 person list now with probably 700 working emails. We utilized the blast feature a lot and actually found it to be really effective.

Q. What did you find useful about NationBuilder? Did you also use texting to contact people?

A. Zach Chasnoff.

In the beginning phase, NationBuilder does also let you do blasts of text messaging too, and in the neighborhood assembly phase we did send out some texts. I don't know if I have a real sense if the texts were more effective than the email blasts. Maybe one of the things I would think about later is that we did a survey for people coming to the neighborhood assemblies, and I think maybe a relevant question would have been how did you receive information about this meeting?

Q. What about Instagram? Did you use it?

A. Zach Chasnoff.

I can't say that we did use Instagram. That is something that I have not jumped into.

Q. I have heard from a couple of interviewees, including the Boston's Youth Initiative, that Instagram seems to be the social media platform of choice for young people. As you go through this process, what might you do differently next year? How do you think you could increase the use of social media in the process next year? How could you gain access to more people?

A. Zach Chasnoff.

We have, Michelle Witthaus the other cofounder and I, just did our "what do we improve for next year list?" One thing that we flagged was stronger facilitation—all around. Harder facilitation—this is about the delegate process—and really asking people harder questions. We let people go, and let them fill out their own project matrices, and let them do their evaluations, but I think there were a couple of projects in particular where we really could have said "hey, is this really absolutely the biggest need of the neighborhood or is there something else on this list that could work a little bit better?" So we could have done a little harder facilitation.

Two, we are working on solving an issue we noted also in the delegate process which was that our numbers for African-Americans were through the roof for our neighborhood assemblies, and through the roof on the votes, they were 58 percent of the vote. In our delegate phase though, it was largely white men who participated, by and large, and I think it is a problem because a lot of the meat and potatoes stuff happened in the delegate phase. What we flagged as the issue was that it is also the most time-consuming phase, so it requires several months of meetings and sitting down, and also all of these outside activities beyond the meetings, like site visits to see where the project would take place. And it seemed like we needed a way for next year to incentivize stronger low income and minority participation in the delegate phase. The delegate phase is where they take the brainstorm ideas and turn them into concrete projects, and this is one thing which is on my list to talk to other cities about, how they have handled some of these issues.

Q. What are barriers to meaningful citizen participation? Are things like transportation, lost wages, food, and child care important?

A. Zach Chasnoff.

We did have food and we did provide child care. It still wasn't enough.

Q. Those are two things that researchers point to as helping to get beyond the constraints or barriers of participation—that someone needs to be home cooking, or someone might need child care in order to participate, so it sounds like you did what you could.

A. Zach Chasnoff.

We did everything that we knew to do in the first year, and I am a full-time community organizer and Michelle Witthaus is a part-time organizer, so a lot of that stuff was not new to us conceptually. But it was not enough either, so now we have to go back to the drawing board on that.

Q. In terms of voting, was there any early or advance voting in the 6th ward?

A. Zach Chasnoff.

What we did was we held a vote for a week, and at multiple places and at multiple times. We had daytime voting, evening voting and we roamed all around the neighborhood. St. Louis is interesting—something that will work better next year in the other wards is that those aldermen actually have dedicated buildings in their wards that they use for community projects. In the 6th ward, we did not have that, and I think although I was happy with our turnout, I think we would have had a larger turnout if in addition to all the moving that we did, if we had just one dedicated place that anybody could come to at any time of the day that week and vote. The other aldermen have community centers that they utilize.

Q. Is the voting on a paper ballot?

A. Zach Chasnoff.

Yes, we are very interested in figuring out electronic voting mediums, but we want to make sure it is done right.

Q. There are some places that have used something like a Scantron form for voting, which helps with the counting process. Would that be helpful to you?

A. Zach Chasnoff.

The counting process was arduous for us. We are interested in a way to facilitate online voting—a trustworthy way.

Q. In terms of the 6th ward, what is your population and were you happy with the participatory budgeting voting turnout?

A. Zach Chasnoff.

The population is just around 12,000. We are happy with the 436 people that voted. It is not a huge number when you just look at it, it is 4 percent of the ward in its entirety. I will say St. Louis has a very disenfranchised voting population, and especially when you are talking about if it is anything that does not have a national election attached to it, or a Mayoral race, then if it is just a local political issue—then some aldermen win with 150 votes, and your competition might have 50 votes, because only a total of 200 people voted in the whole election. When you look at that in terms of St. Louis, getting 400 people out to a completely localized election, then it is double what happens in some other wards on some other issues. I think for us this is a jumping off point. I hope to get it to at least 1,000 votes by next year. I am not sure what other cities do but I would be interested in comparing our experience to other cities.

Q. In terms of the project phase, what are your impressions of the projects that have been suggested?

A. Zach Chasnoff.

So at the delegate phase you are taking what people brainstormed about at the neighborhood assemblies, and you are turning them into concrete proposals.

Q. And that's where you're saying you had mostly white male participation in the process?

A. Zach Chasnoff.

Yes, it wasn't exclusively so, but it was dominated for sure by white males.

Q. Critics of participatory budgeting say that the individual/self-interest will get in the way of the collective/community interests. What do you say to this?

A. Zach Chasnoff.

I noticed things that impressed me about participatory budgeting, and at first it was a concern of mine. I think that the natural human inclination would be that people act on their self-interests and as an organizer I often find myself organizing around people's self-interests. But on the other hand, and here is what I was impressed by, we intentionally mixed up people during the neighborhood assemblies. So, we have in the 6th ward the incredibly wealthy and also those that live in government subsidized housing. We have the whole spectrum, and it is played out in the ward. So we tried to mix people up and have them sit with groups of people that they don't normally live around, and we felt that was important because that would force inter-neighborhood conversations.

What we found during that phase was that there were a lot of people from the wealthier parts of town who would bring an idea that was sort of a "wouldn't it be nice if?" idea, and then somebody from a lower income part of town would say "we desperately need this" and during those conversations the low income people's ideas tend to win out because the others would say, "well, actually now that I am talking to this person I see what the need is, and it seems the neighborhood really needs this a lot more than my idea." That was also replicated at the delegate phase too. Some people brought pet projects and they became delegates to forward that project, and then when they started to look at the analytics—what we give them to measure the neighborhood need—they sometimes changed their minds and said, "you know what, I will save mine for next year, maybe it will be the time then because this other project really needs to happen now." I am still impressed, I still have faith in humanity. People were willing to "back-burner" their initial priorities.

Q. There is a list of characteristics or benefits of participatory budgeting that have been identified. I would like to see if you agree? Do you think the participatory budgeting process contributed to building a sense of trust?

A. Zach Chasnoff.

Yes, absolutely. I think it really built the trust up amongst the delegates. And I think it built trust in the process itself. I know that people who I saw at neighborhood assemblies then came out to vote. I think they saw the projects that they had brainstormed turned into votes. They said, "this is real, you guys are actually doing this." I think during implementation when projects are actually being realized then I think that same trust is going to happen, and I think it is really great. It has fostered this really neat relationship between the alderwoman and her constituents, especially since she was a freshmen alderwoman trying this brand new idea that had never been done before in St. Louis. And I think she brought excitement to that. People were excited and she was able to pull it off with us. I think it was interesting to watch that relationship grow too.

Q.   Do you think participatory budgeting is democratic?

A.   Zach Chasnoff.

Yes.

Q.   Is participatory budgeting transparent?

A.   Zach Chasnoff.

Yes, we saved every single scrap of information so that we had it to produce on demand. There was one woman at a neighborhood assembly who was upset that her project did not get onto the final ballot. I talked to her about how we asked people to volunteer to be delegates, and I remembered that she had even filled out a form, but then never came, and she said "oh, I got busy, and etc." And I said so that is one part of it, but what I was able to do was produce to her the beautification matrix evaluations that people put each individual project through to decide what they were going to do. So I was able to show here was what happened, agree or disagree, and here was the deliberation that happened around this project, in black and white, in the person's handwriting, and so that helped her. She still would have liked to have seen her project on the ballot, but it helped her see that we weren't in some room making arbitrary decisions, that there was a process behind it.

Q.   Is participatory budgeting efficient?

A.   Zach Chasnoff.

Yes, and this is a personal opinion, but I think democracy is messy, inherently. I don't think there is any way to get away from that. Dictatorships are very orderly, easy to manage, right? But they are not ideal. So, is it efficient? I think it is as efficient as it can be. The Participatory Budgeting Project people in New York who are our technical assistance on this, they have done an amazing job of producing forms and finding ways to help streamline this process.

Q.   Does participatory budgeting provide education to citizens?

A.   Zach Chasnoff.

Yes, I think so. We had an interesting educational thing happen where there were several very progressive ideas—it kind of breaks my heart—of what to do with vacant land in the ward. The city has a Landbank that owns the vacant land, and it has this really rigid bureaucracy built up around it, and we were not able to get any of these plans through the city because of that, which annoyed a lot of the delegates. They found out a whole lot about how the city operates, like what does the Board of Public Service do? What kind of funding do they actually have? What do we need to change things structurally, to get some of these ideas through next year? That was the thing that made me the most sad about some of the projects we could not do, but I was happy that people were agitated enough to want to do something about it. I think that was great.

Q.   Do you think that there is hope in the future to work with that Landbank organization to try to ease up some of those restrictions, especially when ideas might be coming from your people?

A.   Zach Chasnoff.

I absolutely do. That's one of our next steps, I don't really know if we can call it part of the PB process, but we are setting up meetings with the city Landbank and we will say this has got to change. Even the alderwoman was annoyed, and having her at the table will help that conversation.

Q.   Does participatory budgeting provide a sense of social justice?

A.   Zach Chasnoff.

I'm not sure, well, yes, I think it does if you think of tax justice along with the social justice lineage, then absolutely. It sows the seeds for other things like this Landbank issue. I think it will sow the seeds for transformational types of things to happen in terms of the social justice arena. It has potential, and I think it depends on how it's facilitated and by whom.

Q.   Does participatory budgeting build community? Is it inclusive of all of the diversity in your neighborhoods? Is there any identifiable group who is left out?

A.   Zach Chasnoff.

There is one small group of Somalians that live on one block in the ward. There were language barriers. We have to figure that out for next year. It is not a huge part of the ward, but it is a significant part and we can't just leave a block of people out. When we were doing door-to-door, we really stuck in that neighborhood a lot and tried to re-knock on doors, and find out when the English-speaking people would be home. I think the alderwoman was able to call one meeting where she had a translator. I think this is another on our to-do list to try to better incorporate those blocks.

Q.   Does participatory budgeting build the belief that meaningful change can occur?

A.   Zach Chasnoff.

That is really hard to answer. It does for me and I would say I noticed that for several of the delegates and this was their first experiment with civic engagement. And I think they were excited about it, and excited for the future. I think it is a great foundation. I don't think everybody is going to look at PB and necessarily see the potential that I see, but I think it has incredible potential when citizens are the driver of economic decisions in their own lives. I think that begins to translate beyond tax issues to all kinds of other issues.

One of the things that I am excited about as an activist and organizer is moving people into post-representational politics, and moving us much closer to a more direct democracy model of citizen engagement. I think PB is huge, a linchpin in getting us somewhere. If we are at Point A and we are trying to get to Point Z, it is a great B and C on that road.

Q.   What advice would you give to another city or ward thinking of adopting participatory budgeting? What would you like other cities to know?

A.   Zach Chasnoff.

One thing that worked for us amazingly well, but had its downfalls too, was running a candidate in the 6th ward around PB. We were able to blow the issue up like crazy from that. So, I would recommend if people are having trouble convincing their alderperson or having trouble making traction on the issue, run a candidate on it. It is a great way to get press. It is a really hard thing for other candidates to argue against. You can't get up there and say "I don't trust your decision-making, but you should vote for me." It doesn't work.

Q.   There is a ward in Chicago that has decided in their second year to not move forward with participatory budgeting, what advice would you give to them?

A.   Zach Chasnoff.

That would be my advice in terms of outreach—run a candidate. If you are not getting anywhere, run somebody on it. Then I would also say this is a good problem, but it caught us off-guard. In St. Louis it spread so quickly and got implemented quicker than we expected, and we did not have the capacity to deal with it. So, I would say to people think about your staff and your funding on several different scales. We thought we would have this long campaign to win implementation, and that is what we were scaled up for, and then it turned out that we were told, "no, you are going to be implementing this and before long you will be implementing in several wards" and so we did not have near the staff or the funding to deal with that and we kind of just made do. That's my other big advice to people as well. This is a growing trend and it is going to spread and grow quickly. So be prepared for it.

Q.   You don't have a participatory budgeting office currently, is that right?

A.   Zach Chasnoff.

Yes, it's complicated. PB St. Louis is a project of the organization I work for—MORE—Missourians Organizing for Reform and Empowerment. So I am a full-time organizer and PB is one of the projects I work on. Michelle works, she has a day job, and this is sort of her part-time thing. I have an office and I run a lot of things for PB out of my office.

Q.   And the 6th ward alderwoman, does she have an office?

A.   Zach Chasnoff.

She's got an office in city hall.

Q.   Do you anticipate that at some point you may need a physical location dedicated to participatory budgeting?

A.   Zach Chasnoff.

I think it helps us to be mobile, so as long as I am grounded in my office that I normally have, then we are going to be setting up hub operations in all of these different wards, so I think it helps us to be able to move around.

Q. Your person that ran, did this person run against the 6th ward person that is in office now?
A. Zach Chasnoff.
    That's right. Yes, Michelle Witthaus ran against Christine Ingrassia, and Christine decided to start to work with us instead of fight us. I am totally happy with it. And it has all worked out, we are friends with Christine, water under the bridge.
Q. Are you running and updating the PB St. Louis Facebook page or the webpage?
A. Zach Chasnoff.
    Michelle Witthaus has done most of the webpage, and we both tend to trade off with the other social media engagement in general. And Christine Ingrassia does her own, none of our alderpersons have any staff at all. And we need a graphic designer for next year.
Q. What will you do next year that is different than this year? In terms of use of social media platforms?
A. Zach Chasnoff.
    I want to expand it, and I want to try new things. Instagram is now on my radar, and I will start thinking about that, and always trying to get better at Twitter. I call myself "Twitt-illiterate" sort of like I know people make Twitter work, but I haven't been able to crack the code exactly yet. I want to go to some social media training, more in-depth stuff. Mostly it is going to be about using what we know works, and then experimenting with other platforms.

References

City of St. Louis, Missouri. 2015. FY 2016 annual operating plan appendix. https://www.stlouis-mo.gov/government/departments/budget/documents/upload/FY16-AOP-ALL-Appendix-As-Adopted.pdf (accessed August 12, 2015).

Gordon, V., J. L. Osgood, Jr., and D. Boden. 2016. The role of citizen participation and the use of social media platforms in the participatory budgeting process. *International Journal of Public Administration.* doi: 10.1080/01900692.2015.1072215.

Participatory Budgeting St. Louis. 2014. http://pbstl.com/how-does-it-work (accessed July 6, 2014).

Appendices

What is Participatory Budgeting?

Participatory budgeting is a new way to make decisions about publicly funded projects in our neighborhoods.

Participatory budgeting gives ordinary people real decision-making power over real money. It's already working in over 3,000 cities all over the world, and now participatory budgeting is being used in St. Louis.

This year, St. Louis Alderwoman, Christine Ingrassia, asked her constituents to decide how to spend capital discretionary funds. Those are funds that can be used for physical improvements that benefit the public, and the 6th ward has committed $100,000.

How Does Participatory Budgeting Work?

Last fall, ward residents like you came to neighborhood assemblies to identify community needs and suggest projects. Then, volunteers joined delegate committees to develop those suggestions into project proposals, and worked with city agencies to estimate project costs. They put together the proposals you will vote on today.

Now is your chance to vote for the projects you think should be funded. The projects with the most votes, up to $100,000, will be included in next year's city budget, to be built or implemented over the next few years.

You'll get to enjoy the improvements you help make happen. And hopefully, you'll be a part of future participatory budgeting efforts in the city!

For More Information:

pbinstl@gmail.com
314-780-3734
or visit
www.pbstl.org

PBSTL Community Engagement Lead
Missourians Organizing for Reform and Empowerment
(MORE)
314-862-2249
www.organizemo.org

Technical Assistance Lead
The Participatory Budgeting Project
347-554-7357
info@participatorybudgeting.org
www.participatorybudgeting.org

Credits:

Special thanks to The Participatory Budgeting Project, MORE, the Budget Delegates and the members of the Ward Steering Committee.

A very special thanks to 6th Ward Alderwoman Christine Ingrassia for taking to initiative and being the first elected official in St. Louis to introduce participatory budgeting to their ward.

Participatory
Budgeting
Saint Louis

2014
Official Ballot

Participatory Budgeting
St. Louis

Alderwoman
Christine Ingrassia

Ward 6

Participatory Budgeting St. Louis

Voting Instructions

- All residents of the ward. age 16 and up, can vote
- You may vote for up to 3 projects
- You can not vote for the same project more than once.
- Mark boxes clearly with an "X" or check mark or fully shade them in.
- Use black or blue ink. Ballots marked with pencil will not be counted.

Parks

- ☐ **Eads Park Improvements**
  Install new park benches and low maintenance outdoor fitness stations.
  Cost:$20,000

- ☐ **Fox Park Restroom Renovation**
  The restrooms in Fox Park will be renovated and made ADA compliant for the benefit of the whole community.
  Cost: $30,000

- ☐ **Perk Up Buder Park**
  Add a child friendly/ADA compliant drinking fountain.

  Paint 5 wooden benches

  Repair existing fence.
  Cost: $15,000

- ☐ **Decorative Bike Racks**
  Installation of approximately 10 bike racks around the ward with an emphasis on the 4 neighborhood parks.
  Cost: $17,000

Streets

- ☐ **Crosswalk Light Jefferson and Park**
  Install an electric cross walk light across Jefferson at Park, which will allow pedestrians from Peabody and Lafayette Square to safely cross Jefferson to the Gate District and Save-A-Lot shopping area.
  Cost: $25,000

- ☐ **Bike Lanes**
  Allocate funds for the placement of bike 10 miles of bike lanes in the ward, with a primary interest on Jefferson; other locations possible.
  Cost:$30,000

- ☐ **Median At Jefferson and Lafayette**
  Installing of a median at Jefferson and Lafayette will not only beautify the street, but will also provide much needed traffic calming at that intersection in between The Barr Branch Library and the gas station .
  Cost:$80,000

Safety

- ☐ **Traffic Calming on Compton**
  Speeding and running stop signs on Compton continues to be a significant safety concern.

  The 6th ward will commission a traffic study to determine the best way to calm traffic on Compton Ave
  COST: $50,000

- ☐ **Street Lighting**
  Good neighborhood lighting brings down crime and beautifies an area.

  The 6th ward will set aside money from the budget to enhance street lighting where it is most needed in the ward.
  Cost: $50,000

- ☐ **Security Cameras**
  Install of mobile security cameras which can be remotely monitored via the internet and can be relocated anywhere throughout the ward as security needs change.
  Cost: $30,000

Choose up to Three (3) Projects

2014 Official Ballot 6th Ward St. Louis

Beautification

☐ **Neighborhood Signs**
Banners for Tower Grove East, The Gate District, Fox Park and Lafayette Square. Designs will be approved by neighborhood residents.
Cost: $40,000

☐ **New Landscaping & Planters**
Beautify the 6th ward by investing in new planters and plants to be placed in cul-de-sacs and end-caps where neighborhood streets end along Jefferson Ave.
Cost:$60,000

☐ **Trash Cans**
Place 10–20 new trash cans with an optional dog waste bag dispenser in high traffic areas within the ward. Locations will include major intersections, bus stops and other high pedestrian traffic areas.
Cost:$15,000.

REAL MONEY

REAL PEOPLE

REAL POWER

Participatory Budgeting Saint Louis

Appendix 6.1 6th Ward St. Louis, 2014 PB Ballot

Street Lighting
Good neighborhood lighting brings down crime and beautifies an area.

The 6th ward will set aside money from the budget to enhance street lighting where it is most needed in the ward.
Cost: $50,000

#1
(206 VOTES)

Security Cameras
Install of mobile security cameras which can be remotely monitored via the internet and can be relocated anywhere throughout the ward as security needs change.
Cost: $30,000

#2
(202 VOTES)

Trash Cans
Place 10–20 new trash cans with an optional dog waste bag dispenser in high traffic areas within the ward. Locations will include major intersections, bus stops and other high pedestrian traffic areas.
Cost:$15,000.

#3
(122 VOTES)

Appendix 6.2 6th Ward St. Louis, Winning Projects in 2014

7   Case Three: Youth Initiative in Boston, Massachusetts

Unlike the participatory budgeting processes in Chicago and St. Louis, which are specific to wards, the process in Boston is city-wide and focuses strictly on youth. The City of Boston, Massachusetts, had an estimated population of 645,966 in 2013. The city structure includes four at-large councilors and nine councilors elected by district. In April 2013, under the direction of former Mayor Thomas Menino, the city committed $1 million of its capital improvement budget to the participatory budgeting process. The intent of the city-wide participatory budgeting initiative was to engage young people in government, specifically in the allocation of and decision-making about the budget (City of Boston 2013; Gordon, Osgood, Jr., and Boden 2016).

The city's Youth Council and its steering committee coordinated efforts to gather project ideas at eight idea assemblies in its first year. In 2014, about 400 ideas were proposed. These ideas were narrowed down to a more manageable list, and developed into viable projects by members of the change agent committees. The viable projects were then vetted and eventually 14 projects were placed on the ballot and seven were funded. Persons of any age were allowed to participate in the project development, but only youth ages 12 to 25 in Boston were eligible to vote on the projects during a week-long voting period. Winning projects for the first year included upgrades and repairs to playground and picnic equipment, purchase of laptops for three high schools, a feasibility study for a skateboard park, installation of security cameras at a park, and installation of new sidewalks and lights in two newly renovated parks (City of Boston 2014; Gordon, Osgood, Jr., and Boden 2016). Under the direction of Mayor Martin Walsh, this same process was repeated in 2015 for the second year of participatory budgeting.

The following interview with Aaron Tanaka was conducted in late spring 2014 prior to the first election process. Tanaka was an employee of the Participatory Budgeting Project and assigned to assist the City of Boston. The interview with Pam Jennings was conducted in early summer 2015 immediately after the second election process. Jennings is an employee of the Participatory Budgeting Project and now assigned to assist the City of Boston with the participatory budgeting process. Selected segments from the interviews with Tanaka and Jennings are presented in Question and Answer format.

Q.   Could I get some background information on you and your involvement with participatory budgeting?

A.   Aaron Tanaka.

My connection to the issue came from my former workplace where I was the director of an organization called the Boston Workers Alliance. It is a grassroots organization mostly working with adults and a lot of what we were doing was ground up, about quality access to employment. In 2011, we first heard of participatory budgeting in Boston and we were one of the first groups that were calling for PB, and we were involved in bringing the idea to the Mayor's office. When the Mayor announced that he was going to be doing PB, I connected with the Participatory Budgeting Project in New York, and I had met Josh Lerner and knew him for a couple of years. We decided to go in and work together to be the providers for this project. PBP is based in New York, and I agreed to be part of the Boston base as a supervisor, knowing that they would hire a full-time organizer that would also be working with me. This is the first year of any form of PB in Boston.

Q.   As a community, do you think Boston was ready for participatory budgeting? From the elected officials' standpoint, citizens' standpoint?

A.   Aaron Tanaka.

I think people who know about PB are all very supportive, and obviously it is hard to be against PB. In this case though PB in Boston is one of the few city-wide processes in the country—so it is the entire city, as opposed to being broken down on a district-by-district basis. It does not require the participation or the endorsement of the city councilors. There is really just the Mayor's office that is involved. So for that reason, yes, I would say people are really receptive to it. The political people who matter are in the Mayor's office. People are all very enthusiastic about it. I think it has been very well received. In the community I think it's one of those things that as people hear about it, people think it is cool and they want to get involved. My organization did some work around popularizing the model before it came to Boston, but it's definitely different to actually have something going that you can talk about.

Q.   In terms of the people who have been involved throughout this process so far, what do you think it is that gets people in the room? Is it neighbor reaching out to neighbor? Is it established citizen groups that have contacts?

A.   Aaron Tanaka.

The way this process started was with the formation of a steering committee and I am on that. In the initial outreach, it was based on my own network, the staff here in Boston, and the relationships the city had with some community and youth organizations, so we did a lot of outreach before we even started. Then we had a bunch of people apply and ended up with a steering committee of about 30 organizations. The majority, over 20 out of those 30 organizations, were youth specific or youth-serving organizations. So we structured the steering committee to reflect the intention of the effort that this would be a youth-led process. A lot of the outreach and interest really moves through two core channels: 1) the non-profit, youth service, youth organizing infrastructure that exists in the city; and 2) the central outreach is done through the city's own youth-related programs and departments—particularly the community center, as well as the Mayor's Youth Council which is a network of young people from throughout the city that are part of this council program. So it has been different groups of people and that has been important. I think the third area that we would like to see more of, which hasn't been as successful at this point yet, but we are hoping to turn that around, is that we would also like to see more direct outreach through the school systems. This is not really happening at this point, although we are hoping to get it there.

Q.   Could you talk about the projects that have been proposed throughout this process for this first time? What projects to you think will most impact the community?

A.   Aaron Tanaka.

It is hard to say what the projects are because we are still in the process of narrowing down the projects, so we have had about 400 projects proposed through eight community assemblies throughout the city, which were attended by hundreds of young people where they give their ideas. It's just a little early. I was at one of the change agent committee meetings, which is what we call the budget delegates here in Boston. The group that I was sitting with were a group that was interested in building a multi-cultural youth arts center in East Boston, so that was cool, pretty interesting. I have heard people talking about bringing Wi-Fi along major transportation routes, on major bus routes for example. I have heard a lot of discussion around cleaning up school bathrooms, which is a big problem—some of these don't even have doors on stalls. I heard a good number of projects relating to urban agriculture—like community gardens, an idea for a fruit tree park. I don't know if that one will make it through. Another memorable one was a memorial for those young people who have been killed in the City of Boston. Sort of to commemorate their lives in a visible way through some sort of art sculpture.

Q.   In terms of the process, when is the vote?

A.   Aaron Tanaka.

It will be June 14th through the 21st of 2014. It is a week-long process, and there is no early voting process.

Q.   And the ballot process?

A.   Aaron Tanaka.

There will be no online voting, there will be a way online that the projects will be available to look at, but this time around we don't have the technical capacity this time around to do online voting. The big issues are that it is hard to do an age verification or residency verification with online voting. We did use a thing called Citizinvestor for people to propose ideas online, but to be honest it really did not get much traction.

Q. Will you use an electronic process for tallying of the votes?

A. Aaron Tanaka.

I don't know.

Q. What kind of social media platforms have you used to reach out to people or to remind people of events?

A. Aaron Tanaka.

There are four channels that we use: 1) Facebook; 2) Twitter; 3) Instagram; and 4) mobile comments texting applications. The fourth one is sort of a mass texting service where people can opt-in and sign up for updates, and that has been good. I was in a meeting today where people were trying to refine some of that system. On that particular thing, we have been most successful just importing people into it. It is harder to get people to sign up on their own, you know "text YOUTH to 877877" or something. We have quite a number of people—over 150—on our texting service at this point, but I think the feeling has been that it has not been as successful in getting people to opt-in as they would like.

Q. Are you using all four of those methods to do everything? Invite people to meetings? Notify them of meeting results? Does it cover everything or is it limited?

A. Aaron Tanaka.

Facebook is the main one for telling people about upcoming public events and opportunities and the rest is on Instagram and Twitter, and they are really retrospective—so check out what did happen. Here are pics from the assemblies. Less so as a way for turning people out at this point. Part of it is that it is all new and we have about 320 youth on our Facebook page, but I think Instagram and Twitter is by far, much less used. So, we are just sort of given limited time and resources, so we are focusing on Facebook. Although my sense is that with young people that they tend to use Instagram more than anything else. It is a trend. Instagram is sort of an image-based medium, but it is much more narrow in what you can do with it, which is why they like it, you don't get meeting announcements, or whatever else.

Q. Are you using traditional methods? Phone calls, flyers, media coverage?

A. Aaron Tanaka.

Definitely phone calls as far as to committee members and the budget delegates, steering committees—we do phone calls. At the end of the day, that is probably still the most effective way of reaching people. We do flyers for some of the major events that we are doing in public places.

Q. Are you able to distribute flyers in schools?

A. Aaron Tanaka.

No, not yet—you can do them outside of school, but what we are trying to figure out is how to move information through official channels through top administrators. At least by the time we get to the voting in mid-June, so that at least in a few schools that are participating fully where we have a presence on site, and the entire school goes and votes, and then absent that, we would try to do it somehow through the schools.

Q. What will you do next year that is different than this year? In terms of use of social media in the process?

A. Aaron Tanaka.

The biggest thing could have been in generating ideas using social media. Really the main way people propose ideas, there was this online thing called Citizinvestor platform. It is an online platform where people can submit their ideas for different projects but in this case it maps on to a specific location on the map. It is sort of a portal where people can submit ideas and for people to indicate their interests or likes so they can vote on them.

Q. It sounds like Citizinvestor is more about suggesting ideas at the initial stage. Is that correct?

A. Aaron Tanaka.

Using this, people could submit ideas outside of coming to an actual idea assembly, and it had a function where people could vote on them online, but that really did not have consequence. We didn't see many ideas in there in the first place; it was not used at all. For me, I kind of wanted to see us use Facebook and other mediums as a way for people to generate ideas, and I think we would have been able to get a lot more ideas in because that is where people are. On the flip side, there is a value to having people come in person to these sessions to get the whole presentation of what the process is, and it's easier to get their actual contact information for future follow-ups. On the flip side of that it can be resource intensive for us. So it is hard to balance.

Q. Are there groups that are left out? Not participating? Is there anybody that has been left out whether by choice or due to time constraints? Are there any groups that are unrepresented or under-represented?

A. Aaron Tanaka.

Yes, I think both when we started this process as a pilot—this was a truncated process—normally it takes nine months to a year, and we had six months to do it. From the get-go we decided that we wanted to focus on communities where traditionally underserved persons were— so we chose five neighborhoods across Boston that we have focused on. So there is definitely a geographic bias around certain communities— communities of color. It is open to everybody, and the Mayor's Youth Council which is one of the main co-chairs of the steering committee and they have a good reputation from across the city as a neighborhood-based representation organization, but as far as a lot of the steering committee organizations a lot of them are focused based on geography. Beyond that there are any number of demographics that could have gotten more focus on them and that we did not necessarily reach. We did do a specific assembly reaching out to groups of young people who are court-involved, we have an organization that works with LGBT youth, and we have not really had much success in reaching the youth that are homeless. All three of those demographics we have made some effort towards, but naturally it is about who is connected to organizations and resources, and so we could have done more on that.

Q. There is a list of characteristics and benefits that describe what participatory budgeting is. Can I ask you about each of these? Do you think participatory budgeting is democratic?

A. Aaron Tanaka.

Yes, or it should be.

Q. Is participatory budgeting transparent?

A. Aaron Tanaka.

Are you asking about the concept or application?

Q. More the application. I want to know from your experience what you think.

A. Aaron Tanaka.

Yes, to a degree, there could be more, but given the speed at which we are having to move we have been focused on the pilot project, and a lot of it has been getting some people involved with experience and knowledge, so that next year it could be more democratic.

Q. Is participatory budgeting efficient?

A. Aaron Tanaka.

Depends on what you measure or what your goal is. So it obviously takes more time for everybody, but if your definition of efficiency is focused on getting to good results or meeting needs, then maybe the time expended requires that in some ways because you weren't getting there anyway before.

Q. Does participatory budgeting provide education to citizens?

A. Aaron Tanaka.

Yes, seeing young people engaged in the budget process and for some it is the first time they ever saw a budget—they just didn't know what a budget was. And then talking about capital projects versus operating funds, it is a very good process.

Q. Does participatory budgeting provide a sense of social justice?

A. Aaron Tanaka.

Yes, I think so. I think because this is a youth specific process that this is sort of an inherent analysis around empowering young people, so I think that it adds an aspect of social justice to that. It is also about our focus which has been on under-represented communities. In that sense it also attempts to re-balance the access to those in political power.

Q. Does participatory budgeting build a sense of community?

A. Aaron Tanaka.

I think that is still to be seen actually because it does build a sense of connection between organizations that are involved at the committee level. Whether that reaches to communities more broadly speaking I don't know. I think this voting process is going to be the most public part of it, and that is the opportunity to really engage broader numbers of people and have them feel connected to each other across neighborhoods.

Q. Does participatory budgeting build trust?

A. Aaron Tanaka.

I think that is still to be seen. I think, yes, in some ways—young people see city government slightly differently, but in a lot of ways we are still in the middle of it. I think after the process, just how it runs, really is going to determine that.

Q. Does participatory budgeting build a belief that meaningful change can occur?

A. Aaron Tanaka.

Yes.

Q. What advice would you give to another city or ward that wants to strengthen the youth initiative in their community? What advice would you give them in moving forward? What has worked? What hasn't worked?

A. Aaron Tanaka.

I think part of the question is when you put young people together with adults, adults tend to dominate conversations. So, from the get-go there is a question of who is on the steering committee, and do you have a set of young people or youth organizations, and then are you creating space for them? So, assuming it is going to be both a youth and adult process, then there could be value in having almost like a parallel process, not fully parallel but certainly having on the ballots the different categories of projects—maybe if you have eight total categories, that you have two of those categories be allocated for the youth process. I think there is an argument to be made both ways, but even having the budget delegates, for example, not having youth and adults all in the same committee. So again if you had separate committees that were just for young people to come up with ideas for whatever number of categories—so like in the schools' committee for example which I assume the adult processes also have, it should really just be young people on those committees. Or the community centers or parks. You could think about what are the categories that should really be dictated by youth, and then allow space for youth on those committees.

Q. Is there anything else in terms of next year that you might do with the use of social media in the process?

A. Aaron Tanaka.

Yes, I think that just to get more people to be in control of the social media platforms. I think it would be good to have from the get-go a few people who are designated to and who are carrying it out throughout the process. We had a social media working group on the steering committee, but just because of all of the other stuff happening it is hard to keep a consistent group of people focused on it.

Q. I've heard that from a couple other places that administrators for social media platforms are limited to one or two people and they are so overwhelmed by other responsibilities that the updating of social media platforms is more of an afterthought as opposed to being very proactive. Has that been your experience?

A.   Aaron Tanaka.

Yes, that is definitely true. There are additional complications around the city's social media guidelines that draw parameters around who can access it, the content, and updates. I am not saying that is the reason we have not been able to keep up, but it is another piece to negotiate through the process.

Q.   Is there anything else that you would do differently next year?

A.   Aaron Tanaka.

The whole idea collection process and to have the social media use directed towards that. I think it would be interesting to be able to do online voting, but there are so many challenges around age and geographic verifications. I think the number of people you could reach will be much higher.

Q.   So right now, when you are meeting in a face-to-face setting or a community meeting, are you collecting email or phone numbers and asking people if you can add them to your list?

A.   Aaron Tanaka.

Yes.

Q.   In terms of the idea collection process, did anyone go away unhappy or didn't feel heard during the process so far?

A.   Aaron Tanaka.

No, the proposal and the idea collection process was fairly pleasant. It's just such a low level thing where it's really just people throwing out ideas, and there are not really a lot of opportunities for them to feel that way. I think the question about what ends up getting on the ballot, there could be people who went to those assemblies who submitted ideas who will say what happened to my idea? We aren't there yet. I think at that stage everyone was very happy.

Q.   Is there anything that surprised you about the process?

A.   Aaron Tanaka.

Not really. It has been a lot of work, a lot more work than I thought or imagined, and it is hard to do in this short amount of time, but otherwise it has been good—pretty straightforward.

Q.   What is the plan for announcing the results after the vote?

A.   Aaron Tanaka.

There will be a lot of people moving all the results through all of our media channels, using the Mayor's media apparatus.

Q.   When will you start on next year's process?

A.   Aaron Tanaka.

Not sure, soon, I hope in the fall of 2014. We will do the voting in June, spend a couple months doing evaluations, and then hopefully start right after that in fall with putting together the steering committee, as opposed to January which we did this year.

In the following section, the interview with Pam Jennings is presented.

Q.   Tell me about what your position is with the participatory budgeting process in Boston?

A.   Pam Jennings.

For the past three years I have been project manager with the Participatory Budgeting Project, and we are a nonprofit organization that provides technical assistance to places that are interested in doing participatory budgeting, and we also advocate for more PB processes around the United States and in Canada. My role as project manager is to oversee and provide technical assistance, along with my program assistant on the east coast mainly, but my focus is New York, where our organization is based. Also over the past two years we have been working with the City of Boston and also the City of Cambridge, Massachusetts, where they have just finished the PB process for their first year. We also do a little bit of work in Canada; we have been working with a town in New Brunswick. My main focus is on east coast PB communities, and we also have staff in Chicago who work in the Midwest region on PB in the Midwest, and then also out in California where we have additional staff.

Q.   So are you physically located in New York?

A.   Pam Jennings.

Yes, our main office is in Brooklyn, and as needed we travel to whichever cities we are working in.

Q.   I had talked to Aaron Tanaka a year ago about the first year of the Boston Youth Initiative. For this interview, I wanted to follow up about the second go-round with participatory budgeting and see how things have gone during this second year. I am assuming the vote has already happened. Can you tell me what else you did this year that might have been different from last year and what you thought of some of those kinds of differences?

A.   Pam Jennings.

We just finished up the vote at the end of May this year. We had four projects that were able to get funded for the million dollars available. There were 10 projects altogether that were on the ballot. So the top projects this year: one was for expansion of public Wi-Fi throughout a couple different locations; one was for installing water bottle refill stations in parks because many of the parks in Boston don't have any water fountains at all; also one was for gym renovations for one of the big high schools; and one was for a couple more stations of their bike share program called the "Hubway" where you can check out a bike, that was the fourth winning project and that was to extend an existing program.

Q.   In terms of the people who participated and the way that you reached out to them, did you try anything new this year?

A.   Pam Jennings.

Yes, we tried a couple of new things this year. Last year we had about 1,500 voters and this year we had over 2,500. And you know the voters are all between the ages of 12 and 25. We actually did a little bit more with experiments with social media and YouTube advertising. We actually had a short commercial that ran on YouTube, and that was cool because we were able to work with some of the support people at YouTube to be able to help us target the audience so we knew we were reaching only people in Boston, in our targeted age group, and we figured out some keywords to help too with that search process, so that was cool because we were able to target YouTube commercials. We also did some experiments using Facebook ads mainly to be able to boost posts. What we were really trying to drive people to was a big vote party that was happening at one of the community centers. We had a lot of other places that people could vote, but we targeted our outreach efforts to drive people to that voting event. And so the event was really great, we probably had 200 or 300 people that attended just that event. A lot of the similar things that we did the same as last year was using flyers and posters and word-of-mouth outreach with young people going out and spreading the word and talking to their friends and passing out flyers. Similar to last year too we also used text messaging to be able to notify people about the vote and to drive people to that event as well. The text messaging has been one of our more successful methods of engaging with young people. On Twitter, honestly, we use Twitter and we post things, but it hasn't been our most robust form of outreach.

Q. So when you are doing the text messaging, how are you getting those phone numbers to text to originally?

A. Pam Jennings.

A couple of things were used. One is that we were in Boston, and the Department of Youth Employment and Engagement is kind of the home for participatory budgeting there, and they have several other youth engagement and employment programs. So they have thousands of people that apply for summer jobs through that program, so we were able to use all of those phone numbers of everyone that applies for summer jobs and be able to send them messages as well. Also, we have our steering committee that has about 20 organizations on it, so we also ask them for help with sharing their contact list as well to be able to engage people that are affiliated with those organizations. But that is one of our biggest challenges. I think with SMS, text messaging, the biggest challenge is figuring out how to build up your contact list.

Q. Did you use Instagram?

A. Pam Jennings.

Yes, we used Instagram and we also have a Snapchat account. People use that a little bit, not a whole lot.

Q. Did you move to any kind of electronic voting this time?

A. Pam Jennings.

Yes, our organization has been really fortunate to develop a good contact and relationship with a team at Stanford University called the Crowdsourced Democracy Team. They help various cities that do PB and they have helped develop a digital voting tool and we use that in addition to paper ballots. So we still have both options, the digital and the paper ballot. The exciting thing was that we were able to work with the Boston Public School System (BPS) and they basically shared the identification numbers of all of their students, and so we were able to use that to verify voters' eligibility with the digital ballot. That allowed people to be able to go onto their regular BPS website that they use every day and there was a link to get access to the digital ballot so we were able to reach some more folks that weren't there in the face-to-face settings.

Q. Did you have any electronic voting last year?

A. Pam Jennings.

No.

Q. Did you do anything digitally for the idea generation phase of the process? Was that different this year?

A. Pam Jennings.

Yes. It was a little different. The first time around we worked with a group called Citizinvestor which is like a crowdfunding platform, and this time around the city was able to put together a form on their own website so that people who were going to the website would be able to just input ideas through that website. Honestly, I don't think online idea collection has been effective, even though we have had options and we have promoted them, it's not really the most robust way that we collect ideas. It's really in the in-person setting that we get the most ideas.

Q. And how many of the "idea generating" meetings did you have this time?

A. Pam Jennings.

I think somewhere around seven or eight in addition to more informal opportunities where we went out to public transportation stations and didn't do the full scale assemblies, but did a more informal format for that.

Q. Aaron Tanaka had said that last year there were some groups like LGBT groups that maybe you wanted to have more participation from, but you didn't get as much as you wanted. Did any of that improve this year in terms of reaching out to groups that you felt you didn't see the presence of?

A. Pam Jennings.

Yes, I mean I think we tried to do a little more with the steering committee this year in terms of incorporating more groups to reach some of the harder to reach communities.

Q. Did you invite them to sit on the steering committee as representatives?

A. Pam Jennings.

Yes, which we did do, and I think we still have some work that we would want to continue to do on that front.

Q. Aaron Tanaka had also said last year that there was room for improvement for the school involvement. So was providing the identification numbers this year, was that a new thing this year that had not happened before? Did they let you do any voting at their schools?

A. Pam Jennings.

Yes, I think we had probably six or seven different high schools that we were at during their lunch period and we were able to really use a combination of the paper ballots, and we have iPads and laptops available for the digital vote, and we did a combination of those things. We captured a lot of votes that way through just being there during the lunch periods. And also, for what it's worth, we had candy and things to attract people.

Q. Was voting held over a week or a longer period?

A. Pam Jennings.

It ended up being about a week and a half.

Q. Have you had a chance to think about what you might do differently next year with regard to the use of social media platforms?

A. Pam Jennings.

Actually our team is meeting on Monday to do some of that reflection. I think we were really excited about the use of YouTube and what we want to do is get that advertisement running a lot earlier so we can get a lot more hits. YouTube definitely worked with us, but it does take a little while for them to hone in on the target audience, so I think with more time on that then we would have been able to get really, really targeted in terms of our audience. But we recognized that it was a successful pilot. We would do some things differently, but we definitely want to keep doing that.

Q. Were you able to collect any demographic data on these young people other than knowing what school district they were in?

A. Pam Jennings.

So the great thing about the identification numbers is that they are all linked to that set of demographic data about the students and BPS has said that they are willing to share a report of that, but we haven't received that yet, but they will. With the digital ballot there is also a survey that follows that up and does ask for some demographic data as well. We are in the process of downloading and analyzing that. I don't have any demographic data to share at this point.

Q. But you feel like that is something you can build on each year?

A. Pam Jennings.

Yes, definitely. I feel like that is a really critical piece.

Q. Do you have an evaluation plan? Is it formalized?

A. Pam Jennings.

I think our main focus is on surveys during each stage of the process, so at the idea collection events we administer surveys, and then for the people that do the proposal development, the change agents, we administer surveys to them, and then we use the voter surveys as well. So surveying has been one critical thing, and then also supplementing that with some interviews and focus groups as well.

Q. Is it still correct in the idea generation stage that anyone of any age can participate?

A. Pam Jennings.

Yes.

Q. I would like to ask you about the list of characteristics or benefits of participatory budgeting. Can you tell me your impressions? The first one is, is participatory budgeting democratic?

A.   Pam Jennings.
        Yes.
Q.   Is participatory budgeting transparent?
A.   Pam Jennings.
        Yes, and I think one of the most interesting parts of the process is when the change agents are doing their work to develop the proposals. What we tried to do this year was give them some more opportunities to be able to meet with the staff people that work in the city. Being able to ask them questions and get information has been transparent in a way that a lot of decision-making typically is not.
Q.   Is participatory budgeting efficient?
A.   Pam Jennings.
        Yes, I think so. We are starting from ideas that come directly from the community and there's not a lot of other ways to get so much input from community members.
Q.   Does participatory budgeting provide education to citizens?
A.   Pam Jennings.
        Definitely, I think that one of the biggest things is the learning, especially again with the change agents.
Q.   Does participatory budgeting build a sense of community?
A.   Pam Jennings.
        Yes, definitely. I think also the steering committee is important with that aspect because we are bringing together groups and organizations that might not normally be in the same room together and they are collaborating.
Q.   Do you think that the process has been inclusive of all of the different types of diversity in your city with regard to youth?
A.   Pam Jennings.
        Yes. I think there may be some groups that we would want to continue to work on the inclusion of. One group in particular is homeless or children in foster care, and also court-involved children. I think we would want to continue to make some additional efforts to engage those groups, but overall the opportunities that are presented are very inclusive of everyone.
Q.   Does participatory budgeting build trust?
A.   Pam Jennings.
        Yes, I think so. Especially with what I was just saying with the change agent process and with the transparency around the information, and the change agents being able to ask questions and seek information and get the answers they are looking for, and understand if something is not feasible, why it is not feasible, and being very open with the proposal development process.
Q.   Do you think participatory budgeting builds the belief that meaningful change can occur?
A.   Pam Jennings.
        That's a hard question.

Q.   Is it harder because it is a youth-oriented process in Boston? Or do you think the youth are more open to the fact that things can change?

A.   Pam Jennings.

I don't think we have asked that question specifically, so I wouldn't want to presume. I certainly think so.

Q.   What have you drawn from your experience with participatory budgeting that you might want to tell other communities that are getting ready to start the process?

A.   Pam Jennings.

One thing that comes to mind is that the PB process requires time. It is not something you can rush through, especially in the first cycle of doing it when you have to set up a steering committee, and that is sort of three months of work that has to happen before you even start going into idea collection. So just making sure that at least nine to twelve months of time is set aside, especially for the first process. In Boston, in the first year, we had a pretty short timeline, and a lot of those learning opportunities that can happen with the change agents, it was shortened. I think this year we were able to have a much longer timeline and we were able to incorporate a lot of skill-building workshops and other opportunities throughout the process, so there was definitely a more robust learning process for the change agents. I think in any city, that it is the group, whether they are called budget delegates or change agents, that is the group where the most learning happens. So making sure that those folks have enough time to meet, and process, and do the community visits, and do all the work that goes into developing proposals, I think that is really critical. I think, too, this time around we definitely had a lot more young people involved in all levels of the process. So we had young people that were facilitating the change agent committees, a couple of additional young people on staff, we had the Boston youth involved with social media. We worked a lot more closely with young people who were either responsible for posting things on social media or we would run things by them if we were going to be posting things just to make sure that the language we used was appropriate and to make sure it was something young people were interested in and cared about. So especially for a youth-focused PB process, engaging young people in every single aspect of implementing and being the change agents was really valuable.

References

City of Boston. 2013. http://www.cityofboston.gov/images_documents/08%20capital%20planning_final_tcm3-37459.pdf (accessed July 6, 2014).

City of Boston. 2014. http://www.cityofboston.gov/images_documents/2014%20101%20days(press%20release)_v7_tcm3-44474.pdf (accessed July 6, 2014).

Gordon, V., J. L. Osgood, Jr., and D. Boden. 2016. The role of citizen participation and the use of social media platforms in the participatory budgeting process. *International Journal of Public Administration*. doi: 10.1080/01900692.2015.1072215.

8 Case Four: Greensboro, North Carolina

Greensboro, North Carolina, is a refugee resettlement city, and had an estimated population of 279,782 in 2013. The population is 48 percent white, 41 percent black or African-American, and 7.5 percent Hispanic (United States Census Bureau 2015). The participatory budgeting process in Greensboro is unique in that the concept has been looked at for quite some time, but the official process is just beginning.

The city council has approved participatory budgeting beginning in fiscal year 2015/2016 after a four-year process that was initiated by a group of community members who worked with the Fund for Democratic Communities. The council resolution authorizing support for participatory budgeting was adopted in October 2014, and is presented in Appendix 8.1. The resolution includes an unusual caveat of requiring the community to raise $100,000 from community foundation grants as a match to the $100,000 that the city has pledged to fund the initial steps in the participatory budgeting process. Further funding and commitment to participatory budgeting will take place in the 2016/2017 budget.

The following interviews were conducted in summer 2015. Wayne Abraham and Larry Morse are community members who have been and continue to be involved in the participatory budgeting process in Greensboro. Elizabeth Dam-Regier became involved on the community-based committee while she was a graduate student, and she has recently moved to another community. Karen Kixmiller is a Budget and Management Analyst in the Budget and Evaluation Department in the City of Greensboro. Selected segments from the interviews with these four are presented in Question and Answer format.

Q. Could you tell me about how you first got involved in participatory budgeting and what your role has been or is currently?
A. Wayne Abraham.
   I first got involved in 2011 when I was a candidate for city council here, and I was introduced by another candidate for city council to the folks who wanted to do this, and she won the election and I didn't. So she is on the city council, and I'm not, which is fine by me. I'm not tragically upset about it. So the committee that was formed to deal with

participatory budgeting, I joined. I was invited to it and I went to meetings, and so over time I just continued to be involved with the committee that has been diminishing in size, but continuing with the process. As people get worn out, you know, when things take four years to make happen, people drop out.

Q.   Given that you are down in numbers on the committee, and in terms of the next step in the process, are you working with any community groups that you hope are going to take a leadership role outside of your current committee structure?

A.   Wayne Abraham.

We have already contacted a large number of community groups all throughout Greensboro and told them that we want them to submit people to be on the steering committee that the city council will appoint. So we are trying to get as broad of a representation as possible. We held two community meetings at the central library and had pretty good attendance and had a wide variety of folks who came. We are continuing to reach out to the ones who didn't come, and still say we are looking for people. Our plan is to have 18 people appointed to an official city steering committee that will create the rule book for participatory budgeting in Greensboro, and get all that done. We preferred sooner, but government processes being what they are, everything gets made longer than it is.

City council is going to vote on July 21st [2015] to officially approve the contract with the Participatory Budgeting Project and the budget. It took us a while to get the matching funds. So all the pieces are falling into place, but it is taking a bit longer than we all wanted it to. We will be expanding the number of people. The goal has always been to have the broadest conceivable participation as possible.

Q.   The two meetings that you mentioned, were those the two meetings that were highlighted on your website for April and May of 2015?

A.   Wayne Abraham.

Yes, they were the two, the one that was a Saturday, and then the other one that was a Monday. Monday apparently was far more popular than Saturday. We discovered that probably 10 people came to the Saturday meeting and 25 came to the Monday meeting—maybe even more. The room was full and we ran out of chairs for the Monday meeting. So we learned, okay, Monday meetings are popular. People don't want to give up their Saturday mornings I guess.

Q.   Was it a Monday evening meeting?

A.   Wayne Abraham.

Yes.

Q.   In terms of those groups that you reached out to, did you do that by letter, in person, or email?

A.   Wayne Abraham.

Mostly by email, we used our city's Human Relations Commission list. Some of them we knew and some of them we talked to personally, but most of them we did that contact with email. We have a thing here in Greensboro called the Greensboro Neighborhood Congress, which has a lot of different neighborhoods that belong to it. They have shown interest finally, now that participatory budgeting is going to happen, in making it something that they participate in. They have neighborhoods from all over the city who have organized themselves. We are doing what we call a "mock" PB presentation for them on Thursday, so they are going to participate in it and do it as an exercise to see what it's like.

Q. Are you bringing in somebody from the Participatory Budget Project to help with that or are you doing it on your own?

A. Wayne Abraham.

We are doing it on our own. We're good at it by now—after four years we know what to do.

Q. In terms of the numbers of people involved fluctuating, do you think that mostly people run out of time, or run out of energy to commit, or do you think there is something else that turns people off?

A. Wayne Abraham.

I don't think anybody got turned off, it's just that it took four years. You wear people out after a time. I think their enthusiasm is still there, and I think we still have support, it's just that we kept having to push to the final goal. So we are really down to only a few of us who meet regularly with the city staff to go over the details of what needs to be done, but I guess we are the remnants. The other people, we give them updates and they are happy about it, but they can't all come to a city council meeting. I mean to meet the staff during the day, because you have to be able to do that during the day. There are only a few of us that can do that.

Q. In terms of city staff, what has the attitude been like from city staff?

A. Wayne Abraham.

Prior to participatory budgeting being approved, I would have to say they were resistant. But once it was approved, they have been very cooperative, very helpful, and actually it has gone very well. They have provided very intelligent advice and guidance on certain issues, and certainly helped organize the community meetings. I think they have come to understand the value of it. It has made them rethink how they have been doing the budget all these years.

Q. One of the reasons for our interest in Greensboro is because of the difference from other cities that have done this where it is initiated by an elected official, and it is about directly spending the council person's money that is given to their particular ward or district for the process. My understanding of participatory budgeting in Greensboro is that this will be city-wide and it had to have full council approval to go forward. Am I understanding this correctly?

A. Wayne Abraham.

Yes, well, you had to have a majority of the council.

Q.   So because of that difference, I was wondering if you have any thoughts about what issues or challenges that particular approach has presented for you in terms of getting the approval of council?

A.   Wayne Abraham.

Well, we had to convince five out of nine to do it, and we did, we got a 5-4 vote. I think once we got 5-4, two of the waverers really in reality will be supportive of it, two I don't think ever will, but they are of the political party that says no to everything. I would think that it would be a conservative value to have citizens decide how to spend their own money, but apparently not. I'm like well, "shouldn't they be happy about this?"

So I think for us, Greensboro has a very large and diverse community. For a southern city, it is very diverse. It is much more ethnically diverse than is the norm because we were a federal resettlement city, so we have a lot of ethnic minorities here that don't exist elsewhere in the south. We have lots of Asian, we have Bosnian. I think our school system has to cope with 104 different languages. Part of our responsibility is to try and reach out to all of these folks who could potentially take part, and that's how our Human Relations Commission can help. I used to serve on it, and chair the city's Human Relations Commission. So I reached out directly to the current chair of it who knows me and said, "look, you really need to be involved in this, this needs to be a project for you, it's totally up your alley, we want everybody involved in this." And their staff person came to one of our meetings with the budget staff, so I think she is now on board with what needs to be done. So I think outreach is going to be not that hard.

I think convincing people that we don't want to do the same-old-same-old is going to be the hard part. Of course people have always experienced the same-old-same-old, so for them to realize "oh, it's really not, no, it's really not going to be that way, and you really do get to propose what you want to."

Q.   I've heard from other cities that it takes quite a while for people to really believe, but once they see the first projects that they actually have voted on coming to completion, they are then believing that it is going to happen, but there still was that doubt. Is that what you expect to happen?

A.   Wayne Abraham.

It may be that way here. I think part of our city council reticence originally, with at least two of them was that one thought "well it will just turn out to be another thing that Greensboro does and nobody really follows through with and does what they are supposed to do" and the other, I think, thought "well I'm not sure we can afford this." I kept stressing that we aren't spending more money, and we aren't asking you to spend any extra. I think we are the only city that has done participatory budgeting the way we have. There's no special tax, there's no nothing. We are just literally carving out money from the actual city budget and allowing citizens to do it, which I guess is unique, but that's the way it is.

I think that for us, the Mayor Pro Tem's support was probably crucial. The Mayor wasn't really that supportive. The previous Mayor was more supportive. The current Mayor, who you would think would be more supportive, she was more skeptical. But the Mayor Pro Tem, who is African-American, she was more supportive, and I think that has what helped carry us through. Also with the city council member, that I referenced when I ran, who won, she is from one of the nicer, more well-off districts of our city, and she has helped push this too. So the combination of those two has helped bring along the others.

The fact that we were able to get two of them to go the White House conference on PB in May of 2014, and two of them went to that, and they got to see PB there. Part of it is educating the council on what this will be about, and the council members who are open-minded, like I said, we got our fight for a vote, but it passed.

Q.   In addition to those council members that went, did any of your committee members go to the White House conference?

A.   Wayne Abraham.

Yes, we had two go. Four total. Folks have really worked hard over these years to make this happen, and I have to give credit to the city council members who are willing to support it. We had to push them, but we got them to do it. I know several of them through my political activity and others know them. So part of it is just personally having a discussion with them about it, so that they will listen long enough to think "oh, maybe it's not so bad." Their original reaction is "oh, what a disaster it will be, how could we have citizens do this?" And you have to make them understand that it's going to be enough ahead of time that it's going to be incorporated into their budget and this isn't going to be a surprise. City staff will be helping them all along.

A lot of it is educating people. And I think some of the public, like the Greensboro Neighborhood Congress, I think we couldn't really bring them on board until now. There was already this small project fund that the city had and they were very adept at using it, and other people really didn't know about it and didn't use it. So the city took those funds and used it to pay for their half of PB. So their funds got taken away from them, but in reality there is more money, because instead of $100,000 there is $500,000 now. So they have some experience in doing this, they just don't realize it. And I think once it got approved, then they realized, "oh, I see how this works" and that is why they want us to come and educate their members about what to do, because they truly do have neighborhoods from all across Greensboro involved. So once we do a "mock" PB process for them, I think it will make it that much easier to get them to get people to come to the neighborhood assemblies. I think having their buy-in to this now is going to be very helpful. They have seen the benefit of it finally.

Q.   Back to the White House conference, one of the things I read about that was that it had two purposes: one was how could technology be used to help the participatory budgeting process along? And the second was that there was a call for more assessment and evaluation. I wondered if you could speak to either one or both of those things in terms of what you have been thinking about for Greensboro. Will you use technology to interact with people?

A. Wayne Abraham.

I think we have discussed that. I don't think we have come up with a solution yet because we really feel like the official steering committee needs to make the decision. But allowing people to vote online might be one way to use technology, and allowing people to review projects online might be another way. So that has definitely been on our minds in terms of how we can use technology.

We had Josh Lerner from the Participatory Budgeting Project on our conference call in our meeting last Thursday, and he talked about possibly using texting technology to let people know about neighborhood assembly meetings and things like that. So there is discussion about that. There is not a resolution yet, but we are thinking about it.

As far as the research and evaluation part, we have put a lot of thought into that. One of our local universities, University of North Carolina-Greensboro, has stepped up and one of their people is actually one of our committee people. They have already thought about it and looked at the national models for this, and have created a research model for doing exactly this. They will be looking at questions such as do we get enough people involved, how does it work, where did it go well, where did it not go well, so that we can do an actual evaluation. They have incorporated that into our grant request. We are planning on at least $20,000 going toward research and evaluation. So UNC-G is going to be doing that for us, and they are very experienced at it. I am very confident that they are going to do a world class job of evaluating who comes to meetings and what happens. I mean, we need to know. We say we are reaching out, but are we successful?

Q. Can you talk more about the matching fund of $100,000 that you are to come up with in order to leverage the city's $100,000?

A. Wayne Abraham.

We had to come up with $100,000 matching funds. The city said it would put up $100,000 because that is what it normally spends on its neighborhood small projects program. So they still didn't spend any extra money. I just laugh, you know you stand there in front of city council and you listen to all this stuff, and I'm sitting here thinking I know this is political grandstanding. I hope they realize it, but they don't.

So our responsibility was to come up with $100,000 and we knew we had $30,000 from the Fund for Democratic Communities, so we had to come up with another $70,000. $10,000 then came from the Community Foundation of Greater Greensboro. And then we applied to the Z. Smith Reynolds Foundation for $60,000, and that was my job—my job was grant applications. So we applied for $60,000 and we got $50,000. That took until May. Fortunately we, in the interim, had applied for some different things. So we got to a little over $98,000. So we have already talked to the Weaver Foundation. We needed just a little more, so we have reached our $100,000 match.

Q. On your grant application to Z. Smith Reynolds, did you have to apply for that funding using the city as the applicant? Or are you an entity that can apply for grants? How did that work?

A. Wayne Abraham.

We had to do it from the city. And they allowed us to do that. I asked them ahead of time how it had to be done. It could have been done from the community foundation if they didn't want to give money directly to the city, but apparently their granting rules allowed that. One of their four programs they fund is literally exactly matching what we want to do: increasing democracy, increasing participation from minority communities. It was tailor-made for what we were after. It was just a matter of filling out the God knows how many pages online and putting everything together. And then we had to do a formal presentation to them in person. We are there, we just have to, and now that we have the matching money, of course, that lends itself to really moving everything forward. City council isn't going to back down now. They issued the challenge and we got the money, and now you have to do it.

Q. Do you think that the Council thought you wouldn't be successful?

A. Wayne Abraham.

No, but you never know. I think they might have gone ahead and done it anyway, but the fact that we have the money pretty much seals the deal.

Q. But they are just committing for one year, is that right?

A. Wayne Abraham.

Yes, they aren't going to do it on-going. But the way I look at it is if there are hundreds or thousands of people that participate in this, I really can't see them not doing it next year. Plus we are trying to create a system where the city can take it over next time and it doesn't have to be coordinated through PBP. We need PBP to help guide us through this the first time. After we've done it, then we will know what to do, and we can do it again. And I think they understand that they'll have to commit that $100,000 to the next round.

Q. Can I get your reaction to the list of characteristics or benefits of participatory budgeting? Is participatory budgeting democratic?

A. Wayne Abraham.

Yes, that is definitely a major value of this.

Q. Is participatory budgeting transparent?

A. Wayne Abraham.

Yes, I think that is also a major value of this. It's something we stress to everyone.

Q. Is participatory budgeting efficient?

A. Wayne Abraham.

I would assume it is, but I haven't been through it yet. I think I can see how it could be in that by having the budget delegates sit down with city staff, then you aren't really wasting people's time, you're knowing up front, is this doable and how much does this cost? So in that respect, I think it would be.

Q.   Does participatory budgeting provide education to citizens?

A.   Wayne Abraham.

I really do think that it will. I think people are going to learn a great deal more about how their city budget is put together, more than they ever imagined. I've worked in the process of sitting down with budget staff for the last so many months. You don't appreciate what they go through until you have to go through it with them. Then you realize you have to go through all these things. It's really not this simple straightforward thing you thought it was.

Q.   Does participatory budgeting provide a sense of social justice?

A.   Wayne Abraham.

I can see how that would be true. I think that part of what we have done—we have had an on-going argument in our city—that some parts of the city get more spent on them than others, and the fact that we are allocating the same amount of money to all five districts allows each district to make its own determination and its own decisions with the exact same amount of money. So west Greensboro is getting as much as east Greensboro, and east Greensboro can't say that "well, west is getting more that we are."

Q.   So in your mind, this is going to illustrate that maybe that argument is, if it was true, it won't be true in this process?

A.   Wayne Abraham.

Exactly. You're getting the same amount as everybody else. We have kind of an east and west Greensboro divide.

Q.   Does participatory budgeting build a sense of community? I assume you're hoping that it will also do that.

A.   Wayne Abraham.

I do, and I'll give you an example. In one of our community meetings, a lady who lives in district 5, but it's in more of an affluent part of district 5, actually said out loud "well we are going to have to have neighborhood assemblies in the other part of district 5." It actually dawned on her that to be fully representative, she needed to make sure that the people who weren't affluent had neighborhood assemblies and meetings and did this process as much as on her end of it. I just thought, "wow, it dawned on you in this meeting." This was going to be a value that was important.

Q.   I heard something very similar from someone in St. Louis who commented that people were very generous about looking at the bigger picture and the real needs of the community. Do you think that will happen in Greensboro?

A.   Wayne Abraham.

I think that's part of what's going to happen. People are going to realize what their neighbors need that they don't have an opportunity to find out about now.

Q.   Does participatory budgeting build trust?

A.   Wayne Abraham.

I think as long as you have very open and transparent voting and projects, and people aren't shut down, and no one says "this project can be funded because" and "that can't be funded because" then I think people will be okay with that. I think it's not knowing that is part of the problem, and I think that when you say "I want my road paved" and well that's more than the entire budget, versus you want a covered bus stop in the area, and that is well within the budget, then I think people will begin to comprehend. I think a lot of it is that people don't comprehend the cost of things. So this is going to give them a perspective on just how much it costs.

One thing we've discussed, and even city staff have mentioned, that people may say "I want a sidewalk here," and one of their responses may be "we have already planned a sidewalk to go here and it will come in this time frame" and the other is that it may dawn on city staff that maybe we need to move this project up the timeline because people here really want it. There's going to be education on both sides I think. City staff is going to realize it, and I think the citizens are going to realize it. I'm actually optimistic.

We had a "mock" PB process at UNC-G, and we were going to award $1,500. We had three city council members come and we had $1,500 to hand out. It was for three projects. So you were only going to get $500 per project, and we had all of these projects proposed that just blew me away. I thought I don't know what to vote for. The creativity of our own people, people don't realize what projects they're going to have to choose among. We had college students proposing a food truck because Guilford College grows its own vegetables, and they wanted a truck to take them to the other side of town that's a food desert. And the IRC—the interactive resource center—that is sort of a day center for the homeless, they wanted a barber chair so they could give people haircuts so they could go on job interviews. And I thought, "and all you all want is $500!" What are we going to do if we have thousands to disburse? I was inspired by that. I just thought this is really encouraging, and we are only handing out $500 in a "mock" exercise.

Q.   Does participatory budgeting build a belief that meaningful change can occur?

A.   Wayne Abraham.

I hope so. I mean that is my goal. I think the people who are involved definitely have their hearts in the right place. We have been able to infuse into city staff those values. If they haven't thought about them before, I think they have come to realize, "oh, we should have day care maybe at a meeting, so that people with families can come" so I think part of it is that it didn't dawn on them before.

Q. Yes, I have heard people say that food always helps to encourage participation, even if you can only provide cookies that sometimes helps. Also
day care, sometimes transportation to and from, and also going out to
where it's easy for people to get to whether that's a church, community
center, or whatever it might be. These things help with participation. So
my question is what advice would you give to a community if they were
thinking about this, or what lessons have you learned, or what would you
do differently?

A. Wayne Abraham.

Well, the first lesson would be don't give up. Perseverance will pay
off. Work your political connections because you're going to need them.
Involve as many people as you possibly can. I guess that would be the
only real advice.

As far as what we would do differently, I'm not sure what we could
have done differently. I think we tried different things. I think it just takes
longer than you would have ever imagined. When you do it from this
perspective, we were getting the city to do this whereas in other instances
somebody decided to commit the money upfront.

Q. Is there anything else in general that you'd like to tell me about your experience with participatory budgeting?

A. Wayne Abraham.

A couple of things I would say. One is that planning to do proper
research and evaluation is going to be essential because it will help you
get grant funding. And two, involving as many people as you already have
in your city who work on inclusiveness will also help you—our Human
Relations Commission, our Latino community center, all of that kind of
thing. If you bring those people in from the beginning that helps you in
the long run. I know that being able to say, here's UNC-G's proposal for
evaluation, so you're going to get a robust evaluation of how you spent
your money helped the others say yes to spending the money. It's not like
they are just throwing the money into the wind and hoping it will be okay,
we are going to actually have research and evaluation handed back to
show that we spent our money wisely, or what happened and what could
be done better. Foundations who care about these kinds of issues want to
know that they are spending their money intelligently.

Q. Tied to that, in terms of collecting data on participants, and because you
have this large difference in terms of ethnicity across the city, do you
think you will meet with any resistance from people who might not be
legal immigrants, that might have immigration issues, that might be reluc-
tant to give their home address, or their date of birth, or whatever you
choose to use to verify residency and age before they vote on projects?

A. Wayne Abraham.

I don't know yet. We were asked this just recently when we did a presentation for the Latino community center, and this came up, and they were
very pleased with what we told them. I think they will help encourage

people not to be worried about that. I think part of what we will do is choose our wording to be "residents" rather than "citizens" so we say "residents of Greensboro" and not "citizens of Greensboro" which was intentional on our part.

Q.   Anything else you want to add?

A.   Wayne Abraham.

We laugh that Vincent Russell was our temporary president for 90 days and of course three years later he is still our president of our little committee group—Participatory Budgeting Greensboro. We tease him about that. He has been really very good about keeping up with everything. Part of what I have enjoyed seeing is that people even in the process of our committee, people who weren't normally leadership people have become that, so we've already grown people into positions they didn't previously think about having.

In the following section, the interview with Larry Morse is presented.

Q.   What is your role in the participatory budgeting process in Greensboro?

A.   Larry Morse.

Five or six years ago the Fund for Democratic Communities brought Josh Lerner and someone else from the Participatory Budgeting Project's New York office to give a public presentation about the concept of PB. I attended that, and maybe another piece of background that relates to my interest in PB is that I used to teach economics, and did so at A&T, North Carolina Agriculture and Technical State University, for 34 years. It is here in Greensboro, and I retired in 2010. So I was intrigued by the idea and thought that it made great sense—that is the idea being PB. So I went off and on to meetings that were largely held by, and brought together by, the Fund for Democratic Communities.

Then, during those meetings, there were maybe 40 to 50 percent of those attending that were actually Fund for Democratic Communities (FDC) staff, and so often when there was something to be done the rest of us, what I refer to as the civilians, we just waited because we knew their staff would pick it up. It was your basic lazy participation. The director, a personal friend of ours, of FDC, saw what was happening in that one meeting and said that she wasn't sure whether the work on PB was really coming from the grassroots or was really being pushed by FDC. She suggested that a way to measure that and see if it was just the former, or if it was just FDC. And she suggested if it was then that is not going to be something that is likely to work. So what we decided was that those of us who weren't staff, we had a meeting, and we decided that, yes, we wanted to go ahead. And so pretty much our meetings after that were without FDC staff, though there were occasionally one or two staff people who attended. And then we, and I was among those who decided we will take this on, and so we started doing more, engaging more, and being more committed to it.

Q. And how long ago was that, then? That the citizens started to take an active role?

A. Larry Morse.

Maybe three years ago. I mean, we have been at this long enough that I lose track of when things actually happened.

Q. In that initial process did you see people come and go, or was there was a different group that maybe are very active now than there were three years ago?

A. Larry Morse.

I think the folks that are active now were among the participants from the beginning. There were certainly some in and out, but I think those of us who stuck with it were there, but there were a couple of people who dropped away. One went to graduate school; he had been very active up until then. Another was a graduate student here, and finished her program. And then, another I guess, would be described as "burnt out."

We did a fundraiser because we got a grant from the Fund for Democratic Communities and they required that we match dollar for dollar with private fundraising, with a requirement that they won't count monies coming in for donations that are in excess of $100—they count up to $100. So we had some funds and one of the things we did with those funds was, as we were getting to a point where we needed more coordinated work and attention to try to lobby council members, and one of the folks who was part of the active group was hired to work part-time to fill that function. And she found that the whole process got—she did it, did it well—but it was a little too much and so after she actually quit doing what she was doing, but after she largely completed what we wanted, then she pretty much stopped coming to the meetings.

Q. In terms of your elected officials, has there been someone who has been actively involved throughout? Or have they come unwillingly?

A. Larry Morse.

None have come to the meetings or the group. There were maybe four city council members who came to a luncheon one time when we invited Josh Lerner down from PBP in New York. There are two council members in particular who have been particularly helpful, and it was Yvonne Johnson, who is the Mayor Pro Tem, she had previously been Mayor, two mayors ago, and she proposed to the council that the Mayor appoint someone or that they create a committee to look at PB and come back with a recommendation to city council. And so she, Yvonne Johnson, and Nancy Hoffmann have been helpful. Yvonne is an at-large candidate and Nancy Hoffmann is from a district—we have a city council, three at-large, five districts, and a Mayor. They have been supportive all along. They were on the committee and made the recommendation to council that ultimately resulted in the resolution that was drafted by the legal department last October approving that the city would try a year of PB.

Q. And that will be for fiscal year 2016/2017?

A. Larry Morse.

For the budget year 2016/2017. We're just not ready—the time frame of this stuff—it was going to be impossible to do it for this cycle.

Q. One of the reasons I wanted to ask about the council involvement is that in other cities it has typically been a council person or an alderman who had a certain set of money that was designated for their ward or district and they would commit that to the participatory budgeting process. Are you familiar with that approach to participatory budgeting?

A. Larry Morse.

Yes, like more in Chicago. Yes, the council members get no money here like the aldermen get in Chicago or the folks in New York get in their boroughs. So it is all a jointly, full-council decision about setting budget priorities, staff coming up with a budget, and then council having work sessions on these, and then approving it.

Q. And what amount or kind of money have the council committed for that budget year?

A. Larry Morse.

The council decided, and it was in our recommendation, and the resolution was largely what we from the PB side had written, and what we came to was that council would set aside, would allocate, $500,000 to go through the PB process, with there being $100,000 for each of the five districts. And, they also approved to spend $100,000, which would be matched from the private, from our side, with another $100,000 to have $200,000 to pay for the PB launch this year. And what we were also recommending and I believe is in the resolution, that we would follow the Vallejo pattern, and we are in the process of contracting with Josh Lerner at PBP in New York to have them work with us.

Q. And that $100,000, where are you anticipating that it would come from on the private side?

A. Larry Morse.

Going into it, we knew we had, from the Fund for Democratic Communities, they had put in reserve $30,000 to be used for this purpose. They have signed a contract with the city. We got another $10,000 from the Community Foundation. And we submitted a request from the Z. Smith Reynolds Foundation which is actually based in Winston-Salem for $60,000, which would have given us the $100,000. We were awarded $50,000. One of the members of the team teaches at UNC-G, University of North Carolina-Greensboro, and she will be doing, with a team of graduate students and some other folks at UNC-G, will be doing the evaluation. So she has $5,000 in-kind for that. And got a grant, that she was hoping would come in at $5,000 and that would fill the $10,000 gap, but she only got $2,800, so we are short. Our expectation is that we can go to another local foundation and that they will help us. We have initiated some conversations with other local foundations, saying we have this big grant from Smith Reynolds and we may need some back-up, and can we come back to you and talk about back-up funds? And so, one of those larger foundations, they can do a small allocation without our making a formal grant application. So we are fairly confident we will get the full $100,000.

Q. What is the next step?

A. Larry Morse.

So we are close enough that we are actively working on getting the contract with the PBP folks in New York.

Q. And you would anticipate that they would send a person to work in your community during the whole process?

A. Larry Morse.

The expectation is that we will hire, or actually—it is not too simple. Since January, the four of us from PB have been meeting once every other week for an hour with the director of the city budget department, his assistant, and occasionally when her schedule allows the City Manager's assistant comes. And we are working out all these details and so we have been in conversation with Josh Lerner at PBP both independently, and then at a couple of the meetings we have had a speaker phone and Josh Lerner has been on the line.

So the end result is that two people will be hired, they will be hired by the PBP New York office. That's cleaner for the city, and then they don't have hiring responsibilities. But there will be two people that will be hired locally, with assistance from Josh Lerner supplying us with a template for the kinds of job qualifications that they have found are important. And those two folks will be here full-time for I believe it is for ten months.

And then we also have I think 30 percent of the time of, I forget the exact title, some sort of coordinator in New York, and then, I think, also 10 percent of Josh Lerner's time. A good part of that will be not so much our consulting with them, but rather that buys time for the two who are here, who aren't PB experts, to have conversations with or maybe have a time or two that a person from New York comes down and works with them for a couple days. That's what that time is for.

Q. I wondered if you could tell me about how you're envisioning this going forward with getting people involved. In terms of citizen participation, what do you see as the opportunities and the challenges for your community specifically to get people involved?

A. Larry Morse.

To begin with, all four of us are firmly committed, as was Yvonne Johnson and the city council, firmly committed to the notion that this PB process would be a vehicle to increase civic participation, civic capital among communities that aren't currently engaged. And we, just as background on the city, we have a little over 100 languages, home languages, of students in the public school system. So we've got a lot of, in some cases, fairly large ethnic communities, and in other cases obviously quite small. Hispanic is the largest.

And maybe, let's see, a week or two weeks ago, I and Vincent got the invitation, but I accompanied him, we went to the Latino Community Connections meeting to talk about PB, and made a presentation about PB and our interest in getting outreach into the Hispanic community. We know that's an area that we need that we definitely want to work on and that's a key function and that will be decidedly from the beginning, that will be one of the things that the evaluation process will be looking at, and that will be one of the measures of our success. This Thursday Vincent and others are making a presentation to the Neighborhood Congress. The Neighborhood Congress is made up of neighborhood associations, and most neighborhoods around the city have a neighborhood association, and they can each send a representative to the Neighborhood Congress. So we expect to be working through groups like neighborhood associations and the various ethnic groups that have soccer leagues or whatever it is they have got, and get access to those communities, and that will be a large part of the work of the two coordinators who will get hired.

Q. Do you know if these neighborhood associations have Facebook pages or Listservs in terms of how they communicate with people?

A. Larry Morse.

All I know is that my neighborhood has a Listserv, and they do have a website. I'm not sure—neither my wife nor I do Facebook, so I don't know if they're on Facebook too.

Q. One of the other technology-related issues is the actual voting process. Have you talked about how you plan to do that, whether it will be a paper ballot or if you'll try to use some electronic voting?

A. Larry Morse.

We haven't, but I think most of us have in mind doing a paper ballot. Back up maybe two years ago, in May, three or four of us went to the PB conference held in Chicago. It was timed to be the weekend when in Alderman Moore's district there was voting going on. We went on a little walking tour and saw the projects. We ended up at a little community rec center and observed the actual voting, and that was a paper ballot.

What we don't have yet is we don't have a steering committee, and therefore we don't have a rule book yet. But one of the things that we are certainly interested in and hope to influence the steering committee with and have the council approve it, is that voting would be for any resident, not be a citizen requirement. Obviously for those living within, or residing within the district whose $100,000 we are talking about, and looking for maybe age 16 or 18 as the minimum voting age.

Q. In terms of those $100,000 allocations per district, is there a limitation then, has that been determined, on the kinds of projects at this point that can be approved?

A. Larry Morse.

Yes, and that's a soft yes. The folks from the city budget side are fine with capital projects, the reason being that even if it extends beyond the budget year because of construction time or whatever implementation time is needed, then at least it's not an on-going financial commitment. If it's programmatic, and involves city staff and additional city staff being hired and so on, then they get a little anxious about that. There appears to be strong interest on the part of the city to keep it on capital things.

Q.   Could you give me your perspective on the characteristics or benefits of participatory budgeting? The first one is that participatory budgeting is a democratic process. What do you say to that?

A.   Larry Morse.
     Definitely.

Q.   Is participatory budgeting transparent?

A.   Larry Morse.
     Yes.

Q.   Is participatory budgeting efficient?

A.   Larry Morse.
     I think in the first year, in some sense, not. But that is recognizing that in the first year there's a real start-up cost getting the system going, and I think after that, which isn't guaranteed, we also have to vote on whether or not we are going to keep going. It will become increasingly efficient as we get facilitators trained and things like that, and have coordination with rec centers and other public places for meetings. I think it will get smoother as we go along.

Q.   Does participatory budgeting provide education to citizens?

A.   Larry Morse.
     Definitely. One of the things we have used earlier to try to persuade city staff, and this is under a previous city manager, when one of the things we were doing during the time while the council PB ad hoc committee was working, one of the things they wanted us to do was to work with their staff, and we had several meetings with them. One of the points that we made to them was that citizens will gain more information about what is involved in the budgeting process and recognize the issue of trade-offs. We expect that Greensboro won't be any different from other cities in which citizens gain a greater appreciation of the work that city staff does and the skills that they have. Because they will—as you know—out of the process as they are developing projects, they are going to have to be working with staff who are going to have to vet the projects and make sure they comply with regulations and so on, and do the costing which citizens can't do.

Q.   Is participatory budgeting inclusive of all of the diversity in a community?

A.   Larry Morse.
     Well that is certainly what we are trying to do. We are looking at a city which, in a typical year, elects its city council on off-election years with 18 percent of the registered voters voting. So we hope to change that.

Q.   And that's typical of the turnout?

A.   Larry Morse.

   Yes.

Q.   Does participatory budgeting build trust?

A.   Larry Morse.

   Yes, with the voting, and I think one of the other things that folks will see maybe become true of residents in general, they will become aware of, is the current confusion about what we did. "Didn't we vote to do this with a bond issue three years ago? Why haven't I seen it yet in my neighborhood?" And the answer is the city has to maintain, doesn't want to go beyond a certain indebtedness to revenue ratio, and so we will delay bonds, and that's why it's not in your neighborhood yet. It's on the board and it's going to happen, but, yes that's part of that civic learning.

Q.   Does participatory budgeting build a belief that meaningful change can occur?

A.   Larry Morse.

   I think so. And one of the things that the four of us have in the back of our minds, and we haven't discussed it with city staff yet, is that voting on budgets is the first step. And then after a couple years, we would like to have participation in the tax setting. So it's making that process more democratic and more transparent.

   In this city, we are going on five years now with no increases in property taxes so we have had commensurate drops in city services and programs, and living with potholes and things like that, so I think a lot of people would like to see taxes raised and we would like to see services back at a level that we used to enjoy.

Q.   Do you think that attitude is just sort of the outcome of the economic downturn of 2008, just to be cautious, or was there a citizen outcry that they didn't want taxes to go up?

A.   Larry Morse.

   I think it was council members just being cautious, or playing on their own, or what they perceived as their own re-election and livelihood. We are in a state that mandates property reassessment every five years and typically what has happened is every five years after that happens, in all the time I've been here, the general assessed values have gone up, and so the millage has been dropped. But not enough to keep the revenue neutral but to allow the—to intentionally have more revenue, but not keep the old millage on and there would be times that would be a relatively large jump in the taxes.

Q.   If you were going to give advice to another community that was interested in participatory budgeting, given all that you know and have been through and where you stand, what might you have done differently or wished you had known at the beginning?

A.   Larry Morse.

   We tried at the beginning to create more grassroots support figuring we could get a groundswell, and then from that go to council, working with council members before doing that. We went out to about 20 organizations, or churches, and made presentations about PB. Our experience was almost universally that attendees thought "that's a great idea" but not a single person was willing to sign up or otherwise help make it happen. So we shifted gears and began focusing instead on working with the city council members. So that's how we got the working committee and things like that. Those were originated from our working with what we knew were supportive members of the city council. So that experience in other communities might be different or maybe we didn't do it right, I don't know.

Q.   I don't know that there is a right or wrong answer, it's definitely an experiment.

A.   Larry Morse.

We didn't get the specific outpouring of "when's your next meeting?" so in that sense it didn't work. In the sense that it spread the idea and maybe will help us again now when it's a reality, but we'll see.

Q.   In terms of the benefits that you see, is there anything else we haven't covered that you're hoping that this is going to do for your community?

A.   Larry Morse.

Nothing immediately comes to mind. I would underscore that for some ethnic identification is important. I'm white and I taught at A&T which is a predominantly black student body, worked with a local un-doing racism group and recognized that it's way more than just black and white and that we have a pretty large, over the last 10 to 20 years, gotten a fairly large Hispanic population as well, and the blacks and Hispanics haven't really come together so well.

And then we've got other groups, I told you about the array of home languages we've got, and some of those are kind of idiosyncratic, as in we have a fairly large Montagnard community here and that's because for a while here we had a group that provided family services to them. So a lot of those who were allowed to leave Vietnam and come to the States got placed in Greensboro because there was a service set up to assist them. But there are all other kinds of ethnic groups and we just, as a city we don't do it all well, about recognizing the role of race and ethnicity in the things that council decides. I suspect that, other than for the black members of council, which at this point there are three of them, the whites when voting on issue X just don't see the elephant in the room, that what we are talking about is race and we aren't willing to talk about that, and the black members are just plain tired of bringing it up. So we have a lot we can build on.

Q.   Are those divisions with your minority populations, are they also along the lines of poverty issues here as well?

A.   Larry Morse.

Yes.

Q. Is there anything else you would like to add?

A. Larry Morse.

How we have done it, I would say in some sense is very flawed, and other than for the graduate student who was with us for a while, we are all white folks, and for what we are trying to do, that is kind of weird. It is, on the other hand, since it's now down to four of us, it was always less than 10 people. It does uphold the idea about a small group of dedicated people can make things change. In principle, we should have done it differently, but in outcome, it has not been so bad. Although, certainly if we had more people of color with us to begin with, the outreach that we are facing and planning for now would have been a different enterprise.

In the following section, the interview with Elizabeth Dam-Regier is presented.

Q. Will you tell me about who you are and your role in the participatory budgeting process in Greensboro, and what got you interested in participatory budgeting?

A. Elizabeth Dam-Regier.

I'm a recent graduate of the Communication Studies Master's Program at UNC-G. While I was at UNC-G, I randomly mentioned in a class that I was interested in community engagement projects. Then I got pulled into a research project in the Communication Studies Department, and I ended up being a graduate research assistant. My second year of graduate school is when we really started to work with PB and that's how I ended up meeting Vincent Russell. My position in the whole process was to use the PB process as sort of a "mock" trial run to try and 1) promote PB in the community, but 2) also teach under-represented youth how to engage in the community and advocate for themselves. So it's a two part kind of thing. Also, we worked with Dudley High School, which is an extraordinarily African-American dominated school. It's something like 95 percent of students there identify as black or African-American. And so we were working with them to use the PB process to show them how to be activists for themselves in their own community and to create activism.

Q. So the high school students participated in the "mock" process?

A. Elizabeth Dam-Regier.

Yes, they were specifically the honor society students.

Q. So the projects they came up with, they did not get to see to fruition?

A. Elizabeth Dam-Regier.

No, it was strictly a practice run to show them how to get the community involved. What was great about it too was that PB actually got passed in October in Greensboro during this whole process, so even though we were going through this process saying, "hey you're thinking of ideas in the beginning stage" and you're thinking of ideas and this is a "mock" process still, and we don't actually fund this. But in the end they saw this process approved, so I could go in and suggest these ideas and it could eventually come to fruition in the end.

Q. Do you think that process in the high school will encourage some parents to get involved with participatory budgeting because of those students when it gets to that point?

A. Elizabeth Dam-Regier.

I would hope so, but we don't have any clear data, and we didn't look for any data regarding parent involvement. I would hope so, but I think a lot of it was our goal to show that even as teens, and especially in the PB process where is not necessarily discriminatory against people under 18, even normal to include them in the voting processes, to show them how they don't really need adults to create change. So it's more about that and less about thinking "oh your parents can help you with this."

Our big outreach event that we ended up doing with the Dudley High School students was that we held a community "mock" process at their biggest football game of the year. In that sense, we did get family members and other community members highly involved. We had city council representation there, kind of accidentally, which was really awesome. I think that in that event it would definitely help that scenario, but again I couldn't prove it.

Q. Do you envision doing the "mock" process again with high school students or anybody?

A. Elizabeth Dam-Regier.

I think the PB organization in Greensboro, absolutely yes. Vincent Russell has been approached numerous times at various PB-related events and conferences because we have done a couple of conference presentations regarding this, where they have asked him to bring people in and do a "mock" process to educate the community. And we also have had a lot of discussions around using PB in less a city-wide political scenario, and on smaller scales, like to education boards and things like that.

Q. You said you were interested in the citizen engagement aspect to begin with, could you talk about how you have seen the process develop in terms of relationships that have been built or strengthened, people or organizations that you weren't maybe expecting to participate but have?

A. Elizabeth Dam-Regier.

To give you a little background to where I am coming from, I am traditionally trained as a graphic designer and I came from Phoenix. I have been living in Phoenix for the past five years, and when I was there I was really into a national designer's organization, and they have this good program. And what I loved about it was that it takes people from all these different professions to solve big problems. Designers, doctors, lawyers, teachers, artists, and all these random people, throws them in one room, and they solve this huge community issue.

So what I see happening in Greensboro is something like that, but that is not happening yet even though PB Greensboro has been working for four years to get this off the ground. I think that is just starting to catch on. I think we are just starting to make those connections. I think a lot of it has to do with the people in the organization, so typically people who are interested in politics oftentimes aren't millennials. We like to be visual activists; we aren't really interested in actually going anywhere to do anything good. We like to do it at home from our computers. So I can see a lot of the people in Greensboro that are interested in physically getting involved in this, and making those connections are an older generation than I. Which is not a bad thing, but what that does I think is that hinders connections, because the one thing the millennial generation is good at is creating connections rapidly through things like social media. And that is the one thing that I think Greensboro PB is really lacking, that I have painstakingly had to negotiate for the past two years.

Q. Tell me about that—what could other cities learn from you in terms of what has been successful? What are you envisioning or what have you seen work so far or what resistance have you seen if it hasn't?

A. Elizabeth Dam-Regier.

Basically, what is problematic is for social media engagement to work in a movement like this is that you actually have to have followers, which we don't right now. We have a Twitter and a Facebook account that no one really knows exists which is problematic because we don't really know how to promote that. The other problem we are running into is that Greensboro city officials, again this is my interpretation, but we also have very different perceptions of what social activism is in this age. So the Greensboro city officials, they have a very different perspective on how money should be allocated for this project. Right? So basically we are getting $100,000 per district for the actual PB voting process to be distributed, and then we have an additional $200,000. I think they are giving us $100,000, but we are trying raise $100,000. Which is great, but that is a relatively small budget. One of the first things they wanted to cut was all the things that I think make people know about it—they don't want to pay for a designer, they don't want to pay for printing cost, they don't want to pay for someone to actually manage that kind of the PR aspect of this project.

Q. So you are saying no printed or paper products, no brochures?

A. Elizabeth Dam-Regier.

They have a very tiny budget for it, but they are trying to cut it. That is the first thing that they tried to cut. And I only know this because I have been approached to be the designer for all that stuff, because I have been designing local PB materials for Greensboro for the past two years. That's my background, I know the process, and I know the people. The first thing is that they don't want to pay someone to do that. For me, that is challenging because if we want anyone to care about this, we have to look legitimate. And I think city officials don't really see that side of the argument because they don't need to look official to be perceived as official. I think that is one of the problems. And when I say social media and design, those kind of go hand in hand for me. All media, marketing, and PR are all in the same bubble.

Q.   In the mind of the council, do you think they are seeing social media as not even an issue, or do they think it is just going to magically appear?

A.   Elizabeth Dam-Regier.

They see social media as, "hey, Twitter is free, right? So why do we need to pay someone to do it?" At least that is the perception that I have.

Q.   So they aren't looking at that as being an investment in that infrastructure that is needed?

A.   Elizabeth Dam-Regier.

Right, they are looking at the typical things you expect city government to look at, which is aggravating. The whole reason we are doing this process is because the city government hasn't been doing what we have been wanting them to do. Obviously the process hasn't been working great for everyone, so we should take a step back and look at a different way of doing things. I'm sure you know if you have worked with any local government that it can be increasingly problematic and difficult.

Q.   You talked before about the disconnect between the millennials and the older generation who would want to go out and want to do something versus you who don't want to do that. Will the younger people come out to an idea assembly at a physical location or would they want to submit their ideas online?

A.   Elizabeth Dam-Regier.

I think if you give millennials access to both, it will increase engagement in both. But if you give them a defined one or the other, they probably won't. Fortunately I do believe that we are going to get incredible engagement from UNC-G students and any other schools that we work with in the community. For instance, Dudley High School will probably have a project, and this is not confirmed or anything, but I foresee a project developing in the future where UNC-G students help coach Dudley High School students in how to participate in the city-wide process.

Q.   Skipping ahead then to the voting process. What are you envisioning for that to be—do you think it will be a paper ballot or have some online component?

A.   Elizabeth Dam-Regier.

I think it will be paper, mostly because an online component, I think the city will see as costing extra money, which it will, to do it right. Absolutely right. I think it will be paper in the beginning, but hopefully after a few years of this process it will be online. So I don't want to just be PB Greensboro forever, I want it to be like New York or Chicago. Why can't we have an entire city-wide campaign and visual components and a website where you can vote electronically and all this stuff? I hope that all happens, but we are a very little fish in a big pond.

Q. Back to citizen participation, in terms of barriers, one of the issues that has come up in different places is that you have to factor in things like people's lost wages, or what if they don't have transportation, or you need to have food or provide child care. Have you discussed any of those things?

A. Elizabeth Dam-Regier.

Absolutely. The big topic that we discussed is actually child care and incentives. We do buy pizza, you have to get them to come in, and that helps in a big way. Greensboro also has a very big refugee population, and the organization that helps those refugees in Greensboro—they have been very vocal at the PB meetings that we have had so far, so I perceive them being very instrumental. Probably interpreters, and not just Spanish interpreters, we are going to need a variety of different of interpreters because not a lot of people can just interpret anything. We have a lot of sign language needs, ASL interpreters are available, but we are lacking interpreters of other languages and that is a big barrier we are facing. Transportation is probably going to be problematic. Greensboro doesn't have a very reliable public transportation system. When it is reliable, it doesn't travel far enough into to rural areas.

We are a relatively big city, but we are in a weird place right in the middle of Raleigh, Durham, Chapel Hill and then Winston, Salem, and then Charlotte—that is the triangle we sit in the middle of. Greensboro is relatively big, but it is very spread out. It is not built on top of each other.

Q. Do you envision going out to some of those more rural areas for meetings? Will you take participatory budgeting to them in some way?

A. Elizabeth Dam-Regier.

Yes, that was something that came up recently at a meeting, we had an attendee ask about that, and ask if we were going to hold all of our meetings at the downtown library. Instead, our hopes are to leave it up to each one of the districts to decide where they would hold their own meetings. Hopefully they would engage the entire community within their district.

Q. Have you been doing, like you mentioned Twitter and Facebook, have you been doing updates for those? Have you been charged with that responsibility?

A. Elizabeth Dam-Regier.

I have not been charged with that responsibility now that I have graduated. They extend invitations to me to come to meetings, but I hold no real responsibility to this organization anymore. I'd love to stay involved but I just don't have the time available. And I recently just moved out of the community.

Q. Do you still anticipate being a part of the process to watch this go through if you can?

A. Elizabeth Dam-Regier.

I still anticipate being, how do I put this, a vendor of sorts if they need me, or a sounding board type of thing. I don't plan on playing any major role within the organization. This should be run by Greensboro people, obviously, or that defeats the whole purpose.

Q. Can you tell me your impressions of the list of characteristics or benefits of participatory budgeting? Do you think PB is democratic?

A. Elizabeth Dam-Regier.

Yes. It is the most unbiased form of democracy that we can implement in the city. It is way more democratic than the processes we have going now.

Q. Is participatory budgeting transparent?

A. Elizabeth Dam-Regier.

Yes. I think if you do it correctly, it's transparent. I think there is potential to have a façade of transparency and really be quite opaque, but I think if it's done correctly it is relatively transparent.

Q. Is participatory budgeting efficient?

A. Elizabeth Dam-Regier.

No, potentially yes, but not particularly. I think participatory budgeting is not necessarily the process you should utilize to implement all budgeting within the city. I think that can be problematic. But what I do like about it is that it gets community members engaged in the political process again, and also creates a better trust with the government when they are engaging in a political process like that.

Q. And trust is one of the characteristics, too, so you would say yes to that?

A. Elizabeth Dam-Regier.

Yes, definitely.

Q. Does participatory budgeting provide a sense of social justice?

A. Elizabeth Dam-Regier.

Yes, absolutely.

Q. Will participatory budgeting be inclusive of all the diversity in your neighborhoods or districts?

A. Elizabeth Dam-Regier.

I think it likes to boast that, but I think that is very challenging. We like to say it is inclusive but when you run into barriers like transportation and language, it's not necessarily as inclusive as we would like it to be. In our community, Greensboro is a fairly diverse city, but right now basically everyone who is running PB Greensboro is white. That is problematic. We all see that. We need to be more diverse, but it is hard to create diversity when you don't have diverse people that want to participate. That is one of the main challenges we have run into. I read an article about that challenge of diversity within PB.

Q. Other cities that have acknowledged this say they aren't giving up, that they are going to try again. You have to identify it, and then have a plan to try again. Is that what you see will happen here?

A. Elizabeth Dam-Regier.

Greensboro is fortunate in that. It has such an activist history that it is easier to light a fire under under-represented communities because of the histories they connect with. We are fortunate in that way compared to other cities.

Q. Does participatory budgeting build a belief that meaningful change can occur?

A. Elizabeth Dam-Regier.

Yes, it absolutely does. What I love about the videos from the PBP website is it shows people who, even if their project doesn't get chosen, they understand the value of other projects being chosen. It creates a very compassionate and other-minded community. It's not necessarily concerned about social justice for them as individuals or maybe their particular community, their ethnicity, or their group, but instills an understanding of social justice for all which is awesome.

Q. Does participatory budgeting build a sense of community?

A. Elizabeth Dam-Regier.

Yes, absolutely.

Q. What advice might you give to another community thinking about implementing participatory budgeting?

A. Elizabeth Dam-Regier.

First, and this comes not necessarily from my experience, but the experience shared from members who have been doing this since the beginning, is don't be delusional about how quick you think this process is going to be. It can in fact be incredibly hard to gain support. Even though in our heads, it makes so much sense. In our case, we also had a bunch of relatively highly educated people getting together for this, and sometimes what makes so much sense and is rational to us, isn't necessarily rational to a community. And we have to present that rationale, which can be very difficult. That is one key piece of advice. The second piece of advice would be, no matter how long it takes, to keep pushing. The fact that it took us four years to get this thing going, the relief we felt when we found out it was passed by the council was awesome. Even though we still had a lot of planning stages to go through before we could implement this, the fact that we actually got city government to say yes to us for something that we were begging for was an incredible feeling. Just that alone, shows you that you can make change and you can create change in a meaningful way.

In the following section, the interview with Karen Kixmiller is presented.

Q. I wanted to include the perspective of a city employee on the participatory budgeting process and what you think your role will be as the process goes forward. Tell me about how you see your role or the role of staff playing out in the participatory budgeting process.

A. Karen Kixmiller.

I am in the Budget and Evaluation department of the city, and I'm a Budget and Management Analyst. I will say, primarily my role has been support in the PB initiative.

So where we are now, we are actually in contract discussions with PBP in New York. We are going to contract with them to facilitate the PB process, and administer the process. For that purpose they will be hiring two temporary staff to be co-located here at the city to manage the process. We expect to take the contract to city council on the 21st of July, 2015. [See Appendix 8.1 for complete Professional Services Agreement between the City of Greensboro, North Carolina and the Participatory Budgeting Project.]

Now leading up to that, you will see in the council's resolution, the requirement was that the community raise $100,000 in funds and the city would match that for the administrative costs. So the community has raised $90,000 in grants from foundations, There are funds for an evaluation piece and there is still a small gap in the community funding, which they feel certain a local foundation will plug that gap. And so, that is one thing in my mind that could potentially be tenuous, although I think now we had a recent city council change favorable to PB. But that if that change had been in a different direction with that council member it might be more tenuous, you know with council staying to the letter of the law, you know "you don't have $100,000 in your hand." But we feel like with this recent change the council is more favorable.

Q.   When you say change on the council, was there someone on the council that changed their mind? Or a new council person?

A.   Karen Kixmiller.

They resigned. We have a new council person.

Q.   So it is somebody that was appointed, not elected.

A.   Karen Kixmiller.

Yes, appointed for the duration of the term which ends in November. And so my role so far, and Larry Davis, the budget director, will be project manager. But of course most of the behind the scenes or background work will probably be from the other staff as well. This is kind of a joint effort with the city manager's office that has been of course keenly interested in the progress of the project, and we work with the assistant city manager.

What we have been doing since the resolution is meeting twice a month with the local PB folk, the community PB, which is about a group of five, to check on progress because it was incumbent on the community to raise those funds, and I was a little nervous that the funds weren't going to be raised in a timely manner to dovetail with our budget process. I was concerned about that. If you've ever worked in the community, you will understand.

Then, you know how it is. I was in planning and then I moved over to budget. You know working with community groups, nonprofits, and boards of directors, etc., there might be the interest and the desire, but there's not always the time or the commitment level. So I was definitely concerned just knowing from past experiences that we would need to see if there would be enough energy to get the funding in. And they did.

We are just a couple of months behind schedule, I would say. Ideally the staff would have been hired by this time, so that they could kind of get a learning curve behind them when it's kind of our quiet time, you know the budget just passed, but it's going to be fine. We have to pass our budget in June, and so we are on day two of the new year.

We don't have to have the projects determined specifically before we pass the budget, but ideally we wanted to know the direction of the voting so if there was something that we had in the budget maybe we could match it up. There might be some synergy.

Q. And you are putting this in place this budget cycle?

A. Karen Kixmiller.

It's going to be, the administration part is in 2015/2016 budget year, and the awards for projects will be 2016/2017 budget year. And the $100,000 match from the city is basically a repurposing of funds that we have used for a number of years on a project called the Neighborhood Small Projects Program. Essentially, it's very similar to what we might be doing with participatory budgeting anyway. Each of our five council districts got $20,000 and neighborhoods were allowed to submit requests for their neighborhood. It was just a nominal amount of money, but one neighborhood had a historic decorative stone sign that was crumbling into the sidewalk, so it would cover something like that, or refurbishing of playground equipment. So basically we just converted that funding to the administrative costs, and then council per the resolution had promised $100,000 per district up to $500,000.

Q. And where will that extra money come from then if you were doing only $100,000 previously?

A. Karen Kixmiller.

I am not certain. I do not yet know.

Q. But it doesn't have to be there this year, it could be there next year, correct?

A. Karen Kixmiller.

Correct. Now we have CDBG funds, we have some housing money, property tax that goes toward planning and housing initiatives, so I don't know if it's going to be from our general fund, our operating budget, or if it's going to be out of other funds, or if it might be a combination depending on the type of project, it might be out of our capital improvement budget. I could foresee that, potentially, depending on the project, especially if a similar or the same project was already in our CIP, Capital Improvements Plan, and the neighbors or residents vote and it just kind of makes that timeline a little quicker on that specific project. I think there could be potentially multiple sources of funding for the projects.

Q. And that is how you are seeing it, that these things could actually be for things like street improvements, not necessarily just the small projects that were previously funded in the neighborhoods?

A. Karen Kixmiller.

Potentially. I could see that if they wanted to do that, for example, I'm thinking about a couple of parks that are in the planning process or had just recently had the planning process, where they might have a strategic five-year plan in the park to do x, y, and z. And if the neighbors vote that they want the ball courts, and they want the $100,000 in their district to be spent on the basketball courts now, that might be in year five of the five-year plan, but that might just shift in priority, and the $100,000 from the PB might go ahead and pay for those ball courts.

Q.   Do you also see your staff role as being a sort of a gate-keeper in that some projects might be presented and really good, though might not actually be viable? Would you have to monitor that?

A.   Karen Kixmiller.

Yes, we have written into the timeline that there will be a vetting process. I actually spoke the other day about this, as we were working on this contract with the assistant city manager and the budget director, about what staff's role specifically will be in this process. We are to start identifying roles and responsibilities not just for myself in budget, because I am kind of the primary budget staff working on this project, but also it's going to take staff from multiple departments, of course, to vet these projects. And so we are actually all at a conference next week, but that is the very next thing in my mind and in theirs as we are moving towards this contract becoming a reality is to really start delineating roles and responsibilities and how far do we go. This is intentionally supposed to be a community-led project. It's funny when I was listening to one of the videos from the PB project website, Josh Lerner was speaking on the video, and I'm sure you've seen the videos, they are very well produced, and after that I looked at everybody and said, I am a "them" and I am a "they"!

Q.   And how did that make you feel? You also live in Greensboro? You are a community member too?

A.   Karen Kixmiller.

I do, yes! I have conflicting feelings in general about my ability to participate publicly in our political process, and working as a city employee, because you have to kind of walk the line. My social media doesn't have my real name on it, my personal email address isn't identifiable, not that I put anything out there inflammatory, but still I don't want anything to be taken out of context or taken as I'm speaking for x, y, or z. But it is challenging and I think that is part of the difficulty I personally am going to have is not crossing the line because having a background in planning, of course, you are in the community. That's what it's all about, I was in comprehensive planning. So really being able to turn the process over to the community, and trust that all is well, and knowing that some might see any intervention or assistance or participation from city staff as muddying the waters, or directing it too much, or tainting the process.

Q.   Or you might have to say "no" to something that might not be a legitimate expense for taxpayer dollars?

A.   Karen Kixmiller.

Absolutely.

Q.   I am sure that is a concern as well. If a project is suggested and it's a go and looking good, do you then envision all of those departments coming together to help with preparing cost estimates?

A.   Karen Kixmiller.

Yes, the process, from what I understand, you know it will have budget delegates for each of the districts who will do an initial vetting of the projects. I was looking at my Vallejo notes. I had spoken with a lady at Vallejo, California, a couple years ago, and I was reviewing my notes this week. There were upwards of 900 ideas generated, and those get filtered down into proposals. I believe in the first pass 60 proposals were submitted to the city for initial vetting, so I do see that we are going to need a staff team from infrastructure departments, parks and rec, arts, and so forth, to look at feasibility as well as helping with cost estimates. The community delegates I believe will do an initial pass of coming up with cost estimates, but again they are going to need staff probably to help with those before they even submit them to staff officially.

Q.   And that looks like a whole other set of responsibilities that employees who are stretched too far anyway have to take on, and I know while you will do it, it still may be difficult. Is that correct?

A.   Karen Kixmiller.

Yes, and again one of my concerns that I have at this point is knowing where that line is and making sure that all who may be involved as staff in the process, as we go down the road know what their roles and responsibilities are. I sometimes have found myself, or it has been pointed out to me, that I hand-hold a little too much, so for me personally that might be a challenge, and it is going to be especially important for me to know where that line is. Because, you know, in another context, if you see the ball rolling and you know somebody needs to pick it up, I'm going to pick it up and hand it to the person who needs it.

Q.   Will you get to have some input into these temporary staff people that are hired by the PBP so that maybe there will be a comfort level that they will do what is necessary?

A.   Karen Kixmiller.

So far, as it is right now, no one from the city is on the review committee for the hiring of staff, and I think part of that again is the staff are being hired by the PBP and part of the concern or feeling is that it is part of their control and part of their duty to find someone they feel comfortable with.

Q.   Right, so based on their expertise, they probably know who they should be looking to hire?

A.   Karen Kixmiller.

Right. But on the other hand, I have sent out probably 80 emails with these job postings personally, myself. And again just going back to what I initially said about having worked with the community and the public, you know people are interested and want to participate, but sometimes the enthusiasm in doing the actual logistics, it can wane.

Q.　On that issue, based on your other responsibilities at the city, what do you see in terms of the challenges of actually getting people in the room in your community and getting them to participate in a meaningful way?

A.　Karen Kixmiller.

So maybe the difficulty of the two new hired PBP staff will be in getting community support, right? I definitely feel like in any community that is a challenge today. People are busy, they lead busy lives, families have multiple commitments. There are so many things that are pulling at our interests these days.

Certainly city budgeting is not sexy. Unless there is something inflammatory or something that makes the news, embezzlement or mismanagement, people don't really care, it's something in the background. I mean they care, but they aren't up in arms about it—it's not at the forefront. It's definitely going to be really incumbent on these community PBP hires, where hopefully the people who are hired have already a great knowledge of Greensboro's diverse landscape and knowledge of Greensboro's nonprofit groups. I think that is going to be a huge key, to really be working and leveraging our existing nonprofit organizations that have a very broad reach in our community, as well as our neighborhood associations, those institutions are going to be key as well in really reaching the people.

As we know just from other political ventures, those who participate tend to be whiter and older and more educated. And honestly the community folks who brought PB to Greensboro are whiter, middle-aged, and very educated. So that has been a concern of mine as well is that the people who have been at the table with this PB process at the city, the community folk who have been participating with the city since October, are very homogeneous, are all white, educated folk.

Our community is actually a minority-majority if you look at our Census. If you just look at the white, non-Hispanic, we are probably at like 45 percent. That is just an estimate. We have a lot of immigrant communities here, we have a lot of Montagnards, and so it's really going to be important if you want inclusion and you want to hear those needs to get into those communities, which requires trust. And honestly if we hire somebody or if the community hires somebody who doesn't already have an intimate knowledge of the city's landscape, that ramp-up and that learning curve is going to take longer than it is going to take to learn how to do PB, because you need that trust. You need to know who are the go-to people in the community. I think that is really key, reaching people where they are, but you have to know which people to reach, and you can't teach that in this amount of time, and we have a 10-month time schedule.

I know one of your interests was social media use, and we have $10,000 in the budget for online, or text gadgets, or apps, or that type of electronic presence. I'm not quite sure exactly how they are going to use it. But, I feel like, at least for my generation, I'm mid-forties, with two kids, and I work full-time. My kids are active in sports, Girl Scouts, etc. even though I work at the city, and I would be interested as just a regular resident, I just can't foresee me committing to weekly meetings, two or three hours a night to a process without some type of controversy or catalyst to get involved. So I think it's really going to be important for them to have other platforms because I just don't have the time to spend driving and sitting in a meeting, and I think a lot of people would participate if they had surveys or if they had interactive questionnaires, chat sessions, chat rooms.

I had mentioned to Josh Lerner at PBP that we do have MindMixer for what that's worth, as a platform that might be able to stimulate community conversation, but I think that's really going to be key to targeting a certain segment of our population. Again, that segment might skew again as whiter, wealthier, so you would need to have Internet. You probably wouldn't want to do surveys on your smart phone, you would need a tablet of some sort, and be educated. So that might be a way to reach that segment of the population, but again with our large immigrant population that's really not going to be an effective method and that is going to take a hands-on approach and trust.

But I do think for that segment of us who are electronically savvy and especially for our younger people, we have a lot of colleges in town to really generate interest from that twenty-something group you definitely have to go the social media or some type of Internet and app presence.

Q.   You mentioned a group of immigrants, the Montagnards? Can you tell me more about them?

A.   Karen Kixmiller.

Yes, from the Vietnam mountains. We were one of their major government resettlement areas, so we do have a large population of Montagnards. There's actually a Montagnard Dega Association here to help those people. I did Census outreach for the 2010 Census, so that gives me an advantage in a way of knowing these communities already, or at least being able to access them, like when I made up a list of the community nonprofits I already had a list in my head of those I had worked with before. So hopefully, whoever is hired would know this. How much time would be wasted having to give them a demographic overview of our city and who the key people are, this would be a problem. I don't even pretend to know all the key people.

We have a growing population of Bhutanese and Nepalese, and actually have a lot of Iraqi immigrants who resettled here, and a pretty large and growing Hispanic population as well. I'll tell you one thing about the Montagnard Dega group, they have six different dialects and languages—you think Vietnamese and they speak French, but no, they have very specific indigenous languages, and that was one thing with the Census I learned. I worked closely with a minister and the senior resource center and did a couple of meetings in their church at the senior center to talk about it where it was in simultaneous translation, and then I worked with the Montagnard Dega Association and gave them materials and they helped translate them into the native languages. But again, if I from the city just showed up to give a presentation on whatever, they would look at me like who are you? It took working with the minister of the church, and finding the minister of the church to get in, to be able to work with that population.

Q.   Do you have money in the budget for translators?

A.   Karen Kixmiller.

We do. That's part of the contract with PBP. What we did, just because with government we have a lot of limitations and we have obviously a lot more policies and procedures that we have to follow. Any kind of contracting that might be a direct payment to an individual for services, we put that in the contract with PBP in New York because they would be able to have the flexibility to hire and pay as needed versus if we as a city organization were to do that, we would have to have a contract started now in the process with agency X, Y, Z and have to put in an RFP [request for proposal]. We couldn't just go and directly contract with those individuals so that process of course as I'm sure you are familiar with is like that in our city. Hispanic language capabilities, and so forth that might be an opportunity for certain types of meetings, or papers or document translations we might be able to provide some in-kind services.

And also the lady who does our contracts here at the city, she has some contacts in the community that provide translation services, she was also in planning. She has some good nonprofit sources that provide in-kind translation and interpretation services. So that the bulk of the money in the budget for that service can be spread wider, if we can get a lot of the in-kind support. I think it's like $10,000 in there.

Hopefully, like in my case with the Census outreach, I didn't have a penny of a budget, literally, not a penny. And it was just getting in with the organizations and getting in with the community and making that relationship, and that was the in-kind translation service. They provided that service for their community because they felt it was important. And I think if you can show that to the community, that they are important— that was a big thing—you are important, you count, as in the case of the Census. Same thing with the budget—you are important, we want to know what you need in your community. Then you will get that support and hopefully you can spend those dollars in other ways or they can go further.

Q.   The commitment from the city at this point is for two budget years only, but they aren't going to go beyond that?

A.   Karen Kixmiller.

Yes, I kind of see this as a pilot to see how well it works. If you think about the administrative costs, and the leveraging of the administrative costs to the value to the community, it is pretty expensive. It costs the same amount of money. It's going to cost about $200,000 to $300,000 to administer and facilitate this. Whether we are giving away $500,000 or $5 million dollars, the basement cost is still the same.

And our community, unlike the other communities, this money probably might come out of the general fund or might be cobbled together if there are projects that are already identified with other funds, but unlike other communities like Vallejo, they had a sales tax that they diverted a certain percent of the sales tax for this. I think 30 percent of that one cent sales tax went for PB.

In the cases of large cities, the wards or aldermen have that discretion to use that money however they choose, if they just wanted to reward people in their community for certain things or if they wanted to put it in their neighborhood or whatever, but they already had discretion. In Greensboro, it's quite different. We didn't have this, all we had was that $20,000, and that's why we had to have the community help find matching funds.

We just lost recently, effective July 1st [2015], revenue because our state has done away with the Privilege Business Tax licenses—a couple million dollars we lost this past year of revenue. It's a little leaner time, and so that is why $500,000 doesn't seem like a lot to the community, but when you have to pull it out of the air it is. When you have to think about down the road, what is this going to offset? There might be again some synergies that this has helped prioritize things we already had in mind, and it can help move those projects forward. But for a city of our size, without already having some type of mechanism for discretionary funding or sales tax that we can divvy up, it comes out of primarily or largely our operating expenses. The community, when the community PB folk first came, wanted certainly a much larger amount of money, but that would be, at least initially, prohibitive potentially, or it would cut into services that we already offer. It would become potentially a trade-off situation.

Q.   Do you think the council has thought through the fact that although the community group was able to get the grant funding required to be matched this year, that may not happen on a yearly basis in the future? So what happens if participatory budgeting is continued?

A.   Karen Kixmiller.

Right, foundations want to spread their wealth, they don't want to keep doing the same thing unless they see really positive results, and we hope our evaluation shows that, but you're right, we can't keep tapping the same resource every year.

Q.   I wonder if you think that would be a requirement the second year, I'm just curious as to what you see, if they recognize that as an impossibility?

A.   Karen Kixmiller.

Definitely when this was brought to council the first time, the original vote was 5-4. And the concern of the four was the cost, and why does it cost so much and why are we contracting with someone from New York to do this? So I foresee that to continue this they might want to do this with our own staff, and in fact that's what Vallejo did in their year two of the process, they reduced the amount of contract they had with PBP in New York, and then they actually added staff. I think they added two staff to facilitate PB. Plus the first year they were using 25 percent time of one of their management analysts, and then the next year when they hired staff that time allotment was going to go down.

But that vetting process, where you have to have the departments look at projects even on city-owned land, you have to ask is this feasible? It is still going to take the same amount of time whether the administrators are on a contract or your administrators are in your office because if they don't have that expertise from parks and rec, transportation, etc. they can't answer those questions. So I think that cost is always going to be there, that indirect cost will always be there.

Our council right now, several of them are on the bandwagon to make us a lean, mean organization, and they are definitely looking at FTE counts, and so I could see some of them not wanting to add staff, and then some of them wanting us to do the process. I know how that goes politically, we don't have money to do it, but we are going to do it. It is like an unfunded mandate in a way. And then in the background of all this, our state legislature is in the process of redistricting our city without our desire and against our wishes. Today in fact. The state legislature, on the bill introduced by a former city council woman, is voting today on whether or not or how to redistrict our city. So I think should that happen, the next time PB comes around it's going to be a very different looking city council.

Q.   And this redistricting would in effect create more districts or totally re-draw them?

A.   Karen Kixmiller.

Re-draw them. The bill that passed the House did not get passed in the Senate, so now they are redrawing them again. We have five districts and we have four at-large representatives or council people, including the Mayor, and they all vote. The original proposal was to go to seven districts with a non-voting Mayor and no at-large, except for the Mayor. And so what that was going to do was put five incumbent council people in one district for the next election in November. Definitely, if that went through it would absolutely change the council representation because five incumbents would be in one district.

Q.   And your next election would be in November 2015? And they all get voted in at the same time?

A.   Karen Kixmiller.

All at the same time. Yes, exactly. That's tenuous politically. So we might have the best PB ever, and when it comes up next year we might have a completely different city council. We could have all brand new council members, seriously. So now the compromised bill is to create eight districts and a Mayor. They won't just leave it alone, it's very curious.

This is a complete aside, but I can understand that as a city if residents or citizens were concerned that their voting rights or the districts were so gerrymandered that they weren't being heard and they brought this to the concern of city council, and city council didn't even consider it, or listen to them so they went to the state for remedy, I could understand that issue. But this was completely outside. There were no protests at city council that there was any problem with the way our districts were. This was a manufactured issue. Now our city has paid lobbyists and attorneys to fight this, whether or not it's good in the end for the districts, whether or not they make better sense than what we have now is kind of irrelevant in that the community wasn't really fighting or arguing that we have a problem. It's definitely a power issue from the state. It's concerning to all of the city council, they might not have a district next year.

Also, our terms for city council are every two years, a clean-slate. Everybody is up for reelection at the same time, which is also very destabilizing. One of the proposals with this bill at the state is a four-year term, but again all at the same time. If you are thinking about the political backdrop, it's really an unknown, because we quite likely will have completely different representation of our community. If five of the incumbents were going to be in one new district, you definitely have a problem. It's not going to be pretty. Just because of the learning curve and everything. That is a real dice throw. Even if PB runs perfectly and it is great and the community loves it, we have a whole different slate who didn't look at this, didn't vote on this, didn't know about it, or conversely even if it's this horrible process, that didn't run well, didn't work well, but there might be champions on the board that say let's do it regardless of the cost. It's very unsettling.

Q. So in terms of timeline, when does the project idea generation happen?

A. Karen Kixmiller.

December. November or December. As far as the timeline goes, neighborhood assemblies will be starting in October and November. We have on the timeline December and January for the projects to come to the city for the city staff to review, and then we would give these back to the community, and they in turn would deliver maybe a second round around March.

One thing the person in Vallejo, California, mentioned to me was that her first year, you have to go into these things naively, you just don't know what the community is going to come up with. It's community led, so you follow their lead. She said the first year they had a lot of projects that got through the process and on the ballot that come to find out weren't feasible, either because the city did not own the right-of-way or it wasn't on city-owned land. Or it was needing operating funds and not capital funds, because that is one thing we want to focus on capital expenses, not operating, meaning we don't want to add staff because that becomes an on-going expense, forever. So she said that in terms of process improvements and looking backward, she said it would be helpful to more strongly vet those projects and to get them in the process a little earlier. In fact, she said if you're in a time crunch to streamline it, it might be better to offer a slate of shovel-ready projects for the community to decide on those, going back to that priority setting, pulling things out of your strategic plans and CIPs, and saying okay well this is what $100,000 would buy and these are the $100,000 projects, which of these would you want? This is a way to do it more streamlined, and you know they are already vetted. I actually prefer that, but this is not my process. I defer to the community. It's up to the steering committee to do the rule book of what and how the process works.

Q.   Are you all there yet?

A.   Karen Kixmiller.

No, we will do that probably in August or September where they make the rules up, and certainly staff would have to have some input there as to what types of projects are feasible, and educate them on the difference between capital and operating and on-going expenses and maintenance expenses. [Segments of the draft Handbook are presented in Appendix 8.2. For complete Handbook see link at http://www.greensboro-nc.gov/modules/showdocument.aspx?documentid=29499.]

Even if you add playground equipment, it has got to be maintained which is going to be an on-going cost to the budget, and you kind of have to think about that as well as a city, and put that in a budget line as well. It's not just clean, $100,000 in and out, done. There will always be on-going expenses of anything you do. I mean I always have to dust my furniture, that's an on-going expense, if I didn't have that furniture, I wouldn't have to dust it.

Q.   Is there any other issue or concern from a staff person's view as opposed to a community person, anything you think that hasn't been thought of that may be a concern?

A.   Karen Kixmiller.

Time commitment. Really understanding time commitments and boundaries. Boundaries and time commitment. A realistic understanding of what this might take as well as what might not be done in lieu of this. Again, I understand the political and the organizational constraints. I worked in planning long enough to know that if city council called and said, "oh, see these downtown buildings that are boarded up, and we need a policy on that tomorrow, and need to know how many there are," then you find yourself that day in 95 degree weather walking around downtown with a camera taking pictures of everything. You don't have the opportunity to say, yes, but those other things I was working on aren't going to get done in time. Yes, they will. That is one of my concerns as a staff member, and certainly it is a personal concern of mine, selfishly.

And the other staff that are going to be a part of the vetting process, at this point they don't know they are going to be involved in the vetting process. This is not even on their radar. It's time that we get a city team together to know what this is going to entail and to set up some parameters for time and work flow, policy and procedure internally, and understand what that means for their other work projects. When I re-read my Vallejo notes and I read that it took 25 percent of her time, I thought "dear God" that is a lot of time. She estimated $95,000 of indirect costs based on other staff time too, that's huge. That's a lot of time. And her city was half the size of ours. So I can do that math.

Q. How spread out is your city geographically?

A. Karen Kixmiller.

About 131 square miles, with 280,000 population. We are southern sprawl down here. We have cheap farm land, and we can throw up a bunch of houses that look alike.

Q. But does it make it harder to conduct community meetings when you are so spread out as opposed to a ward in Chicago where it's compact?

A. Karen Kixmiller.

Yes, it is not compact. And in your district there are known places, identifiable. And here we have a really good network of libraries and recreation centers that are fairly evenly distributed throughout the city, so I see those as being a great resource for meetings that would be a free venue, that would hopefully be a known venue, and that would have bus transportation to it. A lot of them have after-school programs that might be a good way to dovetail, and I have all these good ideas, I just have to give them to somebody. As a single mom, I did the parks and rec after-school programs and that would be a great time to advertise. When I'm there to pick up my kid, I am already there, and if you have the posters out in the lobby when I am coming to pick up my kid and I can look at things and vote on them. It is really going to the people. Or at the libraries that have computers and have that set up so if you are going to have some type of SurveyMonkey or MindMixer to use or to have that on every computer at every library maybe a big sticky note saying "go here" while you are on the computer reminding people to vote.

Q. It sounds like you have got your work cut out for you and a lot of ideas.

A. Karen Kixmiller.

We have a maybe more fiscally conservative and sound way of looking at our future than other cities might. With Vallejo and the sales tax, it's not coming out of a departments' pocket, and that's another point I'll make is that if PB is going to be the wave of the future and the city is going to fund it and if we are going to fund it internally, and if revenue times become leaner, I could foresee a potential for departments feeling maybe resentful because they might have to tighten their belt, and they might have to realign their priorities based on this process. Sometimes that might be a good thing—aligning your priorities to the communities' needs, but as we know there is an A and B that are preferred to go before C. It could be upsetting the applecart for departments and they might feel a little put out in a way—from a budgetary standpoint, as well as workload standpoint—and we really need city department buy-in if this is to be successful.

Reference

United States Census Bureau. 2015. http://quickfacts.census.gov/qfd/states/37/3728000. html (accessed September 5, 2015).

Appendices

City of Greensboro
North Carolina

Financial & Administrative Services Department
Centralized Contracting Division

PROFESSIONAL SERVICES AGREEMENT

CITY OF GREENSBORO
BUDGET & EVALUATION DEPARTMENT
City of Greensboro
PO Box 3136
Greensboro, NC 27402-3136

CONTRACTED VENDOR
NON-PROFIT CORPORATION
The Participatory Budgeting Project, Inc. dba PBP
33 Flatbush Avenue, 4th Fl
Brooklyn, NY 11217
347-834-9456
josh@participatorybudgeting.org

CONTRACT INFORMATION
Contract Number: 2015 - 10298
Estimated Award Amount: $153,703.00
Contract Description: Participatory Budgeting Project Administration
Initial Contract Term: August 1, 2015 - June 30, 2016

This contract is made and entered into on the date signed by and between the **City of Greensboro**, a municipal corporation of the State of North Carolina (herein referred to as the CITY) and **The Participatory Budgeting Project, Inc. dba PBP**, herein referred to as "PBP", **a NON-PROFIT CORPORATION** with offices located as written above.

WITNESSETH:

The City's **BUDGET & EVALUATION DEPARTMENT** has requested responses from qualified firms to provide services for administration of the Greensboro Participatory Budgeting Project; and

Whereas, **PBP** has demonstrated prior experience and performance in providing such services and has submitted a response to provide such services in accordance with the following exhibits and attachments, which are attached hereto and incorporated herein:

Exhibit 1: 1.1 City Council Resolution; 1.2 Scope of Work; 1.3 Responsibilities of City and Contractor; 1.4 Submitted Budget Allocation for Eligible Expenditures; 1.5 Position Descriptions; 1.6 Sample Reports

Attachment A: **PBP's** Submitted Fee Schedule

NOW THEREFORE, in consideration of the foregoing, the mutual covenants contained in this Agreement, and other good and valuable consideration, the parties agree as follows:

SERVICES RENDERED

In consideration of the monetary payment hereinafter described, **PBP** will provide administration services for the **Greensboro Participatory Budgeting Program of Greensboro (Greensboro PB)**. Such services shall be performed and charged for in accordance with the attached Exhibit 1 and Attachment A.

PBP and City mutually agree to the following:

1.   AGREEMENT SPECIFICATIONS

   a)   Specific Duties and Responsibilities

      PBP shall fulfill the duties and responsibilities of this agreement as specified and in accordance with the attached Exhibit 1, including scope of work, solicitation, if any, and proposal submitted; plus Attachment A, Fee Schedule.

   b)   Work Schedule

      Work shall be delivered in accordance with the documentation attached in Exhibit 1 and Schedule A, defined above.

   c)   Term

      Contract term shall be from start and end dates listed above.

   d)   Compensation

      Compensation for services herein shall be provided in accordance with Attachment A, Fee Schedule. Total compensation for services described in Exhibit 1 and Attachment A shall not exceed the amount written above. Bills for fees or other compensation for Service or expenses shall be submitted to the City in detail sufficient for a proper pre-audit and post-audit thereof.

2.   BILLING AND PAYMENT

   a)   Payment

      Payment shall generally be made by the City within 30 calendar days of receipt of a complete and accurate invoice unless PBP is otherwise notified.

   b)   Disputed Items

      If any items in any invoices submitted by the Service Provider are disputed by the City for any reason, including the lack of supporting documentation, City shall temporarily delete the items and shall promptly notify the Contractor of dispute and request clarification and/or remedial action. After the dispute has been settled, the Service Provider shall include the disputed item on a subsequent regularly scheduled invoice or on a special invoice for the disputed item only. The undisputed portion of the invoices shall, however, be paid within the normal 30 day period

   c)   Submittal of Invoices

      In performance of the duties and responsibilities, and the scope of work as defined in this agreement, invoices for payment of services shall be based on fees as provided for in Attachment A, Fee Schedule. Payment requests shall be submitted monthly, within fifteen (15) days of the end of each billing period. Invoices will be based on 100% of the work completed during the preceding billing period.

d) Receipts Required

Where invoices are based in part on reimbursable expenses, PBP shall collect and maintain receipts for said expenses and shall make the receipts available to the City, if requested. The requirement to retain receipts shall generally follow the established rules of the Federal Internal Revenue Service regarding what type of expenditure must be supported by receipts for income tax purposes.

e) Non-Appropriation

In the event that this contract shall be funded from multiple years, the automatic renewal clause shall not apply to this contract should the Greensboro City Council fail to appropriate funds for the additional term of the contract for the ensuing fiscal year. If this non-appropriation occurs the contract shall become void.

3. SUBCONTRACTING REQUIREMENTS

a) Assignment to Subcontractors

PBP shall assign no subcontracting work without written pre-approval of the City. In the event that subcontracting is pre-approved by the City, PBP shall ensure that steps are taken in accordance with the City's Equal Opportunity Program(s) and federal subcontracting policy to assure equal opportunity to subcontractors.

b) Equal Opportunity

It is City policy to provide equal opportunity in the award of contracts to small, minority, and women's business firms. Accordingly, affirmative steps must be taken to assure that small, minority, and women's businesses are utilized when possible as sources of supplies, equipment, construction, and services.

c) Affirmative MWBE Steps

   i.   Include qualified small, minority, and women's businesses on solicitation lists.

   ii.   Assure that small, minority, and women's businesses are solicited whenever they are potential sources.

   iii.   When economically feasible and where the requirement permits, divide total requirements into smaller tasks or quantities so as to permit maximum small, minority, and women's business participation.

   iv.   Where the requirement permits, establishing delivery schedules which will encourage participation by small, minority, and women's business.

   v.   Using the services and assistance of City staff to assure program compliance, the M/WBE Office shall serve as the point of contact for inquiries.

4.   CHANGES TO AGREEMENT

a)   Rights

The City retains the exclusive rights to cancel, stop or reschedule any or all services associated with the Contract.

b)   Amendment

Prior to the performance of any work not detailed by the Fee Schedule as defined in Attachment A, the City and **PBP** will establish a fair market rate for the performance of such services prior to the performance of such services. This Agreement will be amended at such time to reflect the additional rate and shall herein be deemed to be included as a term of the Agreement.

c)   Severance

Should any part of this Contract be declared unenforceable, all remaining sections remain in force to the maximum extent practicable.

d)   Termination for Convenience

The City, in its sole discretion, may terminate this Agreement in whole or in part whenever the City determines that said termination is in its best interest. Any such termination shall be effected by the delivery to PBP of a written notice of termination 30 days prior to the effective date. In the event of such termination, the City shall compensate Participatory Budgeting Project in full for completed work as specified in Exhibit 1 and Attachment A and any other eligible expenses incurred prior to the delivery of the written notice of termination.

5.   STANDARD PROVISIONS

a)   Commercial Nondiscrimination

It is the policy of the City not to enter into a contract or to be engaged in a business relationship with any business entity that has discriminated in the solicitation, selection, hiring or commercial treatment of vendors, suppliers, Subcontractors or commercial customers on the basis of race, color, religion, ancestry or national origin, sex, age, marital status, sexual orientation or on the basis of disability or any otherwise unlawful use of characteristics regarding the vendor's, supplier's or commercial customer's employees or owners; provided that nothing in this policy shall be construed to prohibit or limit otherwise lawful efforts to remedy the effects of discrimination that have occurred or are occurring in the Relevant Marketplace, which includes Alamance, Davie, Davidson, Forsyth, Guilford, Randolph, Rockingham, Stokes, Surry, and Yadkin counties.

As a condition of entering into this agreement, the company represents and warrants that it will comply with the Citys Commercial Nondiscrimination Policy, as described under Section V. A. 1. of the M/WBE Program Plan. As part of such compliance, the company shall not discriminate on the basis of race, color, religion, ancestry or national origin, sex, age, marital status, sexual orientation, or on the basis of disability or other unlawful forms of discrimination in the solicitation, selection, hiring or commercial treatment of Subcontractors, vendors, suppliers, or commercial customers, nor shall the company retaliate against any person for reporting instances of such discrimination. The company shall provide equal opportunity for

for Subcontractors, vendors and suppliers to participate in all of its public sector and private sector subcontracting opportunities, provided that nothing contained in this clause shall prohibit or otherwise limit lawful efforts to remedy the effects of marketplace discrimination that have occurred or are occuring in the City's Relevant Marketplace. The Company understands and agrees that a material violation of this clause shall be considered a material breach of this agreement an may result in termination of this agreement, disqualification of the company from participating in City contracts, or other sanctions. This clause is not enforceable by material breach of this agreement and may result in termination of this agreement, or for the benefit of, and creates no obligation to, any third party.

b) **Relationship**

The Parties in this contract agree that **PBP** is a Business Enterprise and that the relationship created by this contract is that of client and independent contractor. **PBP** is not an employee of the City of Greensboro, and is not entitled to the benefits provided by employer to its employees, including, but not limited to, group insurance and pension plan.

c) **Supervision and Inspection**

In the performance of the work contemplated in this agreement, **PBP** is an independent contractor with the authority to control and direct the performance of the details of the services that are the subject of this contract. However, the work contemplated in this agreement must meet the approval of the City (which shall not be unreasonably withheld) and shall be subject to City's general rights of inspection and direction to secure the satisfactory completion thereof.

d) **Payment of Taxes**

PBP assumes full responsibility for the payment of all assessments, payroll taxes, or contributions, whether State or Federal, as to all employees engaged in the performance of work under this contract. In addition, **PBP** agrees to pay any and all gross receipts, compensation, transaction, sales, uses, or other taxes and assessments of whatever nature and kind levied or assessed as a consequence of the work performed or on the compensation paid under this contract.

e) **Non-discrimination**

PBP agrees that in the performance of these services that it will not discriminate in its hiring, employment, and contracting practices with reference to political affiliation, genetic information, sexual orientation, age, sex, race, color, religion, national origin, handicap or disability.

f) **Participatory Budgeting Project**

PBP covenants that he presently has no interest and shall not acquire any interest, direct or indirect, which would conflict in any manner or degree with the performance of his services hereunder. PBP further covenants that in the performance of this Agreement no person having any such interest shall be employed.

g) **Interest of City and Other Officials**

No person listed below may obtain a personal or financial interest or benefit from the activity, or have an interest in any contract, subcontract or agreement with respect thereto, or the proceeds there under, either for him or herself or for those with whom he or she has family or thereafter:

i.   Who is an employee, an agent, a consultant, an officer, or elected or appointed official of the City of Greensboro or any designated public agency, or sub recipients and;

ii. Who exercises or has exercised any function or responsibilities with respect to assisted activities; or

iii. Who is in a position to participate in a decision making process or gain inside information with regard to such activities.

h)   Maintain and Provide Required Legal Documents

i.   **PBP** agrees to maintain as current all applicable insurance, licenses and certifications required by law and any additional requirements specified by the City. A City Privilege License is required of all businesses contracted by the City unless such businesses are approved by the Centralized Contracting Division for a waiver. Waivers shall be granted only to businesses performing work exclusively outside of the City limits. Work performed includes solicitation and service support.

ii. Evidence of Insurance, license and certification requirements shall be provided to the City's Centralized Contracting Division upon contract award and subsequently made available to the City for inspection at any time upon request of the City.

i)   Governing Law

This Agreement is made under, and in all respects, shall be interpreted, construed, and governed by and in accordance with, the laws of the State of North Carolina. Venue for any legal action resulting from this Agreement shall lie in Guilford County, North Carolina.

j)   Compliance with Applicable Law

Any term or condition of the Contract which by operation or existence is in conflict with applicable local, state, or federal law shall be rendered void and inoperative. City and **PBP** agree to accept the remaining terms and conditions.

k)   Indemnification

PBP does hereby agree to indemnify and save harmless the City of Greensboro, its officers, agents and employees against all claims, actions, lawsuits and demands, including reasonable attorney fees, made by anyone for any damages, loss or injury of any kind, including environmental, which may arise as a result of Participatory Budgeting Project's negligence in performing, or as a result of, work pursuant to this agreement.

l)   Confidentiality

The Recipient, City, will not disclose to any third party, or make any use of the Discloser's, Participatory Budgeting Project's Confidential Information except as required by the North Carolina Public Records Act. The Recipient will use at least the same standard of care to maintain the confidentiality of the Discloser's Confidential Information that it uses to maintain the confidentiality of its own Confidential Information, but in no event less than reasonable care. The obligations hereunder will remain in full force with respect to each item of Confidential Information for a period of ten (10) years after

Recipient's receipt of that item. However, The City's obligations to maintain software as confidential will survive in perpetuity. "Discloser" means the party providing Confidential Information to the Recipient. "Recipient" means the party receiving Confidential Information from the Discloser. "Confidential Information" means non-public information of a party to this Agreement that is identified as or would be reasonably understood to be confidential and/ or proprietary and is marked "confidential" and meets the requirements of North Carolina General Statutes 132-1.2. Confidential Information does not include information that: (i) is or becomes known to the public without fault or breach of the Recipient; (ii) the Discloser regularly discloses to third parties without restriction on disclosure; (iii) the Recipient obtains from a third party without restriction on disclosure and without breach of a non-disclosure obligation; or (iv) is independently developed by the Recipient without access to Confidential Information.

Pursuant to the North Carolina Public Records Act, trade secrets or confidential information as defined by the North Carolina Public Records Act that are identified as such prior to disclosure to the Recipient is not public information and will not be released to the public by the Recipient except as set out below. Recipient will notify Discloser of any public records request, and if Discloser objects to Recipient disclosing any of the records responsive to the request, Discloser will notify the Recipient in writing within forty-eight (48) hours. If so notified, Recipient will not disclose the records until ordered to do so by a court of competent jurisdiction, and Discloser will enter an appearance as a party in-interest and defend Recipient in any claim, suit, mediation, litigation, or arbitration proceeding concerning the release of the records to which Discloser objected. Discloser will indemnify, save harmless, and pay any and all attorney's fees incurred by Recipient, and any attorney's fees Recipient is ordered to pay to any person(s) or organization(s) as a result of Discloser's objection to the release of the public records. Discloser will also indemnify, save harmless, and pay any and all claims for damages, court costs, or other fees Recipient incurs as a result of Discloser's objection to the release of the records requested pursuant to the North Carolina Public Records Act.

6. PROFESSIONAL SERVICES INSURANCE REQUIREMENTS

a) Insurance Requirements

PBP agrees to maintain all insurance requirements as required by law and shall furnish insurance certificate upon request of the City. A certificate of insurance showing Worker's Compensation coverage shall be submitted to the City at the time of contract award.

7. CONTRACT CONTACTS

a) Contract Project Manager (City)

All inquiries regarding the duties and requirements of performance under this contract, including payment inquiries, shall be directed to:

Larry Davis, Budget and Evaluation Department Director
City of Greensboro
300 West Washington Street
Greensboro, NC 27401
336-373-2582

b)   Contract Administration (City)

The City's Centralized Contracting Division administers the creation of contracts and addendums and performs related contract solicitation and contract letting processes. Inquiries related to contract administration shall be directed to:

Susan Crotts, Manager
Centralized Contracting Division
300 West Washington Street, UG 12
Greensboro, NC 27401
Phone: 336-373-4389

c)   Contract Manager (Vendor)

"The Contract Manager for this project is:

Josh Lerner, Executive Director
The Participatory Budgeting Project
33 Flatbush Avenue, 4th Fl
Brooklyn, NY 11217
347-834-9456
josh@participatorybudgeting.org

8.   INTELLECTUAL PROPERTY

a)   PBP hereby exclusively licenses the City to use, reproduce, distribute, perform, and create derivative works of the Operating Manual in connection with participatory budgeting activities of the City set forth in Exhibit 1. PBP agrees that the City shall retain rights in perpetuity to use any and all works and products created in the Greensboro PB as the City may decide. This agreement creates no future commitment for the City to pay for use of any work products or derivatives created in the Greensboro PB. Contractor retains all other rights, including using, reproducing, distributing, performing and creating derivative works of the Operating Manual, in connection with other activities, including participatory budgeting activities of any other government entity or agency.

The City will use the following attributions for all public documents, except that the City will not be responsible for inadvertent omissions of such attributions or actions beyond the reasonable control of the City:

- Produced by the Participatory Budgeting Project - www. participatorybudgeting.org [including PBP logo]

9.   SCOPE OF AGREEMENT

a)   Scope of Agreement

This Agreement is intended by the parties hereto to be the final expression of their Agreement and it constitutes the full and entire understanding between the parties with respect to the subject hereof, notwithstanding any representations, statements, or agreements to the contrary heretofore made. The terms of this agreement shall not be waived, altered, modified, supplemented, or amended, in any manner whatsoever, except by written instrument signed by the parties.

IN WITNESS WHEREOF, the parties have caused this Agreement to be executed by their duly authorized officers, in triplicate originals on the date written above.

NON-PROFIT CORPORATION

The Participatory Budgeting Project,Inc.

_____

Signature

_____

Date

_____

Title

_____

Printed Name

_____

Witness

Exhibit 1

1.1   City Council Resolution authorizing the support of the Greensboro Participatory Budget Program

1.2   Scope of Work

1.3   Responsibilities of the City and PBP

1.4   Budget Allocation for Eligible Expenditures

1.5   Position Descriptions

1.6   Sample Reports

0248-14
ID 14-0568

RESOLUTION AUTHORIZING THE SUPPORT OF THE PARTICIPATORY BUDGET PROGRAM

WHEREAS, Participatory Budgeting is a democratic and transparent process which involves community members in deciding how a designated portion of a public budget is spent;

WHEREAS, Participatory Budgeting involves three steps: first, residents come up with ideas for public projects they would like to have in their community; second, individuals volunteer to develop a proposal for their project with city staff to establish a budget for the project; third, residents are invited to a public meeting to vote on all projects;

WHEREAS, Participatory Budgeting will be launched with professional assistance, the New York-based Participatory Budgeting Project (PBP) is prepared to work with City Council, staff and residents to set up and manage Greensboro's Participatory Budget process. Its director, Josh Lerner, who met with members of City Council on two occasions, has previously provided consulting services and administered this process. PBP's work administering this process in Greensboro will reduce demands on city staff time;

WHEREAS, PBP will require $200,000 for the launch of this process, it will have three full time employees. Funding for this service will be split evenly between city and local foundations, with $100,000 in matching funds from the City in fiscal year 2015-16;

WHEREAS, five City Council districts will take part in the Participatory Budget process, each district will be allocated $100,000 in fiscal year 2016-17, and its residents will develop their own district projects and vote on them;

WHEREAS, the total cost to the City of Greensboro for this Participatory Budget process in fiscal year 2015-2016 is $100,000 which will be the reallocation of the current Neighborhood Small Projects funding. An additional $100,000 will be raised from community foundations. All funding is contingent on future City Council actions.

NOW, THEREFORE, BE IT RESOLVED BY THE CITY COUNCIL OF THE CITY OF GREENSBORO:

The Greensboro City Council endorses this concept and will consider future expenditures as part of the normal budget process as this project develops.

THE FOREGOING RESOLUTION WAS ADOPTED
BY THE CITY COUNCIL OF THE CITY OF
GREENSBORO ON THE 7TH DAY
OF OCTOBER, 2014.

CITY CLERK

APPROVED AS TO FORM

CITY ATTORNEY

Introduction

On October 7, 2014, the City of Greensboro approved a resolution authorizing the support of a participatory budgeting program. Participatory Budgeting (PB) is a democratic and transparent process in which community members decide how to spend a designated portion of a public budget. PB involves three steps: first, residents come up with ideas for public projects they would like to have in their community; second, individuals volunteer to develop proposals for projects with city staff; third, residents are invited to vote on all projects. Winning projects will be funded by the City.

Scope of Services

This document describes the services PBP will provide to the City of Greensboro administration of the Participatory Budgeting Program of Greensboro (PB Greensboro). PBP's mission is to empower people to decide together how to spend public money. PBP creates and supports processes that deepen democracy, build stronger communities and make public budgets more equitable and effective. This document outlines the phases, steps, and key deliverables that PBP will provide.

Phases

1) Planning of PB Process

- Hire project staff and identify additional City support staff needs.
- Deliver all necessary Participatory Budgeting (PB) Info Sessions for government and community stakeholders.
- Form and manage a Steering Committee, with the City.
- Plan and facilitate a participatory workshop to design the PB process with the Steering Committee.
- Develop PB Rulebook based on discussions with the City and Steering Committee, to define how the process will work.
- Develop an outreach plan for engaging residents, and key promotional and information materials.
- Set up a project website and other communications and tech tools, with the City and Steering Committee.
- Assist the City and local researchers with developing an evaluation plan and instruments.

Key Deliverables:

- PB Greensboro Intro Training for City staff – August 2015
- Participatory workshop with Steering Committee to design PB Greensboro process – by August 2015
- Community-Based PB Rulebook – by September 2015
- Full set of sample project management, info, outreach, evaluation, and publicity materials – by October 2015

2) Technical Assistance during PB Process

- Train and support City staff working on PB Greensboro, assembly facilitators, budget delegate committee facilitators, outreach workers, and poll workers.
- Plan and coordinate Steering Committee meetings, public meetings, budgeting delegate meetings, and voting.

- Facilitate communication and information exchange between groups involved in the PB Greensboro process.
- Coordinate outreach to city-wide and local media.
- Manage project website and social media.
- Assist City staff and the Steering Committee with addressing key issues that emerge during PB Greensboro.
- Deliver all necessary presentations explaining participatory budgeting to community stakeholders.
- Provide orientation for budget delegates.
- Moderate and facilitate meetings and group discussions.
- Assist in the collection of data related to documentation and evaluation of the Greensboro PB process.
- Ensure compliance with relevant Federal, State, and local laws, codes and regulations.
- Develop additional promotional and information materials, as necessary.

Key Deliverables:

- **Weekly or bi-weekly conference calls with City staff responsible for PB Greensboro**
- **Training for outreach workers – by October 2015**
- **Training for assembly facilitators – by October 2015**
- **Training workshop for budget delegate committee facilitators – by November 2015**
- **Delegate orientation – by December 2015**
- **Deliver list of initial community ideas for City Staff review - by December 2015**
- **Deliver Proposed community projects for City Staff review – by March 2016**
- **Training for voting site administrators and poll workers – by April 2016**
- **PB Ballot and Community Vote - by May 2016**

(This section intentionally left blank.)

1.3 Responsibilities

Responsibilities of the City

- The City will pay for eligible expenditures under this project, not to exceed the total amount of $200,000, which includes $100,000 in match funds from foundations in accordance with the attached budget in Exhibit 1.4.
- Provide office space, computers, phone lines, cell phone allowance for two PBP staff.
- Post a link to PBP's web site on the City website.
- Post notices of events, meetings etc. on City website.
- Provide access for PBP staff to:

  o schedule meeting rooms,
  o use computer network, (3rd party network agreements required),
  o printers, paper, copier, etc. that will be charged to the grant budget.

- Review monthly progress reports for satisfactory performance of work and deliverables prior to issuing payments to Contractor.
- Review monthly invoices and backup documentation prior for completeness prior to issuing payments to Contractor.
- Vet community projects for feasibility prior to community voting.
- The City of Greensboro is not responsible for contracting outreach workers, interpreters or translators to provide services for PBP events and meetings.
- Neither the City of Greensboro nor PBP will be responsible for providing child care at meetings. Parents/guardians will be solely responsible for minor children if in attendance.

Responsibilities of Contractor

- Provide technical assistance in accordance with Exhibit 1 Scope of Work.
- Complete delivery of services in accordance with the Project Deliverable Timeline (Attachment A).
- Provide monthly accomplishment reports in accordance with Sample Progress Report by the 15th of each month for the prior month.
- Provide copies of signed and approved time sheets for Greensboro PBP staff.
- Provide copies of mileage logs for review with each invoice, charged in accordance with City travel policy, if mileage is a reimbursable program cost for PBP.
- Provide copies of all public meeting logs from prior month with monthly Progress Reports.
- Maintain all records Contractor is required to submit and/or maintain.
- Provide access to all records related to contract upon request of the City.
- Insurance Requirements – Worker's Compensation: certificate of insurance to be provided with signed contract award package.
- Oversee and supervise work of PBP staff.
- Provide for meeting expenses such as refreshments, community outreach contractors, material translations, and interpretation services as needed.

  o Neither the City of Greensboro nor PBP will be responsible for providing child care at meetings. Parents/guardians will be solely responsible for minor children in attendance.

- Pay salaries, benefits, taxes and any other work related expenses in accordance with Budget.
- Provide City staff community projects to vet in accordance with deliverable timetable.
- Present winning community projects based to City staff and/or City Council.
- Participate in weekly or bi-weekly calls with City PB staff.
- PBP agrees to work with designated evaluation team and provide evaluation data as requested.

1.4 Project Budget Allocation for Eligible Expenditures

Project Administrative Budget Limit: $ 195,600

Contract Cost Allocations

Program Funds Allocated to PBP	Total
PBP Community Engagement Coordinator Salary Costs including benefits, taxes and insurance for 10 month position	47,630
PBP Project Asst Salary including benefits, taxes and insurance for 10 month position	31,750
Meeting expenses including material translation, interpretation, refreshments, and venues	6,350
Travel Allowance (see deliverables)	4,900
Contracted organizers for targeted outreach	8,000
Mileage (to and from City offices to meetings, purchase items, etc.)	800
Website and Technology Tools	10,000
Total Program Costs	**$ 109,430**
Administrative Costs Allocated to PBP	
PBP Executive Dir (NYC), 3% time, including benefits, taxes and insurance for 12 mo.	2,553
PBP Deputy Dir (NYC), 3% time, including benefits, taxes and insurance for 12 mo.	2,553
PBP Communications Dir (NYC), 3% time, including benefits, taxes and insurance for 12 mo.	2,553
PBP Project Manager (Chicago), 35% time, including benefits, taxes and insurance for 12 mo.	23,114
Administrative Costs (as approved by City Project Manager)	13,500
Total Administrative Costs	**$ 44,273**
Total PBP Contract Allocation	**$ 153,703**
Program Costs funded by the City	
Mailing	4,697
Printing	8,400
Publicity/Advertising	7,000
Evaluation of Process	10,000
Office Supplies (Misc)	1,800
Computer Equipment and Network Access	5,000
Office Equipment (May include copier/printer rental)	4,500
Cell phone allowance	500
Total City Operating Costs	**$ 41,897**
Total PB Costs	**$ 195,600**

- PBP will invoice the City based on the successful completion of key milestones or deliverables per Attachment A, which may be prorated.
- Fund Allocations may be amended in writing in the future with written agreement of PBP Executive Director and City Project Manager.
- Budget reflects total fundraising as of 7/21/15: Private contributions $97,800; City funds $97,800.

1.5 Position Descriptions

POSITION OPENING: COMMUNITY ENGAGEMENT COORDINATIOR

The Participatory Budgeting Project (PBP) is seeking a highly motivated individual to coordinate local implementation of a new participatory budgeting process in Greensboro, NC. Over the next year, the City of Greensboro will engage thousands of residents in directly deciding how to spend $500,000. The Community Engagement Coordinator will be supervised by a PBP Project Manager and will work closely with other PBP staff, City of Greensboro staff, local partners, and community members to coordinate events, facilitate community engagement, and support participants. This full-time position will be based in Greensboro and will last 10 months, starting in August or September 2015, with potential extension.

ABOUT THE PARTICIPATORY BYFGETING PROJECT

The Participatory Budgeting Project (PBP) is non-profit organization that empowers people across the US Canada to decide together how to spend public money. We create and support participatory budgeting (PB) processes that deepen democracy, build stronger communities, and make public budgets more equitable and effective. Through our work with partners in over 12 cities, we have engaged 100,000 people in deciding how to spend $98 million.

RESPONSIBILITIES

- In collaboration with the PB Steering Committee, lead planning and logistics coordination for large scale neighborhood meetings, meetings of community volunteers to develop project proposals, and community-wide voting.
- Moderate and facilitate meetings and group discussions, and deliver presentations.
- Facilitate communication and information exchange between the groups involved in the PB process.
- Coordinate community outreach, and recruit volunteers.
- Assist community volunteers with developing spending proposals and vetting proposals with city officials and agency representatives.

POSITION OPENING: PROJECT ASSISTANT

The Participatory Budgeting Project (PBP) is seeking a highly motivated individual to support local implementation of a new participatory budgeting process in Greensboro, NC. Over the next year, the City of Greensboro will engage thousands of residents in directly deciding how to spend $500,000. The Project Assistant will support and be supervised by the Community Engagement Coordinator and work closely with other PBP staff, City staff, local partners, and community members to coordinate events, facilitate community engagement, and support participants. This full-time position will be based in Greensboro and will last 10 months, starting in August or September 2015, with potential extension.

ABOUT THE PARTICIPATORY BUDGETING PROJECT

The Participatory Budgeting Project (PBP) is a non-profit organization that empowers people across the US and Canada to decide together how to spend public money. We create and support participatory budgeting (PB) processes that deepen democracy, build stronger communities, and make public budgets more equitable and effective. Through our work with partners in over 12 cities, we have engaged 100,000 people in deciding how to spend $98 million.

RESPONSIBILITIES

- Support the Community Engagement Coordinator in planning and logistics coordination for large scale neighborhood meetings, meetings of community volunteers to develop project proposals, and community-wide voting.
- Conduct community outreach.
- Facilitate communication and information exchange between the groups involved in the PB process.
- Assist community volunteers with developing spending proposals and vetting proposals with city officials and agency representatives.
- Contribute content to blog posts, websites, newsletters, presentations, reports, and other communications.

1.6 Report Examples

Monthly Progress Report Example

GREENSBORO PARTICIPATORY BUDGETING PROJECT: MONTHLY STATUS REPORT

For the month of [date] - [date]

Training and Community Meetings
      Type and # of Meetings
      # of Attendees
      Attach Sign-In Sheet with Meeting Summary
Key Deliverables Completed
      List Tasks and Achievements
Mileage and Expenses
      Attach mileage log and eligible receipts

Attach time sheets of PBP Greensboro Staff
Additional reporting and/or documentation to be provided to the City upon request

---

Mileage Log Example

Mileage Log and Reimbursement Form

Employee Name		Rate Per Mile	$0.27
Employee ID		For Period	From 5/9/18 to 5/9/18
Vehicle Description		Total Mileage	10
Authorized By		Total Reimbursement	$2.70

Date	Starting Location	Destination	Description/Notes	Odometer Start	Odometer End	Mileage	Reimbursement
5/9/2018	Home Office	Northwind Traders	Client Meeting	36098	36103	5	$1.35
5/9/2018	Northwind Traders	Home Office	Client Meeting	36103	36108	5	$1.35
						0	$0.00
						0	$0.00
						0	$0.00
					Totals	10	$2.70

Community Meeting Sign-in Sheet Example

MEETING SIGN-IN SHEET

Project:	Meeting Date:
Facilitator:	Place/Room:

Name	Organization or Community Interest	Council District	Phone	E-mail	Follow-up

ATTACHMENT A: Fee Schedule

- Timeline and Deliverables to be paid in accordance with Exhibit 1.4 Project Budget Allocation for Eligible Expenditures

DELIVERABLES TIMETABLE

Contract Allocation: $ 153,703

Milestones and Deliverables	Target Date	Cost
Phase 1 – Planning	**July – September**	
Contract Execution & Hiring of PB Staff	8/31/2015	4000
PB Intro Training for City staff	8/31/2015	2000
Participatory workshop with Steering Committee to design PB process	8/31/2015	5000
Community-Based PB Rulebook Completed	9/30/2015	5000
Full set of sample project management, info, outreach, evaluation, and publicity materials	10/15/2015	15000
Phase 2 - Idea Collection	**October – December**	
Training for outreach workers	10/15/2015	3000
Training for assembly facilitators	10/15/2015	3000
Neighborhood Assemblies	11/30/2015	25703
Deliver initial list of community project ideas to City Staff for review	12/15/2015	5000
Phase 3 - Assemblies, Meetings, and Proposal Formation	**January – March**	
Training workshop for budget delegate committee facilitators	12/15/2015	3000
Delegate Orientation	12/17/2015	5000
Deliver proposed community projects to City staff to vet	3/31/2016	10000
Delegate Meetings	4/29/2016	30000
Phase 4 – Project Expos and Voting	**April – June**	
PB Ballot	5/15/2015	10000
Training for voting site administrators and poll workers	5/29/2015	3000
Community Vote	5/29/2015	20000
Presentation of Vote Results	6/16/2015	5000
Total		**153,703**

Appendix 8.1 Professional Services Agreement Between the City of Greensboro, North Carolina and the Participatory Budgeting Project

GOALS: WHAT DO WE WANT TO ACCOMPLISH WITH PB?

We believe we can improve our city through PB. While there are many benefits to doing PB, the main goals we strive to achieve are:

EQUITY

We hope to achieve equity through this process. By this we mean fair distribution of funds for each district and within districts. We also want to see resident participation in each district that reflects the demographics of district residents.

EMPOWERMENT

We want to achieve more inclusión through our process. Greensboro is a city that is widespread and there are people who are excluded from participating fully in other processes. We want to engage those residents who are normally not, specifically along traditional elections and voting, in this process. We'd like to see engagement efforts of Greensboro PB lead to higher participation in other things like traditional voting.

COMMUNITY BUILDING

We want to strengthen democracy in Greensboro by helping to create more community leaders through civic education and the hands-on experience of the PB process. Five years from now we want to see an expanded civic leadership come from PB in Greensboro. We want to see an increase in community relationships. Participants should have fun and enjoy the process.

TRANSPARENCY

We want a research and evaluation of the process to help us measure the diversity and change in diversity of participants in the process. We want to build a sustainable bridge of ideas through PB, a bridge that connects us across neighborhoods and districts and breeds collaboration. We want to have consistency in our process. This is important to consider as some districts will have residents with higher capacities for outreach and participation and we want to make sure to provide more resources and capacity building training to districts/neighborhoods with lower capacity.

KEY PRINCIPLES

- We want to empower people to use their voices by participating in civic life.

- We want to have an accessible process including differences in language, age, mobility and other ways so that everyone feels comfortable participating.

- We want to have a focused commitment to process integrity. This means operating with consistency, discipline, transparency, and accountability.

- We want to be able to let Greensboro residents know that "what they see is what they get" with this process.

We ask everyone involved to work with us to achieve these goals.

RULES: HOW DOES PB WORK IN GREENSBORO?

IDEA COLLECTION

- Anyone is welcome to attend the Neighborhood Assemblies and propose project ideas.

- Idea Collection will be done, online, at assemblies as well as smaller-scale mini-assemblies at non-PB meetings of community organizations, churches, civic associations. Each district will hold at least five Idea Collection events. Events will be planned with consideration for inclusiveness and engaging underrepresented populations.

- It is recommended that there be at least one event in each of the following timeframes: morning, weekend, and evening. This will allow for the broadest possible attendance considering a variety of work and life schedules.

RULES: HOW DOES PB WORK IN GREENSBORO?

PROPOSAL DEVELOPMENT

- Proposal Development will be a collaborative process between volunteer Budget Delegates, City staff, and community stake holders.
- Anyone at least 11 years of age, who lives in the district, works in the district, has a business in the district, is a student in the district or has children who are students in the district is welcome to serve as a budget delegate.
- City Staff and the Steering Committee will decide which issue committees are created based on the ideas proposed by the community at large. Potential issue committees may include but are not limited to: Transportation, Streets, Public Safety, Parks, Arts, Libraries, and Sustainability.
- If there are enough budget delegates who feel they face major obstacles to participating fully in issue committees, they may form a demographic committee for the district in which they are located. Demographic committees are meant to ensure maximum participation from community members, who might not otherwise participate, not to divide or separate sectors of the community. Potential demographic committees may include but are not limited to: Youth, Seniors, and Non-English Speaking Communities.
- Each project will have a monetary cap of $30,000 to ensure each district has at least three winning projects.

RULES: HOW DOES PB WORK IN GREENSBORO?

EXPOS

- Each district will hold Project Expos, where budget delegates will present their project proposals to the community and get feedback. These events include an opening presentation and a science fair style exposition where committees display their projects in process with visual aids (e.g., poster displays or videos).

- The Steering Committee will determine the number and location of the expos.

VOTING

- People who live in the district and are at least 11 years of age can vote for projects.

- At the time of voting, voters must present proof they satisfy the eligibility requirements. Examples of acceptable IDs are listed on page 14.

- To facilitate broad participation, each district will hold multiple days of voting, and mobile voting sites.

- There are no city-wide projects. Each district will have its own ballot, and multi-district projects will be represented on their perspective district ballots. For a project to win, it must win on each district ballot in which it is represented.

- Each voter may cast one vote per project proposal, and will receive the same number of votes (determined by district).

- The projects will be ranked by order of highest number of votes to lowest for each district. The $100,000 will be allocated based on this list until it is expired.

RULES: HOW DOES PB WORK IN GREENSBORO?

APPROVAL OF FUNDING

- After the vote, winning projects will be submitted to the City Manager for inclusión in the recommended budget. The City Manager will submit his recommended budget to City Council for adoption. City staff will keep residents apprised regarding project implementation schedules. Staffmay confer with the Steering Committee for additional information regarding specific projects.

- City Staff will keep residents updated on implementation progress and may confer with the Steering Committee for guidance on project details.

AMENDMENTS

- The Steering Committee will review and modify the handbook as needed at the end of each PB cycle, during planning for the next cycle. In the case of urgent issues that cannot wait until the end of the current cycle, the SC may make changes via a quorum vote. Reasonable prior notice of proposed changes will be furnished to the City of Greensboro and budget delegates.

ACCEPTABLE VOTERIDS

Voters must prove they live in the district and are of age to vote. In order to facilitate broad participation, voters may present a wide array of proofs of ID, including but not limited to one or more of those below, establishing residency and age:

- A document with name and current address from a local, state, or US government agency such as a state etc; driver's license or non-driver ID, consular ID, passport, EBT card, military ID card;

- Voter registration card;

- Utility, medical, credit card bill with name and current address;

- Current lease;

- Paycheck or paycheck stub from an employer or a W-2 statement;

- Bank statement or bank-issued credit card statement;

- Student ID;

- School ID;

- Employee ID;

- Permanent Resident Card (Green Card) or other Immigration Documentation;

- Residency Letter or Identification issued by a homeless shelter, halfway house,

- Passport or other ID issued by a foreign government;

- Social Security benefit statements or check;

- Employment Authorization Document;

- Medicare or other insurance document with address;

- Tax forms;

- School records (or naming the parents of children attending school and the parents' address;

- Title to any property (automobiles,house, etc.) with address;

- Birth or marriage certificate;

- Union Membership Card.

Appendix 8.2 City of Greensboro, North Carolina, Segments of Handbook

9 Case Five: City of Clarkston, Georgia

In 2012 and again in 2013, Clarkston, Georgia, was featured in segments aired by PBS called "America by the Numbers," in which local elections were discussed in relation to the recent changing demographics in the city. Located near Atlanta, Clarkston is a refugee settlement city and has a significant number of residents from a variety of countries including Vietnam, Somalia, Iran, and Bhutan. It was noted in the segments that in 2012 all of the city council members were white, but the city's population was 80 percent non-white. This was a dramatic change in demographics; in 1980 the population in Clarkston was 90 percent white. Today, approximately 60 languages or dialects are spoken within the city limits, which covers a relatively small geographical area (Public Broadcasting Service 2012 and 2013; City of Clarkston, Georgia 2015).

Ted Terry won the mayoral election in 2013. At his request the city council approved a modified version of the participatory budgeting process and committed $10,000 toward the process in the 2015 budget. The City of Clarkston meeting minutes describing participatory budgeting are presented in the Appendix. The intent behind adopting the participatory budgeting process is described within the meeting minutes as follows:

> The City of Clarkston desires to encourage more civic engagement from the public and has piloted a community budgeting initiative for fiscal year 2015. This initiative will give residents the opportunity to have a role in deciding how a portion of their tax revenues are expended. Given our limited resources for organizing and implementing a more robust process similar to what larger municipalities have created, it is our intent that the citizen committees manage all aspects of the projects, up to and including implementation, consistent with procedures to be adopted by the Clarkston City Council.

The following interview with Mayor Ted Terry was conducted in early August 2015. Selected segments from the interview are presented in Question and Answer format.

Q. Can you tell me about your community?

A. Ted Terry.

It is a small town with about 1.4 square miles after our recent annexation. One of the things I realized when I was running for office was that like in most cities we have what you call "new" Americans, and their views are different than the residents who have been here for 10 years, who have their citizenship, and who want to vote. And for those people, their views are different from those who have been in Clarkston for 20 or 30 years.

I recognized this from the very beginning, so I did my best to reach out to certain communities and I got a lot of comments like "they don't feel they want to be at council meetings. They are kind of boring sometimes." You have to find what interests people and what makes it relevant to them. There is a certain mind-set about policy formation too. People find that the slow bureaucratic process is not interesting, so I have to think about what will get people involved. What will get them to the table together and make decisions together? I have to think about how to make government more interesting and how to get people there. I want to hear from those people in the community because they already have the answers. They just need an outlet and they have ideas I never would have thought of.

Q. What is your population?

A. Ted Terry.

We were at 7,554 people and we are now at about 8,000. The annexation was decided by referendum, by vote with a 72 percent vote to approve. There were some people against it, but the majority ruled.

Q. My understanding from the Participatory Budgeting Project website is that Clarkston is doing a hybrid project that was inspired by the participatory budgeting process. Can you explain to me what you are doing with participatory budgeting?

A. Ted Terry.

The council passed a resolution saying we were going to do this process. And at that time we allocated $20,000, but as part of the budget negotiations that figure was then reduced to $10,000. You know you have to compromise. It was really a pilot program. There is no staff involvement. The council looks at it as a volunteer effort. It was approached as a mini-grant process—unlike in New York or Chicago with million dollar budgets for PB. So we had three meetings in April, May, and June where people came together and we had committees that formed under certain topic areas. It was during those meetings that the proposals came about, and then once those proposals had been vetted then the final meeting was a presentation meeting, and then an actual vote was conducted.

We did not do a paper ballot. I wanted all the money to go to the projects, so all of the overhead, all of the supplies were donated. But we had a very public vote where there were five large glass jars, one assigned to each project, and each person was given lima beans to vote with.

The initial plan, it was an outcome of a grant from Clarkston Development Foundation—a community trust project based on a similar model to what participatory budgeting is. In the future I would like to have money to contract with PBP or have the community foundation run the project.

We had a caterer who donated food, and in the future we will need to do more of that kind of thing. We need some money in the budget for advertising and marketing but the council may not approve that and they don't buy into participatory budgeting. Also we will need translation services in the future to get the refugees involved. We need to work with an organization like PBP to do things like publicize the results, run things, send out mailers, put up signs, and update Facebook and Twitter.

Q.   What do you see for the future of Clarkston?

A.   Ted Terry.

We got another annexation legislation passed in the General Assembly so in January 2016 we will add another .3 square miles to the city—mainly industrial, and half of that is vacant right now. So there is potential for job growth—mainly light manufacturing. My current vision for that area is for us to create an office of sustainability for us to use to find ways that the city can be more green, whether that is energy efficiency or something else, and also use that as a thrust to bring in green manufacturing. Industrial areas are low service areas, with high revenues. We might add another $1 million in discretionary funds for the city which would allow us to lower the millage rate. The millage rate has been going up for seven years, which is getting to the point of not too high, but high enough that when someone sees it as the highest in the county it looks bad.

We have been able to hire more police officers due to the last annexation. We are moving in the right direction as far as community policing. I would like to fund a citizen's patrol academy where we help our citizens organize neighborhood watches as opposed to letting them organize themselves. I have seen neighborhood watches come and go based on one single individual who is involved. My thought is that it is so important for the neighborhoods that we need a professional to help the structure and academies work well in other small communities. The residents here would love it and it is not a full-blown neighborhood watch. They ride around in a re-purposed police car with cell phones. There are no guns. No badges. All volunteer people. That idea the council will not like either.

The area that we annexed last year, that we police this year, it is a problem area for drug activity, prostitution and human trafficking. The vast majority of our police calls are in that one area that we annexed. We are always going over there. So when there is a break-in in a neighborhood or little small stuff, the whole neighborhood freaks out—why aren't they policing here? We don't need more police for that, we need more eyes and those eyes are free. I think you could drive around all the neighborhoods in Clarkston in 20 minutes, at 10 miles per hour and you could see the whole city.

Q. Do you believe that these characteristics or benefits of participatory budgeting are true for your experience with participatory budgeting in Clarkston? Is participatory budgeting democratic?

A. Ted Terry.

Yes, it is a democratic process. I believe participatory budgeting is a clear statement of citizen democracy, we will step back, and let them decide. And it would be good to get the school system involved and try this—we have a good principal, and good ideas but nowhere to share those ideas. And nonprofits can make a difference too.

Q. Is participatory budgeting transparent?

A. Ted Terry.

Yes, if it is done right.

Q. Is participatory budgeting efficient?

A. Ted Terry.

Yes, because what we encourage the people to do is their homework, as opposed to the city employees having to do all this legwork. If you do it right you get the citizens to do it for you, and as a democratic process, then the best ideas win. Or at least the projects that have people who turn out to vote win.

Q. Does participatory budgeting provide a sense of social justice?

A. Ted Terry.

Yes.

Q. Does participatory budgeting build a sense of community?

A. Ted Terry.

Yes.

Q. Is participatory budgeting inclusive of all the types of diversity in your community?

A. Ted Terry.

Yes, when done the right way. I think the biggest challenge that exists for any democratic process is that we are missing the transient population. The vast majority that participated this year, and in most elections are homeowners that pay taxes, or condo dwellers. There are some apartment dwellers that may have been here for 10 years. They live at that complex—and rent, but most apartment dwellers say "I am only going to be here a year" or "I am just here staying with someone else." The average homeowner moves every four years, the average tenant dweller moves every year. They are not as invested.

The refugees—those that come here and are placed here, we are at capacity for them. Clarkston is at capacity. All 2,000 units we have, there are none that are vacant. They fill up fast. Refugees might go to nearby zip codes, but once they are here and move off of federal or state aid or they can't stay here for some reason, then they may go a couple of miles away, but then come back to Clarkston.

Q. Does participatory budgeting build trust?

A. Ted Terry.

Yes, with government, and it will increase with participation, yes. That is the whole reason I do participatory budgeting to increase participation.

Q. Does participatory budgeting build the belief that meaningful change can occur?

A. Ted Terry.

Yes.

Q. Do you have any advice to others thinking about implementing participatory budgeting?

A. Ted Terry.

In our case, the more to participate the better. Keep in mind you need to allocate funds for community marketing and advertising. This is a brand new topic to people so the challenge is to explain this to others, to let people know what this is, and there must be something in the budget to say okay this is how we are going to tell people what this is. I wanted it to be more resident-driven, but we need to engage more community leaders, get nonprofit heads involved, and aid organizations, then they will then bring their people to the events—those that they are serving. We need to get other people to bring their people.

References

City of Clarkston, Georgia. 2015. http://www.clarkstonga.gov/ (accessed June 29, 2015).

Public Broadcasting Service. 2012 and 2013. http://www.pbs.org/wgbh/america-by-the-numbers/episodes/ (accessed August 13, 2015).

Appendix

CITY OF CLARKSTON

CLARKSTON CITY WORK SESSION

ITEM NO: F7

| HEARING TYPE:
Work Session | BUSINESS AGENDA / MINUTES

MEETING DATE: July 1, 2015 | ACTION TYPE:
Resolution |

SUBJECT: Clarkston Community Budgeting Proposals

DEPARTMENT: City Council

PUBLIC HEARING: ☐YES ☒NO

ATTACHMENT: ☒YES ☐ NO
Pages: 23

INFORMATION CONTACT: Mayor Ted Terry
PHONE NUMBER: 404-296-6489

<u>PURPOSE:</u> To consider and approve the attached Community Budgeting Proposals for implementation.

<u>NEED/ IMPACT:</u> The City of Clarkston desires to encourage more civic engagement from the public and has piloted a community budgeting initiative for fiscal year 2015. This initiative will give residents the opportunity to have a role in deciding how a portion of their tax revenues are expended. Given our limited resources for organizing and implementing a more robust process similar to what larger municipalities have created, it is our intent that the citizen committees manage all aspects of the projects, up to and including implementation, consistent with procedures to be adopted by the Clarkston City Council.

Various committees made up of Clarkston residents, property owners and/or business owners, were allowed to serve as voting members of the committee. Individuals who did not fit in either of these categories were encouraged to participate in the discussion and/or research of proposed projects.

The committees selected five (5) projects to be presented to the City Council for final approval.

The City Council of the City of Clarkston appropriated $10,000 in the FY' 2015 budget which was earmarked to fund the various projects.

<u>RECOMMENDATIONS:</u> No Staff recommendation.

Appendix 9.1 City of Clarkston, Georgia, July 1, 2015 Meeting Minutes

10 Other Perspectives on the Participatory Budgeting Process

Josh Lerner is the Executive Director of the Participatory Budgeting Project, a nonprofit organization in New York City. Lerner and his organization have worked with each of the cities highlighted in the preceding chapters, and Lerner referred us to many of the interviewees who are featured in those chapters. The Participatory Budgeting Project highlighted the work of Carolina Johnson, a Ph.D. candidate at the University of Washington, on its website in summer 2015. Johnson's dissertation work focuses on an international comparison of the experiences in participatory budgeting of four cities, and she agreed to be interviewed in the summer of 2015 about her observations.

The following interview with Josh Lerner was conducted in spring 2014 and focuses on the use of social media platforms in the participatory budgeting process. Selected segments from the interview with Josh Lerner are presented in Question and Answer format.

Q.   I want to focus on the citizen participation issue and the use of social media platforms today. How have you seen the use of social media change over the years and what works? What doesn't?

A.   Josh Lerner.

Where to start? Social media has been useful for connecting people across neighborhoods and across cities. One inherent feature of PB is that it is very local. It involves people coming out in their neighborhoods to talk about improvements for their neighborhoods, but it is also a part of a broader movement and part of a broader planning and budgeting process. We have used social media especially in places like New York and Chicago to connect people across districts so they can see that they are contributing to something bigger. That it is not just about getting new computers for their schools, it is about changing city governments.

That is one use, and social media is a nice platform for that because we and cities can invite people from across neighborhoods, and it is very open, and it is easy for people to join. It is a low cost form of engagement. So that has certainly been useful.

It has also been useful for a deepening engagement between meetings so that people aren't just voting or coming out to one or two meetings, but feel like they are connected to a broader process and to a broader community. So it is one more tool for community building, so that people can see the achievements of other participants, congratulate them, and share their own information. That has been useful.

It has also been useful just as one more vehicle or avenue for outreach for engagement alongside many other approaches. There is traditional media, canvassing and door-knocking, organizing efforts. There are institutional outreach venues, but social media adds to that, and often especially with little reminders. So, people may have gotten an email, or may have gotten a phone call about a meeting and if they see us on Facebook or Twitter that is one more nudge to go.

Q. As you have meetings, are you collecting email addresses so that you can reach out to more people in particular neighborhoods?

A. Josh Lerner.

Yes, we are to the extent of our authority, and that depends on the city. A place like Vallejo where it is a city-wide process, the first year we were contracted to implement it, and so we were able to on behalf of the city, and there we were able to collect everyone's information when they came to events, and when they participated online. We developed a central outreach list which then could be used for informing people about results for getting them out to vote so that was very useful.

In New York and Chicago where there have been district level processes, the challenge there is that the individual elected officials or council members have their own lists and so that has been more of a challenge. We have not always been able to either get access to their lists or permission to contact people ourselves. So there is a kind of a power issue there. So social media has been nice because it is one space in which we can create and invite people to, independently of the council members. So if you get people to participate across districts through social media it is helpful, even if we can't get or use the contact info through email or phone.

Q. Over time, do you see that this has grown—in terms of the use of social media?

A. Josh Lerner.

I don't think it has been growing exponentially, but it has been growing. It is different across media too. Facebook is restricting who sees which posts so that will actually become less useful, as you have to pay more to have anyone see your posts unfortunately. Twitter has not done that yet, to the extent that Facebook has. So Twitter is more open and easy to spread the word.

Then on Facebook, people may or may not see your posts, whereas with Twitter, anyone who follows you will see it. We have used Instagram in a few places too and that has been very popular especially with young people. I think Instagram is really about usage, and the young people are using Instagram at increasingly higher rates and often using it more than Facebook.

Q. One issue brought up in Chicago's 49th ward was the limitation on who has administrative permissions with some of these social media outlets, and it slows down the process of getting info out. Do you talk to the different cities and wards about how to more effectively use social media?

A. Josh Lerner.

Yes, we do that some, we share sample social media content, sample posts or tweets so they can put them out. We have done social media workshops in New York, guiding folks on how to effectively use social media for engagement. Those samples are used by some and not by some. The workshops and the sample materials are available. We contracted with someone externally to do the workshop.

Q. Where I find people having trouble is that the technology is there, but they don't always have the people or resources to keep things updated as they would like to. Do you have any ideas for better using social media?

A. Josh Lerner.

I think that is really the crux of the issue. So, social media is a tool, and if people don't know how to use the tool or have time to use it, it does not get used effectively. That is what we are seeing, that in order for social media to contribute to PB, then there needs to be both training and capacity for it to work. And recognizing it as work, that it is skilled work that requires someone who knows what they are doing, and who has the time to do it, and too often that is not the case. Social media either is left to someone who does not have a lot of experience with it, or it is not even left to anyone, and it is an afterthought. So, what we found is that for it to contribute most to the process, that there needs to be someone who understands social media, helping to do social media engagement. It is fairly straightforward.

There are different ways to do that. So, one is to train local staff. Another would be to provide financial resources to enable there to be central staff to support local processes, and that is one thing that we are trying to build up—recognizing that a lot of the social media outreach and challenges and strategies are actually similar across PB processes. And it is not very efficient to be reinventing the wheel in each city, and figuring out what works and what doesn't, so we are figuring that out across cities, and there could just be much more economies of scale if some of that work was coordinated.

So rather than having, like in New York there will be 20 districts doing PB in the fall, so rather than having 20 people doing 20 different social media messaging efforts—not very well, having one person who is effectively coordinating, that would be less time and more impact. So, yes, our focus is really on realizing that it is a support role that could have a big impact, and that can reduce the cost of the process and can reduce the time involved if there is someone who can do it well.

We found as far as best practices—we have learned that a lot of or one of the common mistakes is that a lot of the folks doing social media around PB, they do it from the perspective of someone who is already interested in the process. As opposed to thinking about the folks they are trying to reach who are not inherently interested in it yet, or at least who are not as interested in it yet as they are. So, a lot of the content we find tends to be—"there was a PB meeting"—so saying something which is exciting for the staff person organizing it, but doesn't really get at "why someone else should care." So we have encouraged them to lift up why it matters, not just that it is happening.

So for example, telling or having a quote or a picture of someone having a meaningful experience at the event and talking about what they learned. Or about the projects that are being put forward and how amazing they are. Lifting up the content of what makes it interesting more than just the fact that it is happening. That is important.

Q. What do you know about digital or online voting?

A. Josh Lerner.

My understanding is that some cities are exploring digital, but not online voting. So, in other words having a computer at the voting sites, and encouraging people to vote on the computer through a process that enables them to better visualize the implications of their vote. So they can have their own balanced budget with their votes, and play around and see if it adds up to a million dollars or not, which is not necessary but can be interesting. Then they can cast their votes on the computer at the voting sites.

There are a lot of computer programs out there. A couple of times a month, we get a random email from some start-up or developer that wants to use their app for PB. So, there are a lot of things that can be done and the main challenge is a resource issue. The tool itself often doesn't have much impact unless there is the capacity to use it. So, there is not that capacity right now. So what we are trying to do is figure out which of these tools have the potential to have the most impact. There are so many things that can be done, but there is the capacity to do one or two.

One thing we have been doing, is we have been piloting SMS engagement for texting, and working with that in Boston, and we think that has really big potential for engaging people, especially youth and a lot of people who don't participate as much in general, those who use texting a lot, and it has very high response rate and usership rates, and so that is one thing we have found strategic for focusing on.

Q. Can you tell me about your digital scanning system?

A. Josh Lerner.

It was developed internally together with some staff at city council that we work with, basically bar codes were imbedded in the ballots, and then people could scan in the projects from each ballot. So, it cut the time for vote counting down dramatically. This is the first time this year we are using it. We have talked about ultimately having it where the whole sheet is scanned, like a Scantron form, which would be even quicker.

Q. On the broader issue about participatory budgeting, I wanted to ask you about a couple of things I have seen going on in other cities. For example, the 5th ward in Chicago decided on not pursuing participatory budgeting further. What do you tell people in a neighborhood when the alderman does not want to pursue participatory budgeting?

A. Josh Lerner.

What we usually say, and it really is to the extent that we can say it is, talk with your council person or work with your alderman. It is really up to the official and if they feel it is something that the community really wants then they are more likely to do it. So, it is up to people in the neighborhood to put that forward.

What we are doing is working to make the process easier and less time and resource intensive, and we find that is probably the single biggest obstacle to adding more PB processes is that it does take a lot of time. It will still take a lot of time, but there are ways to cut that down. So things like having the vote scanning that cuts down some time. SMS engagement can cut down time on calling and following up with people so we are working on both using tech tools and also process design and training tools to make the workload less.

What we have seen as necessary for PB to be successful is having some central support and most of these cities that do PB have a PB office or an office of civic engagement that coordinates the process and that has five or ten staff members supporting it, and so you only get out what you put into it. It requires that staffing to make it successful.

The following interview with Carolina Johnson was conducted in the summer of 2015. Selected segments from the interview, focusing on the broader issue of citizen participation, are presented below in Question and Answer format.

Q. As you have conducted your research in Scotland, England, and the United States, what are the kinds of things that you've seen in terms of what gets people to participate? How do these cities get people in the room?

A. Carolina Johnson.

So first, they have to know about it, and that is a huge issue. It is actually what it takes to effectively publicize an opportunity for participation, so that people don't just see it, but they notice it, and they should know the difference there. We have had some of the most deprived parts or areas of Scotland to participate in PB, and PB happens in places where people are gentrifying, which is just an anecdotal thing I've noticed. Some towns are the classic cases of the working class, rundown, entrenched generational poverty, lots of immigration, lots of artists, and then other people start to come in. You can walk across it all in 2 miles.

In cities in Great Britain, people don't drive anyway; people are on the streets and in the public sphere in that sense, as they go about their daily lives. The district is plastered with signs and banners about participatory budgeting, but people do not see them, so they hear about it by word of mouth nearly exclusively. Once they have heard about it, they will do things such as, "like" the Facebook page, and they "follow" the Facebook page. But they don't do that until they know someone who was involved in the project, and they were personally invited and encouraged to submit a proposal. The word of mouth and all of these pieces were really key in those places, and all of these other forms of publicity then play an important role, but once the word of mouth has activated people to be attentive to it.

Q.   So after people know about it, and they are participating, and going to Facebook and those kinds of things, what else are you seeing in terms of other forms of social media platforms that might be used?

A.   Carolina Johnson.

I'm not seeing much in Scotland. In Scotland, I'd say it is Facebook exclusively. Facebook does get used. People have "liked" the page and it does get used for reminders. In Vallejo, California, again it's reflective of what is already used in the community. There's not a huge social media push. It's more that the social media in Vallejo is targeted to the people outside of Vallejo, so that observers are knowing what's going on rather than in a really important way that the people in the city need it to be.

In New York it's going to be different. If you're looking at district 39 in Brooklyn which has a lot of affluent and often very creative neighborhoods, then you will see different social media getting used a lot more because the residents of those districts themselves are living their lives on social media more.

Q.   Do you think that we will see a change in the future in terms of how those interactions using social media are done to encourage participation?

A.   Carolina Johnson.

I don't know exactly what change, I am sure it will evolve as technology evolves. The key with effective publicity for things like participatory budgeting is you go to where people are talking, so if people are talking on social media, that's where PB organizers should be. If they aren't talking on social media, then talking on social media is not going to help make it a better process. I believe that we will evolve and if PB is being implemented by people who have the resources and are committed to making it a good process, they will evolve. They will try to go to where the people are.

I think it is also worth saying that in most places where people make a real effort to engage youth, youth tend to get on social media more, definitely in places where there are youth committees, like looking at Boston, and how they use social media would be really different than in Vallejo. It's a youth process, and I suspect that the relationship to the geography of neighborhoods is different, so I suspect the use of social media there will be different as well. I know youth committees and youth volunteers have been doing more of the social media outreach. People go where they communicate.

Q.   In terms of Vallejo, what have you seen there in terms of the voting process—is it paper? Is it digital?

A.   Carolina Johnson.

Both, in the last round of voting. You have to vote in person, there is no
remote voting, but at the voting places you can choose to vote on a laptop.
There was a voting system that was designed in collaboration with a group
at Stanford and so people could choose. A lot of people choose and prefer
to vote on paper, and that's just an impression I had. I was at the vote in
Vallejo in October. People would vote on the computer if you asked them
to nicely, but people preferred to actually handle it in their hands.

Q.   Have you been following Vallejo for a few years then?

A.   Carolina Johnson.

I mean I have been tracking it since the first round. I wasn't there for
the vote their first year, but I was there for about a month or so during the
first round of budget delegate meetings as they were finalizing projects
going to the ballot.

Q.   Some say the Vallejo process started because of the bankruptcy issue and
that might have made the process a little bit different from other cities. Do
you agree?

A.   Carolina Johnson.

I don't think it was different as a result of the bankruptcy in the sense
of what people were interested in prioritizing for projects. I don't actually
feel that the main impact the bankruptcy had was different. In Vallejo there
were questions of where should the budget priorities be going. Does it need
to be going to public safety, basic services, should it be going to a community garden? Those conversations are really common across the board.

I'd say the main reason of how the bankruptcy impacted Vallejo was
kicking people into gear to feel like they had to take responsibility for
their own community—that was the real impact the bankruptcy had in the
sense that if they didn't get something through PB at least in the first year
it wasn't clear how they were able to get it otherwise.

I think as it went on people did start to find more or gain more knowledge of other ways they could try and access certain kinds of other
resources. I think another way the projects might have changed is that the
first year there were a lot of projects that would have been giving over or
transferring implementation of a program to a particular organization or
set of individuals, and that obviously became somewhat problematic on
the legal side for the city. There was a lack of clarity in the beginning,
such as what kind of restrictions there should be on whether the people
are voting for salaries for specific individuals as part of the PB process, or
if projects should have an open bidding process?

So I think that the first year there was a little bit less interaction during
the vetting process between the city and the project committees. Then the
second year there was a little bit of a shift in terms of thinking are we just
giving money to an organization to implement something, or just sort of

clarifying the definition of what was a viable project, and was it even a possible project that could be voted on, or how these things were defined.

Q.   Could you tell me your reaction to each of the characteristics or benefits of participatory budgeting based on your academic research and what you have observed in the field? The first is that participatory budgeting is democratic. Do you agree?

A.   Carolina Johnson.

Yes, I think that is a fair description. There are a lot of different ways you can think about being democratic, and participatory budgeting tends to really prioritize democracy in terms of government by the people in a sense. It's generally, the process usually is democratic. It is imperfect, every process is imperfect, and there are different kinds of deficits in terms of how effectively democratic it is.

The process is at least as inclusive as other voting opportunities that we have in this country, usually more inclusive. The public generally has better control over the agenda for what decisions are being made, within constraints. There's always an initial agenda constraining decisions that are made by the steering committee or local government, but within that it is more open to public influence and public priorities than many other local government processes I think.

Q.   Is participatory budgeting transparent?

A.   Carolina Johnson.

In some ways it's transparent, and in some ways it's not transparent—it's like Congress. In a sense there are some parts of it that are extremely public, but some parts that aren't and PB is meant to be deliberative. Deliberation is at its very nature not always transparent, people are not in the room because the discussions, the reasoning, and the shifting positions of people in the room are happening internally in their exchange. And that can be something that people not in that room may feel is not transparent, but again that is a characteristic of many group decision processes.

Generally most people organizing PB aspire to be transparent, and will generally be responsive to questions about the process. There is a lot of negotiation that happens not just within the people in the U.S. model where there are budget delegate committees, and there's obviously a limit to how transparent that process can be because it's deliberative.

You can videotape, but there's also negotiation that happens with government in terms of which proposals are legal, which ones are valid, and that really takes you to how transparent are the existing government agencies that are being collaborated with.

So I know this has been a concern people have that I have talked to in New York, just because New York's bureaucracy is extensive and the different departments in New York are worlds unto their own. So if a project gets sent to a city department to be vetted, whether the project is legal or not, or what the actual cost is, there definitely tends to be some variation in the transparency of the project vetting process. That is actually affected by the culture of the community that PB is operating in.

I do think that PB pushes greater transparency. That putting PB into a community will push the local budgets, the local decision processes, to be more transparent than they were. So in that sense, the claim that PB is transparent as just a blanket statement, I am actually pretty comfortable with saying that. It will generally be more transparent and will be more democratic with variations.

Q. Is participatory budgeting efficient?

A. Carolina Johnson.

In terms of efficiency, it depends on what your objective is for these issues. PB has big criticisms that you can hear from city managers or folks involved in just providing services at the city level, that it is very inefficient. If all you're interested in doing is defining a budget, it is not an efficient process.

If what you're trying to do is get a very granular sense of what are the real priorities of the community, I actually think PB can be very efficient at that. Because it has citizens to do the work, and there are collateral benefits that come out of that. In terms of citizen education, supporting other kinds of mobilization and cooperation, all of those kinds of outcomes of a well-run process, and you can get a lot of prioritization around a lot of different issues, different areas of work in a city, within the PB process.

You aren't just working only on planning one neighborhood necessarily or streets and transportation in isolation from thinking about parks, there is some of that in PB generally, and you have to specialize. But it's a process that allows priorities and needs across a really broad range of issues to come to the surface and aggregates a lot of information about public needs and preference.

And then most people make decisions freely about those. It's a very time intensive process though, time and labor intensive for everyone involved and that is a reality. But it's also again better than people like to think, where if you talk to someone who knows anything about PB they say that seems ridiculous. In two or three meetings a committee can come down on a short list of projects to give to the city out of 120. In that sense, that's only five to six hours of work. It's actually pretty efficient to get a list of the 12 most important parks improvements or street improvements or investments in arts and culture in that community. So it takes a lot of time, but it actually gets a lot done.

Q. Does participatory budgeting provide a sense of social justice?

A. Carolina Johnson.

I think it can provide a sense of social justice when the organizers are committed to making social justice a priority in the process. The process, by putting real money on the table, and by allowing that money to be spent on the things that are most important to the people who participate, really it can adjust the balance of whose voice is having the most impact.

You can see where PB is implemented, you do see different demographics of the people who participate, and that's a testament to the work that is done just in the basic sense of organizing to get them aware that the process is going on.

PB also in some ways, it is getting at tangible things. Some people will complain that it is not a huge amount of money, and that we aren't over-hauling the budget, but at the same time it means that you're targeting issues that people are more impacted by. And in that sense you are getting people who might be coming from lower income brackets, who are more dependent on public services, and they might see more of a purpose in showing up in the room than if it was a higher level budget re-write.

Q.   Does participatory budgeting build trust?

A.   Carolina Johnson.

Sure. A well-run PB process can do all these things. But doing a well-run PB process is very hard, you have to have a serious commitment. If you have a PB process that isn't transparent, it's not going to build trust. But the experience of working across common divides in a community, adding people from different parts of the community working in rooms together, we can build trust between groups of the community.

It can improve trust between citizens and local government. It won't always do that, but it can, if you bring people in who often have a really skeptical view of each other, say community neighborhood groups and folks from the city planning department. They often bring the impact of previous experiences, you bring them into a PB room and they are work-ing collaboratively and productively together, they come out feeling like this isn't an enemy, this is someone who ultimately has similar objectives with different strengths. And that can in a sense build trust, make some-one believe that someone else in their political community is trustworthy and is not out to actually undermine them.

So I think it can again if the process is well-run, if it's badly run it can really undermine trust. Like any engagement process, if you invite people and then don't follow through and don't take them seriously, it under-mines the credibility of future promises.

Q.   Does participatory budgeting build a belief that meaningful change can occur?

A.   Carolina Johnson.

I think that when PB leads to meaningful change, it definitely does that. In communities like Vallejo, it is a good example of a place where PB hasn't solved the city's problems in itself with PB, and so it can be con-tentious in different ways, but modeling the possibility of change or the possibility that decisions could be made differently, or include different people, or lead to different outcomes, I think definitely it can be a catalyst for imagination and change.

Q.   In terms of your experience with observing Vallejo, are there any groups or subgroups of people that have felt left out, or where it seems to be indicated that they haven't had full representation, or maybe as strong a representation as they would like?

A.   Carolina Johnson.

Who is left out and who is aware that they are left out are two different questions. Some people feel left out because they sense that change in the system and they no longer have exclusive or privileged access to decision-making. Some people feel left out because they know who is organizing the process and they are on different sides of the political spectrum, so they decide that they are left out because there's sometimes a sense of partisan divide that is in place. Not often, but that can make some people feel excluded where they sort of decide from the start that they won't be heard.

Then you definitely have people who don't know that it exists or don't believe that it's worth their time to go, and they can be left out, and that may or may not actually have an impact on them. There were issues of getting full and equal participation from every demographic group in Vallejo and anywhere that has done PB. That takes a lot of work to really get everyone in the room.

Q.   Is there anything else that you want to tell me about participatory budgeting?

A.   Carolina Johnson.

My whole answer to the whole story of participatory budgeting is "it depends." There's no one thing that is PB. You can imagine designing it in a lot of different ways. So there is the question of what do we call PB, how is PB really different from any other strategy for community organizing where there is a real commitment on the part of both local government and local organizers to improve the quality of participation inclusively across the community? So that is something that is a little bit hard to pin down. PB needs resources for implementation and staff to support it. If you don't have that it is hard to do it well enough to get all those positive outcomes or benefits you mentioned.

One more thing about Vallejo is that the bankruptcy opened up some opportunities to try and introduce some new things. But I actually don't think PB was a strategy for getting out of bankruptcy. It was attached to it because it was an opportunity, but the political work that the council members who supported it, that is what made it work. They wanted to come up with some other way of improving budget transparency and budget decision-making in Vallejo in part because of the bankruptcy, but even prior to going into bankruptcy.

And then PB came up as an issue with a certain amount of resonance and an appeal, and then they did the hard political work of building a coalition that was willing to vote for it on council. And in some ways it was almost despite the bankruptcy. The bankruptcy raised issues such as we don't have time for this, we don't have resources for this, our priority needs to be getting police back on the streets, getting the firehouses open and running, and getting basic services provided for. So the bankruptcy definitely created an openness and a demand for a different way of doing things from a large part of the community that was feeling fed up with stuff, but it then created additional political blocks in terms of where money was available in the budget.

The way participatory budgeting fits in with the bankruptcy is basically that the bankruptcy meant that people were willing to vote for a new sales tax, and a new sales tax meant there was a new flow of money coming in, and the new flow of money coming in provided an opportunity for that money to be intercepted by the participatory budgeting process. There is a lot of interesting stuff in Vallejo because of the bankruptcy, but I actually think the inception of PB and the political story around it, it isn't entirely that different from the experience of other communities. It's not a totally different narrative, but instead has similar characters and some similar conflicts. (The City of Vallejo, California, Council Resolution #12-064, signed April 17, 2012, is presented in the Appendix.)

Appendix

RESOLUTION NO. 12-064 N.C.

ESTABLISH A PARTICIPATORY BUDGETING (PB) PROCESS WITH THE GOAL OF
ALLOCATING A MINIMUM OF 30% OF MEASURE B FUNDS AND FURTHER DIRECTING
THE CITY MANAGER TO RETURN TO THE COUNCIL WITH A RESOLUTION OF
INTENTION TO AMEND THE FISCAL YEAR 2011/2012 BUDGET TO PROVIDE FUNDING
FOR THE CREATION OF THE PB PROCESS

WHEREAS, after more than four years of severe cuts to city services and programs while in
bankruptcy, there is evidence that Vallejo citizens feel disenfranchised from the political process
and are disillusioned by its lack of performance and inability to improve their quality of life; and

WHEREAS, by re-engaging citizens in the democratic process and giving them real power to
make decisions about how to spend their tax payer dollars, Participatory Budgeting (PB) is one
anecdote to the public's lack of trust in government and feelings that their opinions and
concerns about the operations and administration of their City go unheard and do not matter;
and

WHEREAS, PB is a democratic process in which members of the public directly decide how to
spend part of a public budget through an annual series of local assemblies, meetings, and
project proposals and research that result in a final vote by the public to allocate discretionary
funds to specific projects; and

WHEREAS, PB would directly empower and engage Vallejo citizens in deliberative democracy
to propose, research, analyze, decide and vote on projects that they want in their community,
thereby helping to rebuild civic trust and a sense of community in the City of Vallejo.

NOW, THEREFORE BE IT RESOLVED that the City Council of the City of Vallejo hereby
declares its intent to establish a PB process as set forth in this Resolution with the goal of
allocating a minimum of 30% of the 1% sales tax monies, Measure B funds, collected over a 15
month period from April 1, 2012 through June 30, 2013.

BE IT FURTHER RESOLVED that the City Council of the City of Vallejo hereby directs the City
Manager to return to the City Council with a Resolution of Intention to amend the Fiscal Year
2011/2012 budget in the amount of $200,000 to provide funding for the creation of the PB
process including contracting with a recognized expert in the field of PB and a consultant to
assist with the coordination of the PB process, as well as the cost of materials to facilitate and
coordinate the PB process.

BE IT FURTHER RESOLVED that the City Council will:

- Upon approval of the Fiscal Year 2012/2013 budget and as the 1% sales tax monies are
  received, deposit a percentage of those revenues as set by the City Council as part of
  the approved budget in a reserve account until the PB process is complete in spring
  2013 and the City Council is able to consider the approval of the public's voter approved
  projects.

- Consider qualified and proposed PB projects to be those that satisfy the criteria of a one-
  time expenditure to complete the project; or a program or service proposal that off-sets
  other expenditures in the City's budget so that the cost is $0, pays for itself or increases

the City's revenues. Projects or expenditures that are traditionally funded by the Vallejo City Unified School District, Greater Vallejo Recreation District and/or any other public agencies or entities would not qualify as a project for the purposes of the City's PB process.

- Contract with a recognized expert in the field of PB to consult on the design of the PB process and its facilitation.

- Contract with one full-time and one part-time consultant to assist in the coordination and day-to-day logistics and operations of the PB process.

- Work with the recognized expert in the field of PB to identify and appoint a Community Steering Committee to establish the PB structure and process.

- Establish a Community Steering Committee to assist in the design of the PB process with the following parameters:
  - Each Councilmember nominate three civic organizations that will then recommend individuals to the City Council from those organizations to serve on the Committee. The Mayor shall make appointments to Committee with the consent of the City Council pursuant to Vallejo Municipal Code section 2.02.350 E.
  - The recognized expert in the field of PB will work with the Community Steering Committee and lead PB design process and development of the PB structure.
  - The Community Steering Committee's proposed PB process and structure will return to City Council for consideration and approval before implementation of the process, including rolling out general assemblies, neighborhood meetings and project proposals.

- Appoint two Councilmembers to act in a liaison capacity to the Community Steering Committee.

BE IT FURTHER RESOLVED that after Vallejo citizens vote for PB projects, the City Council will consider approval of the expenditure of Measure B funds on the public's approved and voted on projects.

Adopted by the City Council of the City of Vallejo at a Special meeting held on April 17, 2012 by the following vote:

AYES: Councilmembers Brown, Gomes, McConnell, and Sampayan,
NOES: Mayor Davis, Vice Mayor Hannigan and Councilmember Sunga
ABSTAIN: None
ABSENT: None

OSBY DAVIS, MAYOR

ATTEST:

DAWN G. ABRAHAMSON, CITY CLERK

Appendix 10.1 City of Vallejo, California, Council Resolution #12-064, signed April 17, 2012

11 Lessons Learned: Best Practices for Communities

As public administration has evolved into a values-based discipline, we have witnessed a growing litany of activities designed to enhance democracy, ensure ethical conduct, and incorporate social equality. This volume presents participatory budgeting as one such activity that aims to ensure greater democracy and transparency in the communities where it is implemented. At the same time, we seek to better understand the spaces in which citizen engagement occurs, including both physical and digital arenas.

As discussed in Chapter 2, participatory budgeting has evolved over three phases, with the most recent being characterized as a period of extension and diversification (Global Campaign on Urban Governance 2004). This diversification is the outcome of the intersection of the fundamentals of participatory budgeting and local culture. The five examples presented in this volume demonstrate that there is not a one-size-fits-all approach to implementation. There are, however, lessons learned from each that are valuable for administrators and citizens who contemplate bringing participatory budgeting to their own localities. In the following sections, we distill these lessons into findings and action items. We begin first with a discussion of the nuts and bolts—the dimensions and benefits of participatory budgeting.

Nuts and Bolts of Participatory Budgeting, aka the Five Dimensions

As described in Chapter 2, the five dimensions to participatory budgeting are financial, spatial, participatory, normative/legal, and political. These aspects of participatory budgeting are clarifying considerations for the ways in which a municipality can arrange the process. A truly participatory process will include the public in the consideration of each dimension instead of having politicians and administrators making the decisions first and then asking for participation later. Even more important, participation from the point of ideation is more likely to yield a shared understanding of the purposes and process.

With regard to the financial dimension, decisions must be made about the categories and amount subjected to the process. In some instances they are limited to the discretionary part of a budget or a category of expenditures, such as the parks and recreation budget. Similarly, the spatial dimension delineates the areas (e.g., wards, districts) that will participate in the process. Space, both physical and virtual, facilitates and limits certain kinds of human interactions (Hatch and Cunliffe 2013). Participatory budgeting presents an opportunity for citizens and administrators to come together collaboratively to make decisions; however, collaboration does not occur spontaneously (Amey and Brown 2004). Administrators must be mindful of the impact space will have on all stakeholders and the participatory budgeting process.

In some of the cases discussed in this volume, all residents of a municipality were eligible to participate in the process. In Chicago and New York, the process was limited to the discretionary budget of a particular city council district. Spatial boundaries are equally important as the portion of the budget to be included in the process. Together these two dimensions are considered the boundaries of the activity. Whatever the decisions, the financial and spatial dimensions are the ultimate parameters of the process and must be decided early on.

The participatory dimension is just as important as the financial dimension. Where the latter can be described as the boundaries of the process, the former can be characterized as the enfranchising aspect. Will the participatory budgeting process mimic direct democracy, where every person of a certain age, residency, and so forth votes on possible options? Or will residents elect representatives to make decisions for them, mimicking the representative democracy already in place? The enfranchisement of citizens, when combined with the boundaries, brings clarity to the contours of the process. When done thoughtfully, the process will reflect the values and culture of the locality.

The normative/legal dimension determines the rules of the game. For example, localities need to decide whether input from the public is binding or advisory. Localities must research the extent to which authorizing or enabling legislation is necessary to institutionalize the recommendations or decisions derived from the process. As discussed in Chapter 2, to accept the feedback provided as merely advisory would fall short of the goals and objectives of participatory budgeting. An analogous example is whether or not the locality wants to move the process beyond public participation to public engagement. Public participation is less powerful and simply provides an opportunity for feedback and comments, but engagement moves to active incorporation of that input into final choices (Nabatchi and Amsler 2014, 65S).

Last, the political dimension is an anchoring aspect in that it helps to define the goals and objectives of the process. Paralleling the five dimensions, there are five benefits of participatory budgeting that enhance the quality of governance within a municipality: democracy, education, efficiency, social justice, and community (see Chapter 2 for a fuller discussion of each; Hadden and Lerner 2011; Lerner 2011). As communities examine the feasibility and desirability of participatory budgeting, these five benefits should anchor discussions about the other dimensions. As members of a locality seek to define the financial and spatial aspects of the process, decide on the participatory elements of the activity, and understand the normative/legal implications, they should do so within the framework of the five benefits. Questions grounded in these benefits include:

- Does the process enhance democracy?
- Will residents have an improved understanding of the budgetary and political processes?
- Is efficiency achieved through representativeness of governmental decisions?
- Are the politically disadvantaged or vulnerable populations more likely to participate when compared to traditional process?
- Does the process engender a greater sense of community?

Beyond these broad dimensions, a locality should contemplate additional considerations when exploring participatory budgeting. The section that follows presents a how-to guide that brings greater specificity. This guide is grounded in the experiences of the five localities discussed in earlier chapters.

What Your Community Can Learn from the Experiences of Others

Table 11.1 presents a How-To Guide for Participatory Budgeting that sum-marizes the questions a community might consider when deciding whether to adopt participatory budgeting. If a community wants to pursue participatory budgeting, it would be helpful to think through the answers to each of the questions asked here (Hadden and Lerner 2011; Gordon 2012, 17).

Table 11.1 How-To Guide for Participatory Budgeting (PB)

Questions to Ask	Steps to Take
Could PB work in our community?	Political will and permission from those controlling the budget are critical.
	Explore any necessary statutory considerations.
How do we put PB on the agenda?	Organize public events to explain what PB is.
Who should be at the table for initial discussions?	Find interested organizations and parties: private, nonprofit and governmental; experts at local universities; members of churches, neighborhood groups, and schools; and community leaders.
How do we pitch PB to attract interest?	Stress the following features:
	Democracy—PB is a way for politicians and constituents to connect. It brings new people into the political process. Many participants reported they had never been involved in any community or governmental activity prior to PB.
	Transparency—PB will provide for less corruption and waste.
	Education—Citizens become more active and more informed.
	Efficiency—You have the benefit of local residents' expertise on their neighborhoods, and they will take an interest in seeing the projects through to completion. The citizens will have a sense of ownership.

	Social Justice—Everyone has a voice. Under-represented groups participate, and often projects are directed to those who truly need the most help.
	Community—Regular meetings build camaraderie and community.
How do we deal with resistance?	Address these common concerns and criticisms head on: "You are doing the elected officials job." "There is no money." "The process will be stolen by the 'squeaky' wheels, the loudest and most active."
Where will this money we will use come from?	Elected officials usually commit some discretionary funds, although cities in difficult financial situations can address broader issues.
How much money do we need to get started?	Any amount will work; it depends on the type of projects that will be undertaken. The point is that the citizens have real power over real money that will address real community needs.
What other resources will we need?	You need time, patience, and a lot of planning. PB takes real work; it will not just happen. You may need external experts, and you will have to do a lot of outreach and education. To enrich participation, you may need to offer child care, take the meetings out to the neighborhoods, or have meetings on the weekends when people are available. And offering food never hurts.
Is it important to have clear processes and procedures?	Yes. A truly participatory process involves the public from ideation to implementation, which is likely to yield a shared understanding of purpose and procedures. Clearly defined and documented processes and procedures ensure accountability and transparency.
What will our community really get out of this process?	Transparency. A more efficient budget process in which citizens help make tough choices. Educated citizens who are committed to the community and re-energized to participate in their government. Citizen trust in elected officials and belief in the value of their government.
Are there risks involved?	Without the required effort to ensure representativeness of participants, there is a risk of political elites or more affluent citizens capturing the process.

Sources: Hadden and Lerner 2011; Gordon 2012, 17.

While the findings we present and the action items we recommend in this chapter are a solid first step, more work is needed to fully understand the participatory budgeting process. More research is needed to investigate whether communities that follow our recommendations will successfully increase the level of participation and engagement of their citizens, as well as whether this will strengthen the trust that citizens have in their local government and its leaders. This challenge that contemporary leaders face in engaging citizens and gaining their trust remains one of the leadership challenges of local governments and it requires further study (Nalbandian, O'Neill, Jr., Wilkes, and Kaufman 2013; Gordon, Osgood, Jr., and Boden 2016).

Through the words of the local community leaders, we have gained an understanding of their experiences with participatory budgeting. This research project has demonstrated the challenges of implementing participatory budgeting for each of the communities highlighted in the previous chapters. The following findings and suggested action items are drawn from the interviews.

Participatory Budgeting Infrastructure

Finding 1: Many Jurisdictions Lack Adequate Infrastructure for Participatory Budgeting

Most political jurisdictions in the United States have limited experience with participatory budgeting. For participatory budgeting to be successful, cookie-cutter copies of the process do not need to be enacted by each jurisdiction, but communities should learn from each other and incorporate what works for their particular needs (Lerner 2011). To build capacity and develop the infra-structure necessary for participatory budgeting, there must first be the political and financial commitment from elected officials to see the process through. Decision-making power must be shared with constituents if the participatory budgeting process is to be successful and meaningful (Gordon, Osgood, Jr., and Boden 2016).

For example, Greensboro, North Carolina, has moved very slowly toward adopting the participatory budgeting process because of a lack of both political and financial commitment from elected officials. The process there has been driven by citizens rather than spearheaded by a particular elected councilperson. The community group has worked toward adopting participatory budgeting since 2011, and only in October 2014 did the city council agree to make par-ticipatory budgeting a part of the budgeting process (Greensboro Participatory Budgeting 2015; Gordon, Osgood, Jr., and Boden 2016).

Most communities that are just starting with the participatory budgeting process are increasingly reaching out to nonprofit organizations with partici-patory budgeting expertise for assistance to ensure that limited resources are used wisely (Gordon, Osgood, Jr., and Boden 2016). This is a primary way in which cities can ensure success in their first year of participatory budgeting. Further, no matter the approach or level of support from elected officials, communities must allow at least a year for the process to be thoroughly and adequately implemented.

Balancing Act is a commercially available tool designed to help boost citizen engagement and it has the potential to be utilized within community-led participatory budgeting projects. Balancing Act's typical use has been to illus-trate the complex trade-offs inherent in budgets, but it has also been adapted as an educational tool to crowdsource preferences for allocating a fixed amount of money. It has been identified as a tool to address some of the challenges confronting participatory budgeting such as 1) lack of attendance at meetings; 2) lack of participation within those meetings; and 3) lack of complementary tools to help participants learn about the potential allocations. Balancing Act helps address these issues by 1) broadening the number of people involved with PB, particularly those who are unable to attend the face-to-face meetings; 2) making the meetings more interactive and tech-friendly; and 3) serving as an educational tool to help residents understand the merits of each project and how each might potentially fit in with the limited funds available. In New York City district 5, represented by Councilmember Ben Kallos, participatory budgeting meetings set for early 2016 have started the process of integrating Balancing Act into the process (Amirehsani 2015).

Finding 2: Restrictive Policies Prevent Successful Social Media Use in Participatory Budgeting

Perlman (2012) identified eight categories of restriction on public sector social media practices: employee access; account management; acceptable use; employee conduct; content; security; legal issues; and citizen conduct. Perlman finds that "it is not surprising that nearly all of these elements are restrictive and concerned with regulation of conduct and content, and that they do not speak to the issues of SMS (texting) innovation, use in policy networks, or citizen participation" (72). Yet, actual online citizen participation is a primary measure of whether municipalities are doing a good job of engaging citizens, and ultimately, whether citizens trust their government (Manoharan and Bennett 2013). As reflected in interviews with participatory budgeting community leaders, a balance must be struck between procedural regulations of social media platforms and the need for their constant, consistent, timely, and accurate updating (Gordon, Osgood, Jr., and Boden 2016).

It is not surprising that government organizations might struggle with issues related to the administration of a social media presence. In many ways, a bureaucratic structure is antithetical to social media use. Information and communication technology (ICT) has had a tremendous impact on the method and speed of modern communication. As Carolina Johnson explained, the increased use of social media by municipalities is often largely a response to citizens' expectations. These expectations can create difficult questions about how a local government will manage its social media presence. As ICTs become more commonplace, citizens come to expect more immediate access to information. The concern for any local government interacting with citizens on social media is that immediacy will trump accuracy. From this perspective, it is understandable that some municipalities have tasked the office of the chief administrator to manage their social media presence while others have delegated that responsibility to the internal IT department (Reddick and Norris 2013, 459). Regardless of where and how municipalities administer social media efforts, it is important for administrators to recognize that social media is not a static space but rather an environment designed for collaboration (Kaplan and Haenlein 2010, 65). As Sheree Moratto of Chicago's 49th ward explained, overly restrictive administrative access can compromise the effectiveness of a social media campaign. The immediacy of social media activities requires fewer constraints on procedural regulations.

Finding 3: Social Media Platforms Can Be Effective in Participatory Budgeting But Have Been Underused

All interviewees agreed that social media platforms could effectively encourage participation in the participatory budgeting process and in the actual budget voting process. However, to date, social media use in participatory budgeting has been limited and sporadic. There is a great need and great potential to increase and expand social media platform use to expand and encourage participation (Gordon, Osgood, Jr., and Boden 2016).

The digital divide, the gap between those who have access to and the ability to use ICTs effectively, seems to explain some of the reluctance on the part of administrators and elected officials to embrace social media completely as it relates to participatory budgeting. Sheree Moratto explained that some citizens of Chicago's 49th ward are extremely knowledgeable about ICTs and are willing to engage on social media sites while others struggle with basic computer skills. Administrators must consider the gap between those with access and the ability to use ICTs (van Dijk and Hacker 2003) as they contemplate how to best interact with citizens in virtual spaces.

Finding 4: Security is a Major Concern When Expanding the Use of Social Media and Introducing Electronic or Digital Voting into Participatory Budgeting

The problem of verifying residency and age severely limits the potential of online, digital, or e-voting processes (Gordon, Osgood, Jr., and Boden 2016). We anticipate that these obstacles will be addressed and appropriate security safeguards will be available in the near future.

Recommendations for Creating the Participatory Budgeting Infrastructure

Action 1

Communities that use participatory budgeting need institutional social media platform policies. For example, policies should empower a sufficient number of community leaders with the administrative authority to update social media platforms.

Action 2

Communities engaged in participatory budgeting should understand that actively managing social media platforms is real, important work—not an afterthought. Participatory budgeting will require an investment in training both citizens and staff on the use of social media platforms.

Action 3

Communities should plan for, develop, and use social media platforms to complement the other forms of communication available for citizen engagement and mobilization. Communities should explore and expand ways that people can opt-in to participate and submit initial project ideas online.

Citizen Participation in Participatory Budgeting

Finding 5: A Combination of Traditional Citizen Engagement Approaches with Multiple Social Media Platforms Works Best

The interviewees used a combination of traditional citizen engagement approaches (phone calls, flyers, and door knocking) with multiple social media platforms to garner the highest participation (Gordon, Osgood, Jr., and Boden 2016).

Finding 6: Special Efforts Are Required to Include Under-Represented or Excluded Populations in Participatory Budgeting

Communities undertaking participatory budgeting should be aware that it is possible to inadvertently leave out populations that do not have access to digital technologies. There must also be recognition of what the organization loses when participants are not gathered in person—such as the ability to collect pertinent contact information. During the participatory budgeting process, a community may overlook populations with limited availability and access to social media platforms, including the elderly, the poor, the less educated, and new immigrants (see "Processing Power: Participatory Politics" 2013). Targeted outreach efforts may be required and participatory budgeting meetings may need to be scheduled to accommodate the needs of these under-represented populations (Lerner 2011; Gordon, Osgood, Jr., and Boden 2016).

Finding 7: Social Media Outreach to Citizens Does Not Guarantee Participation

The use of social media platforms alone will not guarantee citizen participation. Content of the messages sent via social media platforms matters, and the sender matters, too. Information overload is partially to blame. However, if the citizen recipient believes the sender to be trustworthy, he or she will be more likely to participate (Jenkins, Ford, and Green 2013). A recent study by Hock, Anderson, and Potoski (2013) found that when city managers make telephone calls to personally invite citizens to meetings, it significantly increases the number of attendees. This approach is not without costs in terms of time and money (Gordon, Osgood, Jr., and Boden 2016).

Recommendations for Increasing Citizen Participation in
Participatory Budgeting

Action 4

Communities should build on existing and active social media platforms that the community uses. Communities should also be encouraged to try new approaches.

Action 5

Communities should identify ways to turn passive observers on social media platforms into active participants (Jenkins, Ford, and Green 2013). Communities should understand that social media platforms are not just top-down processes but are collaborative (Nalbandian, O'Neill, Jr., Wilkes, and Kaufman 2013) two-way forms of communication (Nitzsche, Pistoia, and Elsäßer 2012; Neshkova 2014). Citizens should be able to connect across neighborhoods and districts and see the impact of the whole process.

Action 6

Communities should identify who is being left out and work to include excluded populations in the participatory budgeting process.

Action 7

Communities should understand that message content counts. Communities should remember that citizens might not all respond in the same way to a particular alert or message. Participatory budgeting leaders should have a variety of "scripts" prepared and use them as appropriate. They should remember to ask before posting, "Why does this matter to the residents?"

Assessing and Increasing the Impact of Participatory Budgeting

Finding 8: Assessment is Critical to the Success and Expansion of
Participatory Budgeting

Interviewees acknowledge a clear need to use social media platforms more in the participatory budgeting process, but they recognize that they have a responsibility to do this securely. Additionally, one outcome of the May 2014 White House event on participatory budgeting was the realization that communities need to share more than just examples of success. Concrete demonstrations are needed, along with identification and agreement on the types of assessment data to start collecting so that meaningful comparisons can be made among communities about what works and what does not (Scola 2014; Gordon, Osgood, Jr., and Boden 2016).

As a first step toward assessment in New York City, during the first year participatory budgeting was implemented there, evaluators tracked demographic data such as gender, age, race, ethnicity, length of time a resident lived in the neighborhood, primary language spoken, household income, and educational levels, as well as data about each participant's level of participation in the process, including number of meetings attended, who participated in idea assemblies, who volunteered to serve as budget delegates, and who actually voted. The evaluators surveyed participants about their levels of satisfaction and how comfortable they felt with the process. This information allowed the organization to improve the process in subsequent years and it helped them improve the levels of inclusion of all members of the community in the participatory budgeting process (Kasdan and Cattell, n.d.).

Similarly, in Chicago, demographic data has been collected, along with responses to questions about which outreach methods were most effective in encouraging participation, why individuals chose to participate, and in what manner they chose to get involved (Crum, Baker, Salinas, and Weber 2015, 16; Gordon, Osgood, Jr., and Boden 2016).

In Boston, an evaluation of the pilot year of participatory budgeting was conducted by Tara Grillos (2014). The evaluation attempted to answer the following questions (5):

- What was the process, and how could it be improved on for the following year?
- Who participated and how? Was participation representative of the intended targeted audience?
- What decision processes did participants employ? What were the outcomes of those decisions?
- What impact did the participatory budgeting process have on the youth who participated?

The evaluation consisted of collection of survey data, observations at meetings, and in-depth interviews of approximately 30 people who were involved throughout the steps in the participatory budgeting process (Grillos 2014, 5). Some of the findings included the following: 1) the accelerated time frame for the first year was problematic (8); 2) there was a need for better communication and organization (9); 3) facilitators felt that the youth voice was heard (23) and participants reported feeling that they have more of a voice as a result of participating (29); 4) there was greater awareness of needs across Boston (26); and 5) participants reported they had learned more about how governmental processes work (27) and about democracy (31). Specific recommendations included: 1) expanding into and coordinating with the schools (32–33); 2) extending the timeline (32); and 3) engaging social media specialists, creating a user-friendly website, and involving youth in the social media presence (33).

As stated by St. Louis 6th ward Alderwoman Christine Ingrassia, the participatory budgeting community is small, but the White House event held in May

2014 brought national attention to the issue by bringing participatory budgeting leaders together so that they could talk "about the challenges and potential of participatory budgeting" (Scola 2014, 2). To build participatory budgeting capacity as suggested by the interviewees in this study, Krzmarzick (2013, 1) finds it is very important to

> measure, monitor and make adjustments . . . Project teams posed questions such as, What's working? What's not? What are the risks? What's our return-on-investment? What's our return on engagement? Based on continuous weeks and months of assessing the relative value of their online activities, social media project teams tweaked their efforts to achieve greater impact.

Recommendations for Assessing and Increasing the Impact of Participatory Budgeting

Action 8

Communities should identify best practices, share and exchange information with other communities, and support further research efforts.

Action 9

Both communities and the academic realm should research and develop "technology that might help spread participatory budgeting more broadly, such as voting apps or databases through which communities could share information" (Scola 2014, 2). Communities should explore the potential for electronic or digital vote tallying.

Action 10

Communities should solicit feedback from all stakeholders and incorporate changes into social media platform policies, procedures, and practices as necessary.

Recently, the nonprofit organizations Public Agenda and the Participatory Budgeting Project (2015) worked together with the North American Participatory Research Board to develop a comprehensive and user-friendly toolkit for evaluators and implementers of participatory budgeting. This report identifies 15 key metrics for evaluating participatory budgeting as a community goes through the stages of the participatory budgeting process: planning, idea collection, proposal development, voting, and project implementation (2–3). The metrics are divided into three areas of evaluation: civic and political life; inclusion and equity; and government (4). The 15 metrics attempt to answer the following questions through a variety of data collection measures (4):

- To what extent does participatory budgeting engage a significant and growing number of residents, including those who cannot or do not participate in mainstream political life?
- To what extent does participatory budgeting foster collaboration between civil society organizations and government?
- Is participatory budgeting associated with elected officials' political careers?
- Is participatory budgeting engaging traditionally marginalized communities?
- Does participatory budgeting facilitate participation?
- Is participatory budgeting fostering equitable distribution of resources?
- How are the number of participatory budgeting processes and dollar amounts allocated changing from year to year?
- What is the implementation rate of winning participatory budgeting projects?
- Are additional resources being allocated to projects or needs identified through participatory budgeting?
- What is the cost to government of implementing participatory budgeting?

Each of these questions deserves attention and further research. While some of these questions may be more difficult than others to answer, they can be used to guide a community that undertakes participatory budgeting through its own unique participatory budgeting evaluation process. The evaluation results can then be used to improve the process each year.

Conclusion

In our introductory chapter we echoed calls for a better understanding of how values should influence a public administrator's day-to-day activities. The pursuit of administrative efficiency is generally situated as standing in contrast to the quest for values-based administration. However, it has been artfully said,

> there is no need to reconcile democratic politics and scientific efficiency (i.e., politics–administration dichotomy), but rather to keep the tension between the two alive, because it is at the intersection between them that public administration comes into its own.
>
> (Stivers 2008, 56; as cited in
Rossmann and Shanahan 2012, 65)

To be sure, the pursuit of democratic and public service values in governmental operations is not always the fastest way to produce outcomes. But we should not confuse expedience with efficiency. A process that takes longer to produce a decision that more closely reflects the public's interest is more efficient than one that takes less time and is only somewhat reflective of the public interest. Rather than view the situation as a competition among ideals, we should instead seek efficiency and productivity within "the larger context of democracy, community, and the public interest" (Denhardt and Denhardt 2000, 557).

Public administration "comes into its own" when practitioners and students alike have the competencies and skills necessary to design processes that are sensitive to and reflect a multiplicity of values. We should not be afraid of the inherent tensions in the administration of government. Instead, we should seek to prepare ourselves and our colleagues to address the conflicts we will face throughout our careers.

Ultimately, if we have any hope of solving the ever-increasing number of "wicked problems" (Rittel and Webber 1973; Head and Alford 2008), it must be understood that the path forward is much more likely to yield successful outcomes when the public is involved. Participatory budgeting provides an excellent example of how the public can be part of the solution to an issue rather than bystanders waiting for a decision from politicians.

The benefits of participatory budgeting are manifold. As we heard from the community leaders, at its best, participatory budgeting is democratic, transparent, and efficient. It educates citizens, instills a sense of social justice, and builds a sense of community. We hope that this volume in its entirety has addressed many of the issues specific to successfully implementing participatory budgeting and that it will inspire communities to investigate the potential benefits of participatory budgeting. While it is too early to tell if participatory budgeting and other forms of citizen engagement have staying power, it is clear that the benefits of such initiatives provide clear and convincing evidence that we should welcome and prepare for a future in which members of the public have a dual role: citizen and administrator.

References

Amey, M. J., and D. F. Brown. 2004. *Breaking out of the box: Interdisciplinary collaboration and faculty work.* Greenwich, CT: Information Age Publishing.

Amirehsani, K. 2015, November 13. Email correspondence with Victoria Gordon. See website for more information at http://abalancingact.com/.

Crum, T., J. Baker, E. Salinas, and R. Weber. 2015. *Building a people's budget.* Chicago: University of Chicago, Great Cities Institute.

Denhardt, J. V., and R. B. Denhardt. 2000. The new public service: Serving, not steering. *Public Administration Review* 60 (6): 549–559.

Global Campaign on Urban Governance. 2004. *72 frequently asked questions about participatory budgeting.* Nairobi: UN-HABITAT.

Gordon, V. 2012. *Striking a balance: Matching the services offered by local governments with the revenue realities.* Washington, D.C.: ICMA.

Gordon, V., J. L. Osgood, Jr., and D. Boden. 2016. The role of citizen participation and the use of social media platforms in the participatory budgeting process. *International Journal of Public Administration.* doi: 10.1080/01900692.2015.1072215.

Greensboro Participatory Budgeting. 2015, June 11. Participatory budgeting Greensboro meets funding goal to launch city's first PB process. http://greensboropb.org (accessed June 22, 2015).

Grillos, T. 2014. Youth lead the change: The city of Boston's youth-focused participatory budgeting process. Report provided by email via Pam Jennings to Victoria Gordon, June 30, 2015.

Hadden, M., and J. Lerner. 2011, December 3. How to start participatory budgeting in your city. http://www.shareable.net/blog/how-to-start-participatory-budgeting-in-your-city (accessed July 18, 2012).

Hatch, M. J., and A. L. Cunliffe. 2013. *Organization theory: Modern, symbolic, and postmodern perspectives.* 3rd ed. Oxford: Oxford University Press.

Head, B., and J. Alford. 2008. Wicked problems: The implications for public management. Paper delivered at Australian Political Studies Association Conference, Hilton Hotel, Brisbane, Australia.

Hock, S., S. Anderson, and M. Potoski. 2013. Invitation phone calls increase attendance at civic meetings: Evidence from a field experiment. *Public Administration Review* 73 (2): 221–228.

Jenkins, H., S. Ford, and J. Green. 2013. *Spreadable media: Creating value and meaning in a networked culture.* New York: New York University Press.

Kaplan, A., and M. Haenlein. 2010. Users of the world, unite! The challenges and opportunities of social media. *Business Horizons* 53 (1): 59–68.

Kasdan, A., and L. Cattell. n.d. A people's budget: A research and evaluation report on the pilot year of participatory budgeting in New York City. New York: Community Development Project at the Urban Justice Center.

Krzmarzick, A. 2013, March 15. Social media matures into viable, valuable communications tool. http://www.astd.org/Publications/Magazines/The-Public-Manager (accessed May 10, 2014).

Lerner, J. 2011. Participatory budgeting: Building community agreement around tough budget decisions. *National Civic Review* 100 (2): 30–35.

Manoharan, A., and L. Bennett. 2013. Opportunities for online citizen participation: A study of global municipal practices. *Journal of Public Management & Social Policy* 19 (2): 137–150.

Nabatchi, T., and L. B. Amsler. 2014. Direct public engagement in local government. *American Review of Public Administration* 44 (4 supp): 63S–88S.

Nalbandian, J., R. O'Neill, Jr., J. M. Wilkes, and A. Kaufman. 2013. Contemporary challenges in local government: Evolving roles and responsibilities, structures, and processes. *Public Administration Review* 73 (4): 567–574.

Neshkova, M. 2014. Does agency autonomy foster public participation? *Public Administration Review* 74 (1): 64–74.

Nitzsche, P., A. Pistoia, and M. Elsäßer. 2012. Development of an evaluation tool for participative E-government services: A case study of electronic participatory budgeting projects in Germany. *Administration and Public Management* 18: 6–25.

Perlman, B. 2012. Social media sites at the state and local levels: Operational success and governance failure. *State and Local Government Review* 44 (1): 67–75.

Processing power: Participatory politics. 2013. *The Economist* 406: 63–64. http://search.proquest.com (accessed March 28, 2014).

Public Agenda and the Participatory Budgeting Project. 2015. 15 key metrics for evaluating participatory budgeting: A toolkit for evaluators and implementers. http://www.publicagenda.org/pages/participatory-budgeting-research-and-evaluation (accessed September 11, 2015).

Reddick, C., and D. F. Norris. 2013. E-participation in local governments: An examination of political-managerial support and impacts. *Transforming Government: People, Process and Policy* 7 (4): 453–476.

Rittel, H. W. J., and M. M. Webber. 1973. Dilemmas in a general theory of planning. *Policy Sciences* 4 (2): 155–169.

Rossmann, D., and E. A. Shanahan. 2012. Defining and achieving normative democratic values in participatory budgeting processes. *Public Administration Review* 72 (1): 56–66.

Scola, N. 2014, May 15. The White House brings participatory budgeting in from the fringe. *Next City.* http://nextcity.org/daily/entry/participatory-budgeting-cities-white-house (accessed May 22, 2014).

Stivers, C. 2008. The significance of the administrative state. *Public Administration Review* 68 (1): 53–56.

van Dijk, J., and K. Hacker. 2003. The digital divide as a complex and dynamic phenomenon. *The Information Society* 19 (4): 315–326.

Index

CPSIA information can be obtained
at www.ICGtesting.com
Printed in the USA
LVHW082250130123
737115LV00006B/413